Jorge Ramos has been the anchorman for Noticiero Univision for the last 19 years. He has won seven Emmy Awards and the Maria Moors Cabot Award for Excellence in Journalism. He writes a weekly column for more than 50 newspapers through *The New York Times Syndicate.* Ramos has appeared on NBC's *Today,* CNN's *Talk Back Live,* Fox News' *The O'Reilly Factor,* and PBS's *Charlie Rose,* among others. He is the bestselling author of *No Borders: A Journalist's Search for Home* and *The Latino Wave.* He lives in Florida.

THE LATINO WAVE

THE LATINO WAVE

HOW HISPANICS ARE TRANSFORMING

POLITICS IN AMERICA

JORGE RAMOS

TRANSLATED FROM THE SPANISH BY EZRA E. FITZ

rayo

AN IMPRINT OF HARPERCOLLINSPUBLISHERS

FEB - 2007

TO THE FIRST LATINO U.S. PRESIDENT,

WHO, SURELY, HAS ALREADY BEEN BORN

"Latinos are not from the other side of the moon."
—JORGE I. DOMÍNGUEZ, Harvard University

"Hispanics have edged past blacks and are the nation's largest minority group."
—New York Times, January 22, 2003

"The long-anticipated Latino majority has arrived."
—DAVID HAYES-BAUTISTA, commenting on the fact that over half of the babies born in California are Hispanic

"In little more than fifty years there will be no majority race in the United States. No other nation in history has gone through demographic change of this magnitude in so short a time."
—BILL CLINTON, 1998

"My job is, of course, to promote the diversity of America, to herald the fact that one of the great strengths of America is the fact that we're diverse and that we welcome diversity in this country."
—GEORGE W. BUSH, October 3, 2002

"The nation of many nations."
—WALT WHITMAN, talking about the United States

"[Latinos emphasize] their personal desire to continue being distinct."
—OCTAVIO PAZ, The Labyrinth of Solitude

"Everyone talks about the latinization of America, but few people talk about the Americanization of Latinos. It is a two-way street."
—HARRY PACHÓN, Tomás Rivera Policy Institute

CONTENTS

ACKNOWLEDGMENTS

THIS BOOK STEMS, of course, from many things.

The conversations I had with Raul Yzaguirre of the National Council of La Raza, Roberto Suro of the Pew Hispanic Center, Arturo Vargas of the National Association of Latino Elected and Appointed Officials (NALEO), and Harry Pachón of the Tomás Rivera Policy Institute greatly influenced this book's analysis and conclusions. They, after all, are the true experts on this subject.

Sonia Colín and Janet Murguia allowed me an inside look at the campaigns of George W. Bush and Al Gore as they sought to gain the Hispanic vote in the 2000 presidential election. Their testimonies are invaluable and, without them, such a perspective on both the Republican and Democratic parties would not have been possible.

Many of the ideas and arguments presented herein have previously been explored by others. Therefore, I have made a very thorough and concerted effort to attribute, cite, and quote all arguments, ideas, and facts that aren't my own. The vision put forth by other Latinos has enabled me to approach the complicated subject of the Hispanic condition.

The book *Latinos: Remaking America* was fundamental for me as I oriented myself along the lines of the most important issues affecting Hispanics today. I am thus indebted to those who helped in its publication: Ricardo C. Ainslie, Elaine Bernard, E. Richard Brown, María S. Carlo, Jorge Chapa, John H. Coatsworth, Wayne A. Cornelius, Rodolfo O. de la Garza, Louis DeSipio, Jorge I. Domínguez, Celia Jaes Falicov, Paul Farmer, Juan Flores, Patrícia Gándara, Merilee S. Grindle, Jacqueline Hagan, David E. Hayes-Bautista, Pierrette Hondagneu-Sotelo, Peggy Levitt, Luis C. Moll, Lisa J. Montoya, Gary Orfield, Mariele Páez, Barbara Zurer Pearson, Nestor Rodriguez,

Richard Ruiz, George J. Sanchez, Roberto C. Smith, Catherine E. Snow, Doris Sommer, Alex Stepick, Carol Durron Stepick, Carola Suárez-Orozco, Marcelo M. Suárez-Orozco, Silvio Torres-Saillant, John Trumpbour, Diego Vigil, Mary C. Waters, Hongjian Yu, and Ana Cecilia Zentella.

The research and data presented here have been invaluable resources: they show the Hispanic reality in a quantitative form. There are several studies I cite frequently, and without them this book would lack a solid factual basis: "2002 National Survey of Latinos" (Pew Hispanic Center/Kaiser Family Foundation); "Latinos in Higher Education: Many Enroll, Too Few Graduate" (Pew Hispanic Center); "Latino Viewing Choices" (Tomás Rivera Policy Institute); "Immigrants Dispel Negative Stereotypes" (Public Agenda); "Mobilizing the Latino Vote: 2002" (National Council of La Raza); "Latinos Potent, but Vulnerable, Force in U.S. Economy" (National Council of La Raza); "Overall U.S. Economy Gains from Immigration" (National Academy of Sciences); "Immigrants and the Economy" (National Immigration Forum). The studies and analysis done by the Brookings Institution, the Center on Urban and Metropolitan Policy, the U.S. Census Bureau Public Information Office, the Urban Institute, and UCLA's North American Integration and Development Center were also highly valuable.

The autobiographies of María Arana, Ilan Stavans, and Richard Rodríguez are extraordinary reflections on Latinos' incessant search for identity, and I used them as constant guides and references. These writers have already entered and exited from the torment. The books *Strangers Among Us* by Roberto Suro, *The Buried Mirror* by Carlos Fuentes, and *The Cosmic Race* by José Vasconcelos were central in establishing context and a long-term vision.

I have the greatest bosses on Earth at Univision. Ray Rodríguez, Frank Pirozzi, and Sylvia Rosabal, the vice president for news, understand only too well what it means to be both a journalist and a writer, and have graciously granted me the space and support I needed to be both. Thanks, Ray. Thanks, Frank. Thanks, Sylvia.

The enthusiasm of my editor, René Alegría, is contagious. He is the true force behind this book, as well as behind Rayo, Harper-Collins's Hispanic imprint. René is my friend; he knows how to listen, and he posesses an extraordinary capacity for observation. All of his edits invariably improve upon the original, and how many other writers can say this about their editors? Andrea Montejo, in charge of much of this book's publication process, is incredibly patient, tolerant, and attentive to detail. If her fellow compatriots followed her example, there would already be peace in Colombia.

Bill Adler, my agent, has a marvelous eye for new tendencies. It's the human contact—direct, without the use of the Internet, fax machines, or cellphones—and his insatiable curiosity that makes him so special. When he speaks, I listen.

And, to make a long story short, it's the experience of spending the past 20 years of my life in the United States—as an immigrant and as a Latino—that has enabled me to write this book. How does one thank an entire country? How? One way or another, I thank you.

THE UNITED STATES is becoming a Latino nation.

By the year 2125, there will be more Hispanics than non-Hispanic whites in the United States. Decades before, in 2050, whites will have become just one more minority in this country. Most of us will not be around to see such developments, but the process has been set in motion, and looks to be irreversible.

The Latino wave is advancing unstoppably, inexorably, imperturbably. Each passing year brings roughly 1.5 million new Hispanics into the United States, via immigration (both legal and undocumented) and new children born in the United States to Latino families.

It's this constant growth that affects everything. Hispanics made up 5 percent of the total U.S. population in 1970, 9 percent in 1990, 12.5 percent in 2000, and 13.5 percent in 2002. The figure will rise to 18 percent by 2030, 22 percent by 2050, 29 percent by 2075, 33 percent by 2100, and 36 percent by 2125, at which point Hispanics will outnumber non-Hispanic whites in this country (35 percent). The watershed period from 2120 to 2125 will mark—if the trends hold true and my calculations are correct—one of the greatest demographic transformations ever: a future snapshot of how a minority became a majority. The Latino wave.

This demographic revolution is, of course, a cultural one as well. This is no exaggeration. The growth and influence of the Latino community will significantly change the power structure within the United States as well as the way in which we live on a day-to-day basis. Nothing—absolutely nothing—will remain untouched by this Latino presence.

Like it or not, there is a wave sweeping across the United States, washing over everything, and even those who refuse to believe this are going to get culturally soaked.

The United States is witnessing a veritable demographic revolution, and this will have far more important repercussions than the war on terrorism, the state of the economy, or even the oftentimes disastrous forces of nature. What is unfathomable is that many people haven't even noticed that it is happening.

I don't intend to inundate you with statistics in this book. What I want to do instead is help illustrate not when or where Latinos will transform the United States, but how. You don't have to be a visionary to realize that Latinos already wield enough power to significantly influence an election and choose the next president of the United States, and the next, and the next. . . . Conclusion: the Hispanic vote can easily decide a closely contested election. It already has.

For now, the political force of the Latino voting community lies in its ability to define close races in states that have a lot of electoral votes. It is easy to argue that the Florida Latino community gave the election to George W. Bush in the year 2000, and that the Latino voters in Colorado, Nevada, and New Mexico reelected the president in 2004. As soon as you factor in the number of Latinos who are in the process of becoming full, voting U.S. citizens, the Hispanic vote takes on an entirely new dimension. The Hispanic vote will cease to be a weightless player on the political scale, and instead become the veritable "big boy" in states and regions where the Latino population has historically congregated. In the next century, every critical decision that this country makes will have to pass through the filter of the Latino vote. That's where the numbers, and this country, are heading.

Political parties and organizations that have thus far refused to adjust their strategies and agendas to include the concerns and needs of the Hispanic population will quickly become irrelevant. It's only a matter of time. Even today I'm constantly shocked when a public official or political party ignores the Latino community. They just don't seem to realize that ignoring the Hispanic community today will have enormous political consequences in the future, for the majority of this community is on the verge of gaining the right to vote.

There can be no doubt that both parties—Democrats and Republicans—are fervently seeking the Hispanic vote. But at times I get the impression that the top brass of each party is still oblivious to the fact that Hispanics are already starting to change—and sometimes dramatically—the political tasks and the electoral map of the United States.

On January 22, 2003, the day that I wrote the first few words of this book, the *New York Times* ran a front-page story proclaiming "Hispanics Now Largest Minority, Census Shows." According to the Census Bureau, as of July 1, 2002, there were indeed more Hispanics (38.8 million) than African Americans (38.3 million) in the United States.[1]

The seemingly inexorable transformation of the United States into a Latino nation will be complete sometime during the first quarter of the next century. The possibility exists, of course, that some cataclysmic event will put an end to this process of Latinization. As doubtful as it is, a catastrophe of some kind—a major new terrorist attack, a third world war, the explosion of a nuclear device, a terrible natural disaster—could affect current trends in Hispanic growth. Also doubtful but possible, a radical, xenophobic politician could attempt to close the southern border of the United States using military force or some sort of new advanced technology. If either of these highly unlikely scenarios occurs, the seeds of change have already been planted. Even if the United States were to shut itself off from the rest of the world, the changes would continue from within: thousands of Latino babies are born every day, the use of the Spanish language is spreading steadily, and Hispanic customs continue to influence non-Hispanic citizens.

But what does this Latinization really mean? It does *not* mean that the country is going to end up resembling Latin America—at least not in the near future. What it does mean is that the experiences, customs, and traditions of U.S. Hispanics are having, and will continue to have, a fundamental influence on the country's future. The Hispanic presence reemphasizes the multi-ethnic, multiracial, and multicultural condition of the United States. Multiculturalism, not monoculturalism, is the prevailing trend. And tolerance for diversity—currently exemplified by Latinos—is one of this country's principal characteristics.

There are no Latinos living outside the United States. By definition, a Latino is someone who was born in Latin America (or is of Latin American descent) but currently lives in the United States. And this itself confers some very distinct characteristics, brought about by the collision of two or more worlds and typical of Latin American citizenry. A Latino is, by definition, a mix of cultures, languages, identities, possibilities, and times, both past and future.

Some of those reading this book may think that Latinos are a nation within a nation. But this is exactly where the dilemma surrounding U.S. Latinos comes from. We are not a separate nation. We are different, yes, but we are also indisputably American. We make up a part of this nation and we're not going anywhere.

It would therefore be true political suicide to forget, underestimate, or push aside the growing Latino electorate. The time when politicians could single out and stereotype the Latino vote (because immigrants don't vote) has long since passed. Latinos born in the United States will soon be an undeniable majority within the Hispanic population. Today, the party that ignores or underestimates the young, second-generation Latinos who are not quite yet of voting age is putting a rope around its neck.

This is a complicated matter, it's true. Hispanics are not a homogenous group, and gaining an understanding of them—and gaining their votes as well—will take much conscientious effort.

So now the fundamental question is this: What is the future of the Latino population? Are Latinos going to assimilate themselves just as the European immigrants did before them? Or are they going to maintain some of the characteristics that differentiate them from the rest of North American society and continue to remain distinct?

According to Harvard professors Marcelo Suárez-Orozco and Mariela Páez, Hispanics face three possible scenarios in the future. The first is that they will replicate the experience of earlier European immigrants and be assimilated; the second is that, based on racial differences, some Latinos will fully integrate with whites in two or three generations while others will remain at the margins of U.S. society; and the third is that Hispanics, by virtue of their vast numbers, will create their own sociocultural space and forge new strategies for adaptation. I have the most faith in this third scenario.

This book's thesis is that Latinos are different, that Latinos are distinct. Yes, they are rapidly integrating themselves into this society—especially along political and economic lines—but they will not completely and fully assimilate culturally. Latinos are creating their own space in this country, and their particular cultural differences will continue to influence the rest of society. These uniquely Hispanic cultural characteristics are forever changing the face of the United States. Latinos are shattering the proverbial concept of the melting pot.

Of course, the Latino wave has a countercurrent, an undertow. Just as Hispanics are Latinizing the United States, Latinos are also becoming Americanized, as argued by Harry Pachón of the Tomás Rivera Policy Institute. The Americanization of Hispanics is a phenomenon mainly affecting those Latinos who have lived here for two or more generations. Nevertheless, from where I stand—and this is what I'm attempting to prove in this book—the Latinizing current is the dominant one.

But why are Latinos different? It has to do with numbers, culture, and a tendency to stay connected to one's roots.

Latinos have maintained close ties with their countries of origin through constant migration, the close geographic proximity of Latin America, and technological advances such as cellphones, e-mail, and supersonic jets, which form a permanent bridge. Their rapid growth—through high birth rates and immigration—allows cultural patterns to be constantly reinforced, instead of gradually disappearing, as happened with the European immigrants who preceded them. Living in L.A. and driving to Tijuana to visit your girlfriend or picking up a cellphone to call your mother in Mexico City today just isn't the same as living in New York in 1910, with an entire ocean separating you from your family in Sicily.

This is the defining characteristic, the principle difference between Latinos and the other immigrants. It is this connection with our Ibero-American past and present that sustains and nourishes the Latino community in the United States. So it is not enough for a politician to stammer out a few words in Spanish, dress like a mariachi, and offer us *tacos* and *mojitos* in order to get our vote. Rather, it is knowing where we come from, what makes us different, what our problems and needs are, and how we are changing the face of the country.

Democrats and Republicans are caught up in a struggle to win the hearts and votes of the Hispanic population. Never before has such a great effort been made to capture Latino support. Nobody can ever again forget this segment of the American population, especially if they want to win the election.

It can be argued that Latinos decided the 2000 presidential election: the 537 votes that decided Florida could well have come from Cuban American voters who were heavily influenced by George W. Bush's speeches in Spanish. And Latinos also determined the 2004 elections, giving Bush a clear advantage over Kerry in the states of Florida, Arizona, Colorado, New Mexico, and Nevada.

Whoever is looking much further down the line knows the real change in this country has nothing to do with terrorism or the economy, nor with future elections, but rather with the immense growth and influence of the Latino community. And whoever doesn't want to see or listen should cover his eyes and ears.

When my son Nicolás had just turned 6, he would challenge his sister Paola—a 17-year-old girl with marvelous basketball skills—to pickup games in front of the house. As you might suspect, despite all his efforts, Nicolás never won a match. Nevertheless, after every single game, Nicolás would say to Paola, "When I'm older, I'm going to win." And nobody doubted that. Nicolás always had a well-developed spirit for competition, and one could tell he would be taller than his sister.

I'm relating this family anecdote because it bears the same message as this book. Like Nicolás, Latinos will continue to grow, to educate and prepare themselves, and someday—a day that, unfortunately, none of us will be able to witness—they will outnumber all other ethnic groups in this country.

This dramatic demographic shift will have enormous political, cultural, and economic consequences for this country. The growth of the U.S. Hispanic community will eventually overtake all in its path. The vast numbers of individuals in the Latino community will warrant a greater political representation for Hispanics and the issues important to them. The issues important to U.S. Latinos are more and more important for the United States as a whole, and this needs to be clearly understood.

One final, important clarification: This book is not marked or influenced by any sense of political favoritism. I have tried to treat both parties—Democrats and Republicans—equally in my analysis. I'm not interested in garnering votes or supporting this or that candidate. Rather, I'm trying—more than anything—to help myself (and others) understand.

THE LATINO WAVE

CHAPTER ONE

MAKING HISTORY:

HOW LATINOS DECIDED THE 2000

AND 2004 PRESIDENTIAL ELECTIONS

HISPANICS REELECT BUSH

The big news from the 2004 presidential election was that some 9 million Hispanic citizens used their votes to reelect George W. Bush. No, the election was not decided in Ohio. It was decided long before that in states with high percentages of Latino voters: Florida, Arizona, Nevada, Colorado, and New Mexico. Bush won those five states, and because of it he was able to gain four more years in the White House.

Never have so many Hispanics voted in an election. They represented roughly 8 percent of the total votes counted, and 3 million more voted in this election than in 2000. And never before had a Republican candidate won such a high percentage of the Latino vote: 44 percent, according to the exit polls. This represents a surprising increase over the 31 percent won by Bush in 2000, according to *The New York Times.*

In other words, many Hispanic Democrats decided to jump ship and vote for the Republican candidate during the 2004 election. This shift explains Bush's victory, and it also shows that, for the first time, Democrats were beginning to lose the command that they'd had over the Hispanic vote for decades.

John Kerry, the Democratic candidate, only managed to win 53 percent of the Latino vote, which was nowhere near the 67 percent won by Al Gore in 2000. What happened?

"Kerry had no strategy for winning the Latino vote," Raúl Izaguirre, president of the National Council de La Raza and one of the most well-respected Hispanics in the country, told me. "He never connected with Latino voters; part of it was his personality, but also it's because, from the very beginning of his campaign, he never had a coherent strategy for convincing Latino voters that they should side with him."

Izaguirre, who represents a nonpartisan organization, felt that Bush, on the other hand, did have "a very effective strategy for winning the Latino vote, with good, creative, and emotional TV ads. The president managed to connect with Latino voters."

The results are impossible to ignore.

If Kerry, for example, had spent more time addressing the Hispanic and Spanish-speaking voters in Colorado, Nevada, and New Mexico, he would have won the election. I'll explain.

Bush won Colorado by a 107,000 vote margin over his Democratic opponent, Nevada by 21,000, and New Mexico by 6,000. In other words, if 67,000 Hispanic voters had sided with Kerry instead, he would have won an additional 19 electoral votes, giving him a total of 271, enough to reach the White House.

How could the Democrats have underestimated the importance of the Latino vote when it came to winning the presidency? Those 67,000 votes—which represented less than 1 percent of the total Latino vote—could have been won with relative ease had the Kerry campaign simply conducted more interviews in Spanish, run more ads on Spanish-language radio and television, and linked itself with the ultimately successful senatorial campaign of Colorado's Ken Salazar. But for some reason, they didn't. Why?

When Bush was a candidate in 2000, he gave more than 100 interviews to the Spanish-language media. In 2004, Kerry ought to have matched or exceeded that. Instead, he gave a mere 25 such interviews. In other words, Kerry hamstrung himself and was unable to counteract the pointed, unequivocal messages emanating from the White House.

In many ways, Kerry committed the same general errors that Gore did. Gore lost in 2000 because of the Hispanic vote in Florida; Kerry lost in 2004 because of the Hispanic vote in Colorado, Nevada, and New Mexico, among other states.

The Democrats were confident in their belief that in 2004 they would win the Latino vote by a wide margin, which is why they didn't spend significant amounts of resources to guarantee that. Proof of this can be found in a July 26, 2004, memorandum from the Democracy Corps group, whose members advised the Kerry campaign.

The memo—directed at all Democrats involved in attracting Latino voters—noted that the Republican Party considered increasing Bush's support among Hispanics to be one of its highest priorities. In fact, in a July 17 interview with NBC's Tim Russert, Bush pollster Matthew Dowd unequivocally stated that one of the campaign's chief goals was to win at least 40 percent of the Latino vote. This was no secret. What's surprising is that the Democrats—despite knowing their opponent's strategy—did so little to even maintain their traditional advantage over Republicans among Hispanic voters.

The memo sent by Kerry pollster Stan Greenberg (one of the founders of Democracy Corps, the other being James Carville) established that "Bush is not only failing to reach that goal, he is failing to hold on to what he had—with his support dropping to just 30 percent." In a triumphant tone, this report asserted that Bush was losing support among the Hispanic population in Florida, as well as southwestern states such as Nevada and New Mexico.

This information was based on a poll conducted by the Democratic Party that stated that 61 percent of Hispanics would be voting for Kerry and only 30 percent would be voting for Bush. It added that "Bush's approval rating among Hispanics has suffered steep declines over the past five months," and that even "after Kerry is attacked here on abortion and gay marriage, his support among Hispanics does not drop a point."

Nevertheless, even at that late summer date, Democrats were concerned that the Republicans might be able to convert many Hispanic voters based on the president's conservative moral values. "Hispanic voters are more socially conservative and potentially conflicted on issues like abortion and gay marriage," the report cautioned. And this is exactly what happened shortly thereafter, with the Democrats being unable to do anything effective to contradict the Republican message. The Democrats saw that they were in danger of losing the Hispanic vote four months before the election, but evidently they did not give the warning serious consideration.

The assessment done by Democracy Corps seems to be supported by two other independent polls: one done by *The Washington Post,* Univision, and the Instituto Tomás Rivera, which polled 1,605 people between July 6 and 16; the other poll being conducted by the National Annenberg Election Survey from July 1 through 21 of 3,715 registered Hispanic voters. The first poll gave Bush no more than 30 percent support among likely Hispanic voters, while the second asserted that the number of Hispanic voters identified as Latinos had risen 6 percent from 2000.

This was good news for the Democrats. But instead of seizing the opportunity to reinforce their support among the Hispanic community, they let it slip away.

This memo was fundamental within the Democratic campaign. Some Kerry advisors believed that the Latino vote was without a doubt assured, and thus they decided not to expend any extra effort toward recruiting more Hispanic voters. This proved to be a fatal error. Such thinking permeated the Kerry campaign, and ultimately eroded it.

What the surveys said in July was very different from what the voters said in November. Why? First of all, there were about 3 million more Hispanic voters in 2004 than there were in the previous election, and it was difficult for pollsters to know who and where they were. Secondly, unlike the Democratic Party, the Republicans did not depend on external groups to plan, produce, execute, and distribute their publicity among the Latino community, which made their message more pointed and effective. Finally, the majority of Latino voters— who had been born in the United States—were not really all that different from the rest of the population, and thus they reacted favorably to Republican messages of patriotism and conservative moral values.

The organization that did the most to support Democratic efforts to secure the Latino vote was the New Democratic Network (NDN). In the spring of 2002, the NDN created a Hispanic project whose objective was "to communicate the message that, with the Democratic agenda, Hispanics everywhere will have a better life." They spent some $6 million on advertisements, messages, and conferences that reached out to Hispanic voters during the 2004 campaign, much more than either of the two major political parties. But, in the end, their frustration was palpable.

In an email sent 10 days after the election, the NDN's founder, Simon Rosenberg, and his colleagues, María Cardona, Sergio Bendixen, and Joe García, issued a stinging critique of John Kerry and the Democratic Party:

> It is our conclusion that the Kerry/DNC coordinated campaign never took the [Hispanic] vote seriously enough. We now know that there was talk at the highest levels of the campaign that Bush would not make gains from his 2000 number—35 percent—and that little money or attention was needed to speak to Hispanics in the final months. From what we saw, despite having a determined and talented Hispanic team in place, the campaign's decision makers did not spend the money or make the commitment needed to swing this vote, potentially allowing states like Nevada and New Mexico to slip away.

In the months leading up to November 2, there were many, many voices crying out with the message that the election would be determined by the Latino vote. And whoever did not heed these voices would lose. "These results are explained, in part, by what Kerry declined to do," summarized Raúl Izaguirre, agreeing with the NDN's conclusions.

These results are also explained by what Bush did do. The Republicans knew full well that Hispanics tend to have very conservative moral values, especially on the issues of abortion, religion, and gay marriage. According to exit polls, 80 percent of voters listed "moral values" as a determining factor in their choice, and they preferred Bush to Kerry on the subject. Hispanics were no different.

Ralph Nader, the independent candidate, and his running mate, Peter Camejo, who is of Venezuelan origin, carried 2 percent of the Latino vote.

After the electoral dust had settled and spirits had calmed, Kerry and the Democrats came to realize that the Latino vote truly was what ultimately decided the 2004 presidential election. But by then, it was too late.

Here is how the battle for the Hispanic vote began:

Early in 2004—Wednesday, January 7, to be exact—President Bush proposed issuing temporary work permits, a move that would benefit millions of undocumented immigrants for years. This was the first indication that the Bush campaign would go on to win the election that November with the help of Hispanic voters.

In a White House speech, President Bush admitted that current immigration policy was not working, and he spoke at length about the enormous contributions that immigrants have made to U.S. history, culture, and economics over the years. Bush also said that the United States needed foreign manual labor to continue growing, and that for humanitarian reasons and those of national security, he was in favor of granting temporary legal status to thousands of undocumented workers. The objective, he said, was to unite immigrants seeking work with employers who were unable to secure American employees.

Republicans have rarely spoken in such terms.

The problems with Bush's immigration proposal are that it's not entirely realistic, and that it only offers temporary legal status to workers and their families. What happens after the special visas expire, and there is no way to renew them? Bush left the details up in the air.

It would take an infantile sense of naïveté to think that immigrants who worked legally in the United States for years would pack up and go home once their temporary visas expired. This just won't happen.

Any serious immigration proposal must include the possibility of becoming legal residents and eventually U.S. citizens. But these possibilities were not provided for in Bush's plan.

Bush's proposal was unilateral. He made the announcement himself from the White House without consulting any members of the Hispanic Caucus—the group that has done the most over the years to protect immigrants' rights and is most familiar with the issue—or any of his neighbors. Mexican president Vicente Fox was given much of the credit for bringing the proposal about, but the reality of the situation was that the U.S. chief executive only phoned Fox the morning of his announcement so that he could tell him, in a 15-minute conversation, what he was going to say that afternoon. There were no negotiations at all with Mexico before the proposal was unveiled, which is why it seems so incomplete.

Nor does Bush's plan solve the problem of undocumented immigration in the long term. On the contrary, it only delays and complicates the issue. Under his plan, millions of undocumented workers would become legal for a period of time—three, or perhaps six years—after which they would simply return to being undocumented. This will not solve a thing.

Temporary legalization could also become a trap. These temporary workers—like the *braceros* of the 1940s and 1950s—could easily be exploited and manipulated by the employers who sponsor their permit applications. And when their visas expire, they could be deported fairly easily by the new INS, since it would know where to locate each and every worker.

Bush's proposal says nothing, absolutely nothing, about stopping the violence and death that takes place along the border between Mexico and the United States. On average, one immigrant dies every day along this political line.

Nor does Bush explain how he expects to regulate or control undocumented crossings of the United States' southern border. Every day, an average of 1,000 immigrants cross over illegally from Mexico into the United States, or violate the terms of their visas by remaining on U.S. soil after the expiration date. It is patently absurd to speak of national security and immigration reform when the United States' southern border so closely resembles a colander.

The only realistic way to confront the problem of undocumented immigration is through an agreement with Mexico and Central America. But even so, as long as there is such a great disparity in wages between the United States and Latin America, it will continue to happen. For that reason, any logical reform must include an investment program—similar to the European Union—designed to equalize wages throughout the American continent.

The majority of Latinos rejected the president's plan. According to a poll conducted by Sergio Bendixen for the organization New California Media, almost half—45 percent—did so because the plan contained no provisions for people to eventually become permanent legal residents or citizens. Additionally, 63 percent believed that Bush was more concerned with winning the Latino vote than with actually addressing the problems of undocumented immigrants.

In order to bring the Bush plan's deficiencies into sharp relief, the Hispanic Caucus drew up their own proposal, which addressed such things as family reunification, permanent legalization, the protection of immigrants along the border, and aid for undocumented students. According to Bendixen's poll, 85 percent of Hispanics favored the plan devised by Democratic and Latino congressmen. The issue of immigration clearly shows that the two parties were quite literally fighting for the Hispanic vote.

Bush's proposal skirted the problem's real issues. It offered no permanent solutions for the 8 million undocumented workers currently in the country, nor did it establish a plan for a safe and orderly flow of immigrants. But on a campaign level, it was seen as a positive move by Latino voters. And Bush had beaten Democrats to the punch in a key election issue.

It happens every four years. Every election year, that is. Presidential candidates and top political figures turn their attention to the Latino community after a period of almost total disregard. Why? Because they know that the vote needed to win the White House is the His-panic vote. And the 2004 election was no exception.

I call it "Christopher Columbus Syndrome." Every four years, both political parties and the English-language media "rediscover" Hispanics. Oftentimes they treat the community as if it hadn't existed before, or as if it had only recently arrived. Many don't realize that the majority of Hispanics were born in the United States, and their ances-tors lived here even before the country was founded.

Hispanics are changing the face, the culture, the politics, and the economy of the most powerful nation on the planet. Here at the start of the 21st century, they make up 42 percent of the population in New Mexico, 33 percent in California, 32 percent in Texas, 25 percent in Arizona, 16 percent in Florida, 15 percent in New York, and 12 per-cent in Illinois.

Plus, Latinos had the power to decide the 2004 presidential elections. They were the most highly sought after swing vote in the country. Whichever candidate won their support also won the White House.

Ways to woo Latino voters were innumerable, and they took on countless forms. The most obvious and hackneyed of these was to speak to them in Spanish.

Former Vermont governor Howard Dean, who led the list of potential Democratic nominees in early 2004, tirelessly repeated the phrase already made famous by the late labor activist and leader of the United Farm Workers, César Chávez: *"Sí se puede . . . sí se puede . . . sí se puede . . ."*

General Wesley Clark spoke passable Spanish, and he was able to string together a few complete sentences. But his secret weapon was his grandson, Wesley Pablo Oviedo Clark. His only son had married a Colombian woman.

John Kerry didn't speak much Spanish, but his wife, Teresa Heinz Kerry, did. A multimillionaire of Portuguese descent, she was fluent in five languages and represented his link to the Latino community. Kerry also had the support of former HUD Secretary Henry Cisneros, one of the most influential Latinos in the country.

John Edwards, Joe Lieberman, and Al Sharpton spoke no Spanish. Dennis Kucinich did, but he was so far behind in the polls that it wouldn't have mattered even if he were able to write like Gabriel García Márquez.

Hispanic voters had grown more and more sophisticated in recent years, and they demanded that the candidates look for solutions to their most pressing problems. For example, there are high drop-out rates among their young students; they suffer a disproportionately high unemployment rate, lack sufficient health care, and battle discrimination; millions are running the risk of being deported. Which is why each of the Democratic candidates came up with distinct proposals to address these uniquely Latino issues.

It had become clear that, in 2004, winning the Latino vote was going to take more than *mariachis, tacos,* and a few rounds of *"Viva México . . . viva Puerto Rico . . . viva Cuba libre."*

I'd never heard John Kerry speak Spanish before. But there he was, in May 2004, carefully reading a speech in Spanish on the serious problem of school drop-out rates among Hispanic students (1 out of every 3 does not finish high school).

He had left the other candidates—Howard Dean, John Edwards, & Co.—back in the pack, having come from behind to emerge as the Democratic candidate for the presidency.

Now he had to focus on winning the presidential election, and to do that he would need to have the Latino vote securely in his pocket. The setting was appropriate: the Woodrow Wilson High School in East L.A. The date couldn't have been more significant: May 5— Cinco de Mayo—the day on which Mexicans celebrate their military triumph over invading French troops in 1862. Kerry's Spanish had a slight accent, somewhere between Italian and Portuguese, but his words were clear and understandable. He'd been learning the language, he said, by listening to tapes in his "free time."

At the end of his speech, the mostly Latino audience erupted in applause. Kerry had kicked off his campaign to win the Latino vote

. . . and he'd done it in passable Spanish. Also, Kerry tried to address the recent criticism that his campaign was dragging its feet in terms of courting Hispanic voters, and that Latinos were not well represented in the upper echelons of his campaign.

After the speech, I was able to sit down alone with the senator in a classroom for half an hour to chat. The blue seat in which he sat was rather small—it was designed for a teenager and not a 60-year-old man standing 6-foot-4. But Kerry didn't complain; he crossed his ankles and spread his knees, forming a large letter V with his legs. His jacket was off and he was wearing a light blue shirt and a red tie marbled with gray. Kerry's famous jaw was relaxed and moving effortlessly. His flat, almost pressed forehead didn't move. His eyes seemed small set in a face dominated by a solid aquiline nose and framed by his thick gray hair. But those eyes were engaging, and he never looked away.

I wanted to talk about Kerry's thoughts on the issues relevant to Hispanics and Latin America. But the Abu Ghraib prison photos had just been released, and the subject was inevitable.

"I've seen some of them, and they are very, very disturbing. I think it's going to create enormous difficulties for our objective in the region. . . . My immediate impression is that someone has to accept responsibility and apologize for what happened." The next day, President Bush would do just that.

"I think the way the president went to war is a huge mistake," he continued, agreeing with the 48 percent of Hispanics who believed that "Bush misled the American public about how big a threat Iraq was to the United States before the war began." "I believe the president also broke his trust with us about how he said he would go to war as a last resort, and I think we are paying a very big price for it now."

Eventually we left the subject of war behind us, but Kerry—both in English and in Spanish—continued his efforts to differentiate himself from Bush. Topics such as Cuba and the undocumented immigrants in this country gave him a perfect opportunity to do so.

According to his campaign, "John Kerry supports a proposal that will allow undocumented immigrants to legalize their status if they have been in the United States for a certain amount of time, having been working, and can pass a background check." But the candidate stopped short of calling his plan an "amnesty." "You can call it what you want to," he told me. "It's going to help people be able to become citizens and to come out of the shadows."

During the interview, Kerry emphasized the fact that his proposal allows for the permanent legalization of undocumented immigrants, whereas the Bush proposal did not. "Is (Bush's) immigration reform good for the Latino community?" he asked rhetorically. His antici-pated answer was an emphatic "No."

The two candidates also differed markedly over their positions on Cuba. Like Bush, Kerry unequivocally supported the U.S. embargo. But unlike the president, Kerry would allow Americans to visit the is-land nation. "I think that would help change Cuba," he told me. "We ought to do more kinds of efforts that sort of break down the walls of resistance to Cuba.

"The question is, how do we get the change [in Cuba]?" he con-tinued. Kerry had visited the country once but left without having re-quested a meeting with Fidel Castro. "I think that it is important to encourage people to get there." This idea stands in stark contrast to the rules imposed by the Bush administration, which limit visits by Cuban expats to once every three years and prohibit visits by U.S. citizens for purposes of tourism.

Without much effort, we moved from Cuba to Venezuela. "Is Hugo Chávez already a dictator?" I asked. "I think he is fast, fast on the road to being exactly that," Kerry answered. "Yes, I think he is breaking the rules of democracy. He is fighting against the referen-dum. He is imprisoning and intimidating people . . . Democracy is at risk."

Kerry has never been what you'd call a tireless Latin American traveler. Besides Cuba, he's visited Nicaragua once, as well as Brazil and Argentina. (Ah, and one of his daughters spent a year learning Spanish in Chile.) Does this demonstrate sufficient interest in Latin America? "Yes, I'm super interested in the region," he replied, citing his 20 years in the senate, where he served on various committees re-lated to narcotrafficking and subversive activities. And then came an explanation: "I've probably been to Latin America more times than I've been to Israel or Europe in terms of official business."

Kerry had never visited Mexico. But he grew uncomfortable when I told him that he'd been accused there of being a protectionist for questioning the benefits of NAFTA. "No, I'm not a protectionist," he responded. "I believe we need to elevate the environmental standards, I think we have to elevate the labor standards, all across the world."

We moved from the subject of Mexico on to the southern United States. Kerry knew that the election could be decided by Hispanic voters in states like Florida, New Mexico, Arizona, and Nevada. "I think they could," he remarked. "I think it's entirely possible . . . and that's why I want to talk to Latinos all across the country."

And what about the accusations that Hispanics were underrepresented on his campaign staff? "I think that we've got an extraordinary amount of diversity on my campaign," he said, almost defensively, and he went on to enumerate a long list of Hispanics who had participated in his campaign, including former HUD Secretary Henry Cisneros and Los Angeles councilman Antonio Villarraigosa.

Despite such names, recent polls of Hispanics were sending a strong warning to the Democratic Party. Since Ronald Reagan, every Republican candidate who had won at least 30 percent of the Latino vote had gone on to win the presidency. And the most recent poll—conducted by *The Miami Herald*—indicated that if the election were held that spring, Bush would win 33 percent of the Hispanic vote. Unless history were rewritten—and if the percentages of Latinos supporting Bush remained as they were—the Republicans would again win the White House in November.

Did this worry Kerry? "No," he said, "and I'm not being arrogant about it. It doesn't worry me because many people don't know me yet. The election is six months from now, and [the Republicans] just spent $70 million distorting and misleading people about my record."

Kerry struck me as a complex man. During our conversation, he acknowledged that he and other soldiers "were responsible for the loss of many lives." "How did that affect you?" I asked. "Well, I think that affects anybody who carries a gun in another country, shooting other human beings . . . But I did my duty, I'm proud that I served my country, I'm proud of my service, and I've learned a lot of lessons. And I think that I will make a much stronger commander in chief, a much better Head of State, because I've had the experience of war."

A Catholic, Kerry personally opposed abortion, but he defended a woman's right to choose to have one. Brevity wasn't one of his virtues, nor was simplicity one of his characteristics. Kerry was multidimensional; he was used to approaching problems from many different angles. He was—we could say—a cubist politician. This contrasted sharply with the clear and well-defined lines of his Republican opponent.

Kerry was clearly concerned that Hispanic voters didn't see Bush's faults for what they were. "George Bush is the greatest say-one-thing-do-another president in the modern history of our country," he said. Then he added—in Spanish—that "President Bush has broken almost every promise—almost every promise—to the Latino community."

Time was up, but Kerry didn't want to leave. Standing up, and free from the tortures of his tiny blue seat, he insisted that his campaign would be diligently seeking the Hispanic vote, and that it would be spending much more money on Spanish-language ads. His advisors came in two and three more times looking for him, and when they came a fourth time, Kerry could stay no longer. The campaign hurricane was pulling him back in. I watched as his gray-haired head floated away on a sea of backs.

Another event, another group, and another language needed their candidate.

Cuban Americans could once again decide who lives in the White House. I say "once again" because after the 2000 elections President Bush himself publicly acknowledged that Cuban votes played a vital part in his 537-vote victory in Florida. In other words, Cubans chose the president in 2000, and they would repeat the feat in 2004.

It was no surprise, then, that both candidates made frequent visits to Florida to promote their strategies for accelerating the fall of the Cuban dictatorship. Both candidates supported the embargo. But while Bush tried to tighten the economic noose around Castro—limiting Cuban Americans to one visit every three years and limiting money sent to relatives on the island to $1,200 per year, among other things—Kerry felt that opening up the possibility of visits by all U.S. citizens would do more to bring about the end of the regime.

What was certain was that the Cuban vote would be largely determined by each candidate's stance toward the Cuban dictator, and not by his stance on the economy, the war, or other domestic issues.

Unlike the majority of Hispanics, who tend to vote Democratic, Cubans more often look to Republicans. But this is not to say that the Cuban voting block is a monolithic one. In fact, it can vary from Cuban to Cuban.

Support for the embargo, for example, continued to be strong in 2004. A poll conducted by Florida International University showed that 66 percent of Miami-Dade and Broward county Cubans were in favor of it. But other surveys suggested that the embargo was losing support, especially among the younger generations of Cubans and those who hadn't been living in the United States as long as others.

Kerry's strategy was clear. He wasn't hoping to win the Cuban vote. That would have been quite ingenuous. But if he plumbed the depths of the different generations and political strata of Cuban Americans, he could potentially scrape together a few more votes than Gore did in Miami, Hialeah, Fort Lauderdale, Coral Gables, Key Biscayne, Orlando, and Tampa . . . enough to give him a Florida victory.

Kerry also hoped to take advantage of Cuban disenchantment and frustration at the fact that Bush was the tenth U.S. president to have failed in his attempt to end four decades of Cuban dictatorship. Bush's foreign policy was, according to Kerry, "stunningly ineffective," especially with regard to Iraq and Cuba. Translation: Bush had been unable to bring democracy to either nation.

Cuban American displeasure with Bush surged in 2003 when 12 *balseros* were repatriated to Cuba. This happened shortly after Castro's government arrested 75 dissidents and independent journalists and sentenced them to lengthy and unjust prison terms. Bush's decision caused so much displeasure among the Cuban expat community that his brother, Florida governor Jeb Bush, said "it's not right" to have repatriated the *balseros.*

When I was in Miami several months after this incident, I had the opportunity to speak with Governor Bush, who acknowledged that his difference of opinion with his brother made headlines because "it's not often that I find myself in disagreement with the policies of the administration." Nevertheless, the central issue continued to be how to bring the dictatorship to an end, especially since many Cubans— knowing that Castro has killed, tortured, and imprisoned thousands of his opponents—consider him a greater threat than Saddam Hussein.

"What has the administration done to bring democracy to Cuba?" I asked Governor Bush.

"They have maintained the embargo, which is important," he replied in near-perfect Spanish, before adding that the White House has "exhorted our friends in Latin America and Europe to condemn human rights [violations] in Cuba."

Then I posed a new question. "In light of the fact that no weapons of mass destruction have been found in Iraq," I asked, "how do you explain to the expat community the reasons for liberating Iraq but not Cuba?"

"We don't know if we are going to find such weapons in Iraq . . . this is an ongoing process," he said, responding to the first part of my question before going on to focus on the island. "In the case of Cuba, I think that it's important to keep the pressure on Fidel Castro, because change won't come about with him in power. And I think that the president recognizes this as well."

Ultimately, Castro's fate seems to be a matter of secondary concern.

Restrictions on trips and the monies sent to Cuba are not going to bring about Castro's downfall. Even with a limit of $100 per person per month, Cuban expats continue to send millions of dollars back to friends and family on the island every year. And the fact of limiting visits to once every three years has minimal effects, since thousands of

Latin American and European tourists flock to places like Havana, Santiago, and the beaches of Varadero regardless.

In other words, the measures implemented by President Bush will reinforce the embargo and pacify the more conservative sectors of the Cuban community, but they aren't going to bring a dictator to his knees.

It is true that Castro is going to have fewer dollars at his disposal . . . some $1.5 million less per year, according to a State Department spokesman I heard on the radio. This forced the Cuban government to prohibit the use of the U.S. dollar on the island after November 2004. Now, all the money that reaches the island will have to be converted to Cuban *pesos,* and the dollars will end up in the hands of the government.

But it's not going to be Communist Party officials or military officers or Fidel and his brother who are going to be most affected by Bush's impositions. It's those who already don't have enough to eat. The North Korean regime has shown us that when hunger exists in a tyrannical state, the leaders aren't the ones going hungry. Kim Jong-il's dinners are frequently accompanied by the most expensive of French wines.

Plus, in the case of Cuba, Castro has been able to buy Venezuelan oil at well below market value and sell it on the international market, earning many millions in profits.

Neither strategy—Bush's nor Kerry's—would bring democracy to Cuba. The only thing that the two candidates have shown is that Cuban expats are not a monolithic block, and while they are decidedly anti-Castro, there are other, more subtle divisions.

In the 15 years that I've been living in Miami, I've never seen the Cuban community so divided over an issue as they are regarding visits to the island. Many Cubans—especially younger Cubans and those who have only recently arrived—want to be able to travel freely to and from Cuba to visit family and for emergencies. The Miami airport echoes with the cries of frustrated Cubans who are angry that their families are being divided. "We want to go! We want to go!" they clamor.

Bush and Kerry fought hard over the Cuban vote, but Castro will not be overthrown because of the number of visits that Cuban expats are allowed to make. If they really want to do away with the Cuban dictator, Bush and Kerry know how to do so. But neither candidate was willing to run the risks of paying such supremely high consequences. Nothing changed: the United States had yet another presidential election, and Fidel Castro remained squarely in power.

In the end, the 2004 presidential campaign became a forum for seeing which candidate had the best strategy for doing away with Castro . . . and seeing which one cried out the loudest. But the true fight wasn't the one against Castro; it was the one for the hearts—and votes—of Cuban Americans.

Once it became clear that Kerry would be the presidential nominee for the Democratic Party, a short list of potential vice presidential candidates emerged: North Carolina senator John Edwards, congressional leader Dick Gephardt, and New Mexico governor Bill Richardson.

When compared to the other two men vying for Kerry's selection, Bill Richardson could offer something new and unique: the overwhelming support of Hispanic voters.

The argument went something like this: in a country so politically divided between Senator John Kerry and President George W. Bush and so polarized over the war in Iraq, the Latino vote in five key states (Florida, Arizona, New Mexico, Colorado, and Nevada) would ultimately decide the election. It was Hispanic voters in Florida who decided the 2000 election, and Hispanic voters would decide the next election as well.

The importance of the Hispanic vote lay in its ability to determine an election's outcome despite the fact that Latinos were a minority. In the 2004 elections, neither of the candidates would be able to reach the White House without a significant portion of the Hispanic vote. It represented new territory in the country's electoral panorama.

Al Gore won 67 percent of the Hispanic vote in the 2000 elections, but it wasn't enough. If John Kerry wanted to win in 2004, he needed to claim at least 70 percent . . . and only Richardson would have been able to help him reach that goal.

I met with Governor Richardson in Albuquerque in June 2004, and we spoke at length in Spanish. His mother, María Luisa López, was born in Mexico, and because many Hispanics follow the custom of using the last name of both the father and the mother, he was frequently called Bill Richardson López. He was born in Pasadena, California, but grew up in Mexico City. That's why his Spanish is nearly flawless; he also has a great command of French.

Richardson was a man of the world. Without a doubt, that fact helped him greatly when he served as U.S. ambassador to the United Nations and as a negotiator during international crises regarding Iraq, North Korea, and Cuba, among other countries. He'd been nominated for the Nobel Peace Prize no fewer than four times. He was Energy Secretary under Clinton, and he was elected and reelected to Congress several times. In other words, few politicians in the country had such experience at the congressional, state, national, and international levels as did this 56-year-old former baseball player.

Things could have been going better the night I spoke with Governor Richardson, but he maintained his usual sense of good humor. At the last minute, Kerry had canceled a visit to New Mexico so that he could fly back to Washington for a vote (a vote that—by the way—was never held). The sudden change of plans had deprived Kerry of a chance to participate in an Albuquerque tax event, as well as the chance to have a private meeting with Richardson. That would just have to wait.

I, however, had a question that just couldn't.

"You could be the vice presidential candidate," I told him. "Are you interested?"

"I am," he replied without hesitation. "But I promised the people of New Mexico that I would serve as their governor for four years, and I've barely been in office for a year and a half. So I would have to break my promise to them if I were to do so. I've said that I'm not interested in the job . . . [but] I keep seeing my name on lists. Who knows. It's a decision that Senator Kerry is going to have to make based on three goals. One: does this candidate [for vice president] represent Senator Kerry's views? Two: is this candidate prepared to serve as president should the need arise? And three: how many votes will he bring to the ticket? One of these days, a Hispanic will be the vice presidential—or, perhaps the presidential—candidate."

"Do you think the United States is ready for a Hispanic vice president or president?" I asked.

"I think that it is," he said. "This is a very tolerant country. We've had a Jewish candidate (in Joe Lieberman). And with Kennedy we had a Catholic candidate. And I think the American public is ready for a Hispanic or a female candidate."

Did Kerry and the Democrats realize that these elections would be decided by Hispanic voters? At times it seemed like the Republican Party was much more cognizant of this fact. Nevertheless, Kerry had an option—let's call it the Latino option—that Bush wanted. He could choose a Hispanic running mate, but Bush could not.

A few days after our conversation, Bill Richardson officially withdrew his name from consideration. He did so, he said, in order to fulfill his promise to the people of New Mexico. But everyone knew that in reality, he had done so as a courtesy to John Kerry so that he could tap John Edwards without creating any tension within the Democratic Party.

Kerry had a unique opportunity to make history—and to win the election through the Hispanic vote—but he let it slip away.

John Edwards's voice was still hoarse. The previous night, June 28, 2004, he had spoken at the Democratic Convention in Boston, and his throat needed a good rest. But he was in good spirits—that day was his first as his party's official candidate for the office of vice president, and we were sitting down for a 20 minute chat. He perched himself on the edge of his seat and, smiling, looked directly into my eyes.

Edwards—with his boyish looks and not a single gray hair even at 51 years of age—had an easy, amiable character, and no desire to fall into a series of personal attacks against President Bush. Nevertheless, he didn't hesitate to hash out his clear differences of opinion with the country's chief executive.

"Do you think that President Bush lied about the war in Iraq?" I asked.

"I don't have any way of getting into President Bush's head," he replied. "I know that he had said things that in hindsight turned out to be not true."

"Was he lying?" I pressed.

"I don't know," he answered, "because lying involves intent . . . What I know," he added later, "is that there was authority given to this president and he misused the authority; that's what I know."

Iraq was an inevitable topic. But in this interview I wanted to get Edwards's thoughts and opinions on Latin America, a part of the world that he'd never visited.

Edwards—who told me that he wanted to learn Spanish—came from a state, North Carolina, that had seen many of its jobs go south of the border. And this attorney—the first member of his family to attend college—had openly opposed free trade agreements between the United States and Mexico, Chile, and the countries of Central America.

"Is it fair to label you a protectionist?" I asked.

"No, it's not true," he answered. "The truth is we want environmental and labor standards that allow us to have trade, and help the economies in Latin America and here in this country." Edwards believed that these provisions—environmental and labor standards—ought to be included in new free trade agreements, as well as added to the ones already in place.

From there, we moved on to Cuba.

After labeling Castro a "brutal dictator," Edwards said, "We have to keep the embargo in place, because of [Castro]." However—like Kerry—Edwards felt that "it is a good idea to allow principled travel to Cuba."

And then we left Cuba behind us and moved on to other countries. First, Venezuela:

"Do you think Hugo Chávez has abused his power?" I asked.

"I think he has done things that are inconsistent with democratic principles and that should be of some concern to us," he told me. "But at the end of the day, I know they have a referendum coming up . . . and the democratic process needs to be allowed to work there."

Next up, Puerto Rico:

"Do you think Puerto Rico should become the fifty-first state of the Union?"

"I think that should be left up to the people of Puerto Rico." Nothing more.

Edwards had borne witness to the inexorable process of Latinization that his childhood home was undergoing. He'd grown up in the 1960s in a small town called Robbins, North Carolina. His father was a millworker, and the majority of the population was white. Now, according to what Edwards himself told me, half of the population of Robbins is Hispanic.

"Do you think that Latinos will decide this election?" I asked.

"I don't know who will decide it," he mused in his southern accent, "but I think they'll have an enormous role in what happens with this election. And I think that's a good thing—and I don't mean just good for the Democrats—because the Latino community, I think, represents in so many ways the values of America."

The interview came to an end on a very personal and emotional note for Edwards. He and his wife Elizabeth (who is four years older than he and is also an attorney) had had four children. But one of them, Wade, died in a car accident in 1996.

"Is he the reason why you got into politics?" I asked, cautiously. Edwards collected his thoughts and words and lowered his voice:

"My son Wade was sixteen when he died. He was an extraordinary young man. He and I were very, very close. Did a lot of things together. I coached his team, his soccer team. We climbed Mount Kilimanjaro together. I was very proud of him. But beyond that, with your permission, I would rather keep that personal."

And that's how it was.

• • •

As the candidates continued on up and down the campaign trail, the country continued to debate the costs of and reasons for going to war in Iraq. With only a few days left before the summer 2004 transfer of power from the United States to the Iraqi provisional government, serious doubts remained as to the United States' true motivations for overthrowing Saddam Hussein's regime.

The nonpartisan 9/11 Commission concluded, "We have no credible evidence that Iraq and Al Qaeda cooperated on attacks against the United States." These findings did no small amount of damage to the case for war.

The commission's principle assertion—that there was no "collaborative relationship" between Saddam Hussein and Osama bin Laden's terrorist networks—threw the Bush administration's credibility into serious doubt, at least as it pertained to the war in Iraq. And the doubts were legitimate: if Saddam, despite being a terrible dictator, had nothing to do with the planning and execution of the attacks that cost nearly 3,000 people their lives on 9/11, then why did we decide to attack him?

The Bush administration, recognizing that its credibility was standing on very shaky ground, released several pointed statements to the media: "This administration never said that the 9/11 attacks were orchestrated between Saddam and Al Qaeda. We did say there were numerous contacts between Saddam Hussein and Al Qaeda." But in fact, there was much more to it than that.

The president himself, in his now-infamous May 2003 speech on the deck of the USS *Abraham Lincoln,* a MISSION ACCOMPLISHED banner in the background, quite literally said that, with the fall of Saddam Hussein, "We have removed an ally of Al Qaeda." And Vice President Dick Cheney, in September of that same year, maintained that "there was a relationship between Iraq and Al Qaeda that stretched back through most of the decade of the 90s."

Both Bush and Cheney gave many Americans the impression that there was a tight link between Saddam Hussein and Al Qaeda. In fact, they were so convincing that several polls showed that millions of Americans believed without a doubt that Saddam Hussein was behind the 9/11 attacks. There was no governmental campaign to correct this false impression because, clearly, this confusion helped to reinforce U.S. support for both the war and for Bush.

According to the administration, the other reason for going to war in Iraq was because of the purported weapons of mass destruction (WMD). But no such weapons ever appeared. It seemed that UN weapons inspectors and various other efforts to disarm Saddam more than a decade before had, in the end, been effective. Without any WMDs, it was difficult to make the case that the Iraqi regime posed a clear and present danger to the United States.

There can be no doubt whatsoever that Saddam Hussein was a ruthless dictator, and one responsible for the deaths of thousands of Iraqi citizens. Nor can there be any doubt that the future of Iraq will be a brighter one without him in power. But if Saddam had nothing to do with the 9/11 attacks and if he didn't possess any weapons of mass destruction, the question becomes this: how can we justify the deaths of hundreds of U.S. service people? How can we explain the deaths of what Amnesty International figures to be 10,000 Iraqi civilians? How?

If the war against Iraq had directly resulted in a significant decrease in terrorist acts against the United States and its allies, it would be easier to understand the reason to go to war. But no lesser authority than the U.S. State Department itself publicly acknowledged that there were more terrorist threats and attacks against U.S. citizens in 2003 than there were in 2002.

After seeing the decapitation of three Americans—Daniel Pearl, Nick Berg, and Paul Johnson—in the Middle East, and seeing how U.S. soldiers in Iraq were being attacked day in and day out, the words of French president Jacques Chirac seem to have been proven true: that the war, far from reducing the terrorist threat, had created "a thousand little bin Ladens."

But Chirac and the 9/11 Commission were not the only ones critical of the war in Iraq.

Sixteen months after the first bombs fell on Baghdad, the U.S. Senate Intelligence Committee concluded that the information on which the decision to go to war was predicated had turned out to be false.

"In the end, what the President and the Congress used to send the country to war was information provided by the intelligence community and that information was flawed," stated the committee's 511-page report. And this was no partisan judgment: the report was researched and written by nine Republican and eight Democratic senators. It admitted that the majority of the reasons for going to war were "either overstated, or were not supported by, the underlying intelligence reporting."

Surprisingly enough, the committee's findings were not called into question by the White House. Nevertheless, Bush continued to defend his decision to go to war in Iraq while on the campaign trail.

What is perhaps most interesting about all this is the possibility that if this information had been known before—and not after—the war began, many of the senators who voted in favor of the invasion would not have done so. Seventy-seven senators voted to overthrow Saddam Hussein, but several of these, including John Rockefeller, publicly stated that they would have made just the opposite decision had they known all the facts.

But it's too late now.

The blame for this delay in finding out the truth doesn't lie solely with the CIA and other intelligence and law enforcement agencies. It's also the responsibility of Congress and the press.

If Congress had dared to seriously question the reasons for going to war in early 2003 and not in mid-2004, thousands of soldiers and civilians—both American and Iraqi—could perhaps still be alive today. It is also possible that a more peaceful and multinational method of removing Saddam Hussein from power could have been found. Perhaps. But many congressmen were afraid of being labeled unpatriotic—and of losing their bids for reelection—and so they decided to remain silent.

National media sources were also wrong to not have asked the tough, uncomfortable questions of the Bush administration. Many journalists ate up the official reasons for war as if it were an act of faith. Those journalists were also afraid of being labeled un-American, and so they decided to walk the line that was given to them. Many supposed facts that were printed or broadcast were never able to be confirmed. Still, they were presented as if they were absolute truths.

When I asked the director and producer Michael Moore why his documentary *Fahrenheit 9/11*—which was harshly critical of the Bush administration's belligerent tactics—has had so much success outside of the United States, he replied that it was because the U.S. media hadn't done their job well. If they had, he surmised, films like his wouldn't be necessary.

Possessed of this information, Hispanics reacted decisively against the war. According to the poll conducted jointly by Univision and *The Washington Post,* the majority of Hispanics had opposed the idea of war from the beginning, and the majority continued to oppose the war after it had begun. Why?

There were two fundamental reasons. The first was that a good deal of the information coming from Latin America and Spain was against the war, and this information was able to filter into the U.S. Spanish-language media. Plus, with the help of telephones and the Internet, Latinos kept in constant contact with friends and family in countries whose populations were decidedly antiwar. But the second reason is much more empirical: up until the 2004 elections, 12 percent of the servicemen and women killed in Iraq were Hispanic, yet only 9 percent of the total armed forces is Latino. In other words, a disproportionately high number of Latino soldiers were dying in the war.

The Democratic Party was convinced that it would win the Latino vote by a large margin. The July 2004 poll—conducted by Univision, *The Washington Post,* and the Instituto Tomás Rivera—of 1,605 registered Latino voters in 11 states projected that Kerry would win their vote by a margin of 2 to 1.

Another poll, conducted in October by the same organizations, yielded similar figures. According to those results, Bush had not improved his image among Latinos during the previous three months. Why?

The poll showed several general trends. The majority of Hispanic voters disapproved of the way Bush was handling the situation in Iraq (62 percent), matters of immigration (55 percent), and education reform (46 percent). Only when they were asked about the war on terror did Bush receive a majority of support among Latino voters (54 percent).

The most disconcerting thing about these two polls is that their results were so drastically different than what the exit polls showed on November 2: Bush had done much better than expected among Hispanics.

The divisions within the Hispanic vote were a reflection of what was happening in the presidential campaign in general. The country was divided with respect to Bush, and the polls proved this.[1] In the 20 years that I've lived in this country, I've never seen such a polarized political landscape.

Politics had ceased to be a professional matter and had dipped into the realm of the personal. People either loved Bush or they hated him. During my coverage of the campaign, I frequently met members of both parties who seemed genuinely angry with those who didn't hold beliefs similar to theirs. And the TV ads—dirty, personal, and negative—clearly reflected the campaign's sentiments.

During the campaign, it was not surprising to see President Bush eating *tamales* or enjoying a production of flamenco dancers at the White House, nor was it surprising to hear Senator Kerry giving a long speech in Spanish. The fight for Hispanic voters was nothing new. But what was different about 2004 was the amount of resources, intensity, and organization that both parties put into it.

The Republican Party created an organization called Viva Bush, and not a day went by in which the Puerto Rican "Specialty Media" director and campaign spokeswoman Sharon Castillo did not send out reams of information in Spanish on her candidate's activities and statements.

Additionally, Sharon and her team were in charge of coordinating the multitude of requests for interviews in Spanish-language television, radio, and print media that came in for Laura Bush, members of the Cabinet, and other Republican Party members. One example: George P. Bush, the president's popular and charismatic nephew, cut his honeymoon short so that he could direct the Spanish-language media during the Republican Convention in New York. Former Treasury Secretary Rosario Marín and former ambassador Otto Reich also contributed to a team of dozens of Hispanic spokespersons serving the Bush-Cheney ticket.

"Since his days as governor, President Bush has demonstrated an incredible commitment to the Latino community," Sharon Castillo told me during an interview. "It says a lot that he has so many Hispanics working in his campaign and in his administration." This message was key. The Republican Party constantly reminded voters that Bush had the support of people like Hector Barreto, who was chief of the Small Business Administration, Housing Secretary Mel Martínez, White House attorney Alberto González, and Rosario Marín as treasury secretary.

Three months before the election, the Republicans had spent some $2.4 million in Spanish-language publicity and had produced seven commercials for TV and five for radio. This amount was a significant increase over the roughly $2 million they had spent during the 2000 campaign.

On the other hand, the Democrats had Mexican director of Hispanic Media Fabiola Rodríguez-Ciampoli. "Don't write about me," she asked. "Better to write about John Kerry."

Using three or four daily reports, Fabiola and the rest of the "Unidos con Kerry" team tried to "amplify" their candidate's message for journalists working in Spanish. "The Hispanic vote is vital to this campaign," she remarked. "It's a reality that nobody can deny."

The Democrats had produced four television ads, and at least two for the radio and one for print media. And the $1 million that they had spent in Spanish-language publicity leading up to their convention in Boston alone broke the record set by Al Gore during the course of his entire campaign.

Kerry, his wife Teresa Heinz Kerry, and his vice-presidential candidate John Edwards had given dozens of interviews to the Spanish-language media. Teresa Heinz Kerry spoke Spanish well, with only the slightest of Portuguese accents. Kerry dared to pronounce a few sentences here and there, and Edwards didn't even try. But the access they gave to the Hispanic press went far beyond what Bush had done. Similarly, dozens of spokesmen—like Henry Cisneros, former civil servant Aída Alvarez, and the 18 congressional Hispanic Democrats—participated in so-called "radio tours" and interviews with local TV stations via satellite.

The Democrats' efforts were, at times, supremely sophisticated. They could count on the extraordinary support of the New Democratic Network when it came to promoting their messages. On many occasions, one almost got the impression that it was the NDN—backed by the power of experience and a massive checkbook—and not the Kerry-Edwards campaign who decided what messages were aired to the Hispanic community.

Without a doubt, the NDN knew where the Hispanic voters were. Toward the end of the campaign, for example, they sent TV messages to the key states of Colorado, Florida, Nevada, and New Mexico. Similarly, they sent radio spots to the Hispanic communities in Michigan, Ohio, Pennsylvania, and Wisconsin, and they targeted Puerto Rican voters in cities like Cleveland, Orlando, Philadelphia, and Tampa. Only an organization extremely well versed in all things Hispanic could orchestrate efforts like this.

Fabiola Rodríguez-Ciampoli and Sharon Castillo had followed the model that Sonia Colín had first set in motion back in 2000, when she was serving as George W. Bush's Hispanic press secretary. It was thanks to Sonia that Bush gave more than 100 interviews to Spanish-language media sources and often spoke in Spanish, albeit with many grammatical errors.

Both Viva Bush and Unidos con Kerry reflected the beliefs of both candidates that, in a very closely contested election, Hispanic voters could prove to be the decisive factor. And regardless of who emerged ahead on November 2, Hispanics as a group had already won. Never before had so much money been spent courting the Latino vote (some $9 million on TV ads alone) nor had there been such interest (by the English-language media, as well as both parties and their candidates) in the culture, problems, and aspirations of this country's Hispanic population.

The danger is that this interest will prove fleeting and perhaps opportunistic. But—at least at the time—it was both needed and welcome.

There are times when silence can speak louder than words. And this is precisely what happened during the first presidential debate between President George W. Bush and Senator John Kerry, which was held in Coral Gables, Florida, on Thursday, September 30, 2004. During the 90-minute debate neither candidate said so much as a single word dedicated to international issues and foreign policy.

It would be easy to blame PBS's Jim Lehrer, who moderated the debate and chose the questions. But Lehrer—who did an extraordinary job navigating the debate swirling around Iraq—may simply not have felt that Latin America was newsworthy enough at the time. And I'm afraid this reflects the same lack of interest that other U.S. citizens may have about the region.

Ultimately, blame for Latin America's absence from the debate must fall on the candidates themselves. They'd spent months claiming that the region must be a foreign policy priority, but when the opportunity came for them to show it, they remained silent. Both of them.

What good is it to have a debate about U.S. foreign policy—especially at the University of Miami in south Florida—if you aren't going to talk about the new restrictions of travel to Cuba, the possibility of an immigration accord with Mexico, the free trade agreement with Central America and the Dominican Republic, the civil war raging in Colombia, the threats to democracy in Venezuela, the dynamism of Brazil, the trial of Augusto Pinochet, the economic crisis in Argentina. . . . What's the point?

Miami is a bridge of sorts between the United States and Latin America, but it briefly ceased to be so during the first presidential debate. After 90 minutes, both candidates had the opportunity to speak on any issues they pleased, yet neither one chose Latin America. Yes, they had spoken about Sudan, China, Iran, and North Korea, but nothing was said about El Salvador, Bolivia, Peru, or Ecuador. The message was clear: Latin America wasn't really their priority.

But it would be a serious mistake to ignore Latin America. Just as we were shocked to wake up on 9/11 to learn that terrorists had struck this country, so might we wake up one day with a crisis in a Latin American nation that has grave consequences for us here.

These are the facts: Latin America produces more unemployed workers and immigrants than those with good jobs and health insurance. This fosters violence, delinquency, protests, despair, and a lack of faith in a country's institutions. This also explains the resurgence of Leftists, Populism, and Authoritarianism in the region—with Hugo Chávez being a prime example—as alternatives to democratic systems of government that have failed to provide the people with enough to eat.

The former president of El Salvador, Francisco Flores, said it best: Latin Americans' frustration with high crime rates, poor salaries, and the low prices their exports fetch are putting in danger the very democracies that we've worked so hard to create.

Interestingly enough, on the same day as the U.S. presidential debate, the president of Colombia, Alvaro Uribe, and the president of Bolivia, Carlos Mesa, were in Coral Gables to speak (among other things) about the dangers that narcotrafficking presents to the entire American continent. Suffice it to say that Americans consume the vast majority of the drugs that these and other countries produce. But this grave reality wasn't worth a single mention from either Kerry or Bush.

Since 9/11, the United States has been turning its back on its southern neighbors. And doing so is already having serious short-term consequences. President Bush, for example, wasn't able to secure the support of either Mexico or Chile—his two principal business partners in the region, and who also happen to sit on the UN Security Council—when he decided to go to war with Iraq.

Things look equally gray in the long term. Anti-U.S. sentiments are corroding Latin American societies. This helps to explain their op-position to the war in Iraq and Bush's new policy of preemptive strikes. But it also serves to foster the opinion that the United States is acting in a more and more unilateral manner: keeping with its own interests and without regard for the concerns of its friends and allies.

According to a study done by Latinobarómetro, 6 out of every 10 Mexicans, Argentines, and Brazilians had a negative opinion of the United States. And they weren't the only ones. The study, which sur-veyed 19,000 Latin Americans in 18 countries, showed a clear and growing anti-American sentiment in the region.

Relations between the United States and Latin America are cycli-cal. Sometimes, America embraces Latin America in a suffocating bear hug; other times, it completely forgets about its southern neighbors and acts as if they don't even exist. In 2004, we were experiencing this latter form of treatment.

The first Bush vs. Kerry debate confirmed our worst fears: that as far as the U.S. was concerned, Latin America did not exist. As in the 1950 Luis Buñeul film, Latin America had become *The Forgotten Ones*.

Nor was there any mention of Latin America or Latino issues in the second debate, held in St. Louis, Missouri. But in the third debate, held in Tempe, Arizona, on October 13, both candidates touched on the controversial issue of undocumented immigration.

The moderator for this debate, CBS's Bob Schieffer, said that he had received more emails on this subject than any other.

"I see it as a serious problem," said Bush. "I see it as a security issue. I see it as an economic issue, and I see it as a human rights issue." After explaining why people who earn 50¢ per hour in Mexico decide to come to the United States, where they can earn $5.15 in the same amount of time, Bush said that he was in favor of granting undocu-mented immigrants temporary work permits. But he also made clear that he was not in favor of amnesty, as it would not be fair to those people following legal channels.

"We need an earned legalization program for people who have been here for a long time," said Kerry, "[who have] stayed out of trou-ble, got a job, paid their taxes, and their kids are American. We got to start moving them towards full citizenship, out of the shadows." Clearly, Kerry's stance was a much more ambitious one, but even the most optimistic of Democrats didn't think that it would gain enough support to pass Congress.

Despite this progressive stance on immigration, Kerry's statements with respect to drivers' licenses for undocumented immigrants have had a negative impact on his image in the Hispanic community. In an interview with Telemundo, Kerry said that he would not grant driving privileges to an undocumented immigrant. Statements like this confused many.

Cecilia Muñoz, vice president of the National Council de La Raza, reacted by saying that Kerry's comments with regard to drivers' licenses "tainted" his immigration proposal. They were broadcast throughout the Spanish-language media and demonstrated to many that Kerry was not well enough versed in Hispanic issues, that he did not realize the importance placed on this particular issue by the Latino community.

The Saturday before the election, both President Bush and Senator Kerry appeared on the Univision program *Sábado Gigante.* It represented one more sign that both candidates realized that the Latino vote could prove decisive three days later.

Bush and Kerry were separately interviewed by Mario Kreutzberger—better known as Don Francisco—the host of the world's longest-running variety show. Most Americans have probably never heard of Don Francisco or seen *Sábado Gigante,* but the program began in 1962, and every Saturday, some 100 million viewers tune in across 42 separate countries.

"It's an international phenomenon," Marcelo Amunátegui, the show's producer, told me. "Politicians have to appear on entertainment programs to get their message out. And I'm not surprised that both Bush and Kerry accepted our invitation . . . they know that 'el hispano' will be very important when it comes time to vote."

But why would the candidates accept an invitation to appear on a show full of contests, singing, and comedy? Simply because no other Spanish-language program is so wide-reaching and influential.

"*Sábado Gigante* is, above all, about entertainment. It's a show where people can loosen up," a calm and relaxed Mario Kreutzberger told me in Univision's Miami offices. "Besides being able to express their ideas, the two candidates—Bush and Kerry—demonstrated their personalities . . . they spoke about love, music, God, and their wives. That's important. And they know that they will be treated with respect, seriousness, and reason."

What Bush and Kerry did was nothing new. In 2000, Bush and Gore also spoke with Don Francisco. Appearing on *Sábado Gigante* has become something of an inevitable political rite for U.S. presidential candidates. And in very closely contested elections, this 62-year-old Chilean man could either open or close the door to the White House. In other words, neither Kerry nor Bush could have afforded to say no to Don Francisco.

Don Francisco recorded his interview with Kerry in Philadelphia, on October 19. Two days later, he was in Washington to interview the president. But the White House did something extra that day: it granted two other interviews, to Enrique Gratas of Univision and Pedro Sevcec of Telemundo. And the effects were immediate: Bush's statements were headline news on both channels. They would be the last interviews that Bush would give to Spanish-language media during the campaign.

But in order to try and counteract the impact of these interviews, the Kerry campaign lashed out at the fact that Bush had only granted six minutes to each of them. In a report titled "George Bush's Six Minutes of Fame," Fabiola Rodríguez-Ciampoli stated, "If the Hispanic community does not deserve more than six minutes of the president's time, George Bush does not deserve four more years in the White House. . . . Throughout this presidential campaign, John Kerry has granted more than 20 interviews to Hispanic radio, television, and newspapers, including 20 minute interviews with Univision, Telemundo, and the popular show *Sábado Gigante.*"

But to be honest, neither six nor twenty minutes was enough. It would take much more time than that to discuss the enormous problems currently facing the Latino community. This is the way things are: more than 9 million Hispanics live below the poverty line; more than 13 million have no health insurance; the average family income has fallen by more than $2,500 during the past three years; they have a disproportionately high unemployment rate; they represent 12 percent of all casualties in Iraq; roughly 8 million undocumented immigrants pay taxes yet still live under the threat of deportation; there has never been a Hispanic senator or a Hispanic Supreme Court justice; one-third of all Latino students never finishes high school . . . How could issues such as these be discussed in six minutes? Or twenty?

Even so, the fact that both candidates knew Don Francisco represented a key way to win the Hispanic vote and, by extension, the White House was significant. It was no laughing matter.

And the show on which the candidates appeared was the third highest-rated episode of the year.

Millions of Americans went to bed on November 2 without knowing who the next president of the United States would be. Nevertheless, they had their suspicions: Bush had a 130,000-vote advantage in Ohio, and only a shocking development in terms of the uncounted votes could give Kerry room to hope.

Ultimately, however, Kerry decided that those uncounted votes still would not have been enough, and he conceded the race, first in a phone call to the White House at 11:02 A.M. on Wednesday, November 3, and then again, three hours later, to the nation.

Speaking from the Ronald Reagan Building in Washington, Bush accepted his victory by recognizing the enormous effort made by Kerry and the Democrats, and then by asking for unity among Americans, something very difficult and not at all assured after the most heated and divisive election in U.S. history.

More than 59 million people voted for Bush . . . 3.5 million more than Kerry. Bush consolidated his victory with 51 percent of the popular vote and 286 electoral votes, while Kerry won 48 and 252, respectively.

What was Bush's victory based on? According to many Democrats, it was fear that swung the election to him: fear of another terrorist attack, fear of changing horses midstream, fear that Kerry wouldn't be a solid and confident leader. All of these fears were hammered home by the Republican Party. The election was more about fear than about hope and change.

At an early September speech in Des Moines, Iowa, Cheney said that if John Kerry were elected president, "the danger is that we'll get hit again." Later, he tried to clarify his statement, but many interpreted his words as an attempt to instill yet more fear into the voting population. If Kerry wins, Al Qaeda could strike again, he seemed to be saying.

Exit polls indicated that the two major issues in the minds of voters were terrorism and moral values. Of those polled, 86 percent said that terrorism was, for them, the most important issue of the election. But 80 percent said that moral values was the central theme. And for those who voted for Bush, "moral values" meant opposing abortion and gay marriage.

The United States woke up on November 3, 2004, just as divided as it was the day before. But the new picture of the country—dominated by Bush's 31 "red" states—suggested a nation much more conservative than the Democrats could have imagined. Bush's victory confirmed the perception that people tend to vote for candidates who remind them of themselves.

From the mountains of information that surrounded the 2004 U.S. presidential election, two particular stories deserve to be rescued: the story of Mel and the story of Ken.

While much of America was submerged in the Byzantine details of Ohio election law, the 40 million members of the Latino community were thrilled to learn that two Hispanics—two!—had been elected to the U.S. Senate. No Hispanic candidate had been elected to the Senate since 1964, and there have been only three in all of U.S. history. But history changed on November 2, 2004.

Republican Mel Martínez, a 58-year-old Cuban who served as housing secretary during the first Bush administration, defeated his opponent, Democrat Betty Castor, after a hard-fought and often dirty campaign. Mel, who came by himself to this country at the age of 15 under the so-called Operation Peter Pan, also represents the first immigrant elected to the U.S. Senate.

Before the election, I asked Martínez if he ever dreamed about becoming a senator. "I always think about it; that is the dream," he answered. "My goal is to be a point of Hispanic unity."

The challenge was an enormous one. Because of the extreme diversity within the Hispanic community itself, a true national leader has not emerged—as Jesse Jackson did for the African-American community—nor has a single Hispanic agenda that all Latinos can support.

"Can a Cuban American lead Mexican Americans and Puerto Ricans?" I asked. "It's possible," he replied. And in some ways, he's already done so: Martínez served as the Orange County Chairman. "Many Puerto Ricans, Cubans, and Mexican migrant workers live there," he explained.

One of his main concerns is the disregard that most Americans seem to have for Latin America. "It's a mentality that exists in this country," he explained. "A sense of apathy, a huge lack of interest in Latin America. But I can be the voice of Puerto Rico in the Senate, I can speak about plans for Colombia, Cuba, and Venezuela, and I can improve our convoluted relationship with Mexico. . . ."

Martínez believes that immigrants like himself can achieve anything in the United States . . . even the White House. "If the Constitution were changed to allow immigrants such as yourself or Governor Schwarzenegger to reach the presidency, would you be interested?," I asked. "I'm 58 years old . . . it's no longer for me," he said as a means of explanation. But he immediately added a caveat: "But here in the United States, you never say never."

The other Hispanic who reached the Senate November 2 was the Democrat Ken Salazar. A Mexican American, Salazar won one of

Colorado's seats by defeating his Republican opponent Pete Coors, of Coors Brewing Company fame. The Salazar family has been living in Colorado and New Mexico for 12 generations; in other words, they were here before the lands were handed over from Mexico to the United States in 1848. Ken's ancestors didn't cross the border . . . the border crossed them.

This Hispanic combination in the Senate couldn't have been more balanced: a Republican and a Democrat, a Cuban and a Mexican, a conservative and a liberal. U.S. Latinos—who have suffered a lack of leadership for so long—now have two leaders to fight for them. But the interesting thing is that both candidates were successful in their campaigns by emphasizing their assimilation into the mainstream and not their "hispanidad."

Nevertheless, there is no doubt that Ken and Mel will have their ears finely tuned to the concerns of the Latino community. Ken's acceptance speech in Denver was greeted with cheers of *"Sí se puede . . . sí se puede."* And in one of his interviews after being declared the winner, Mel affirmed that "the first thing we must do is attend to the matter of immigration."

Their presence in the U.S. Senate is a unique opportunity to make Latin America a priority for U.S. foreign policy. No Latin American president or other functionary will be able to visit Washington without passing by the offices of those two Hispanic senators.

Plus, they both have a solid command of Spanish, especially Mel (though it's been said in the press that Salazar is able to converse well enough in Spanish with his 82-year-old mother). After all, *Florida* and *Colorado* are Spanish words.

And whatever issue might affect the continent—from immigration reform to free trade agreements to combating the violence in Colombia or the crisis in Venezuela—will at long last have a pair of true inter-Americans to debate the issue on the Senate floor.

One of the first battles that these new senators will have to confront is the anti-immigrant climate that has swept the country since the 9/11 attacks. We need only to look to Proposition 200 for evidence of this: Prop 200 was approved that same day, November 2, by a majority of voters in Arizona, and it threatens any public official, police officer, or doctor who offers public services to an undocumented immigrant with criminal charges. It reeks of discrimination, ignorance, and racism.

While most Americans voted their fears and saw confusion and uncertainty in the wake of the election, the Hispanic community rediscovered hope. Latino parents now have two more examples they can point to when their children say they don't know what they want to be when they grow up: "If Mel and Ken can do it, *m'ijo,* you can too."

After the 2004 election, Hispanics had 2 senators, 24 representatives,[2] and a governor, Bill Richardson of New Mexico. The challenge has been laid out for the future of Washington: the confirmation of a Hispanic Supreme Court Justice, and a Hispanic candidate for president in 2008.

The 2004 vote is the best example of how Latinos are becoming Americanized. The Latino vote seems more and more to be mirroring that of the rest of the country. According to Roberto Suro, director of the Pew Hispanic Center, "the bottom line to me is that with these results, it's no longer sensible to think of Hispanic voters on a national basis as a core constituency of the Democratic Party."

Before the 2004 election, Latino voters favored the Democratic Party by a margin of 2 to 1. But afterward, Republicans were almost on a par with Democrats: 44 percent voted for Bush and 53 percent voted for Kerry. Hispanics, it turned out, were more conservative than many had realized.

Republicans realized that when it came to issues like abortion and gay marriage, many Latinos' beliefs coincided with their own. In fact, exit polls showed that a full 44 percent of Latinos felt that abortion should be made illegal. This represents a clear increase over the 32 percent of Latinos who felt the same back in 2000.[3]

Similarly, in 2004, 33 percent of Latinos considered themselves conservative, compared with 26 percent who considered themselves liberal.[4] Like the rest of the United States, Latinos are becoming more "traditional." [5] And this held enormous benefits for President Bush and the Republican Party. They understood the conservative tendencies of voters—both Latino and not—and took advantage of that fact on election day.

The most surprising thing about this tendency is that it took many Democrats by surprise. Right up until the election, most polls had Kerry enjoying a 2 to 1 advantage among Latino voters . . . an advantage that ultimately never materialized.

Latino voters are resembling the general electorate like never before. This Americanization of Hispanics on a political level—which is just one more way to measure assimilation into the United States—contrasts sharply with Harvard professor Samuel Huntington, who fatalistically predicted that Latinos were not adapting to U.S. culture and that they were a threat to the country's cultural continuity.

The conclusions we can draw from the 2004 U.S. presidential election are that once again, the race was decided by the Latino vote—this time in states like Colorado, New Mexico, and Nevada—and that the Latino vote (as a *New York Times* headline suggested) was declaring its independence from party lines.

No longer will any one party be able to say that the Latino vote belongs solely to them. As such, the fight to win it will be more heated—and crucial—than ever. As the New Democratic Network said in a November 12 email, "Hispanics are a swing vote. They are no longer a base vote of [the Democratic] Party. . . . Given the size, growth rate, and distribution of Hispanics, it is safe to say that if we do not reverse the gains made by Bush and his team in future elections, Democrats will not be able to become the majority party in our lifetimes, and perhaps beyond."

HOW LATINOS ELECTED BUSH IN 2000

The Latino vote put George W. Bush into the White House. Which is no great surprise, considering that he occasionally refers to himself as "Jorge Bush."

Bush knew that Hispanic voters were different from whites, blacks, and Asians, and he treated them differently. It's thanks to this that he won Arizona, Colorado, Nevada, Texas, and Florida. Put another way, Bush won 5 of the 10 states where over 10 percent of the population is of Latin origin. The 2000 White House was won with an accurately targeted political strategy that proved critical in his victory over Al Gore. Bush had good reason to focus his efforts on Latinos. They—and no other minority—gave him the final push he needed to reach the White House.

Bush has never underestimated the growing importance of the Hipanic vote. When he first won the election to be governor of Texas in 1994, he did so with 29 percent of the Hispanic vote, which was enough to defeat the popular incumbent governor Ann Richards. This 29 percent may not sound like much, but it is a considerable increase over the 23 percent of Texas Hispanics who voted for his father, George H. W. Bush, in the 1988 presidential election. When you are talking about thousands of votes, 6 percent is a huge number.

Bush quickly grasped that his political future in Texas could very well depend on capturing the Latino vote, and during his gubernatorial reelection in 1998 the figure had risen to a surprising 38 percent.[6]

You don't have to be a professional analyst to see that Bush instinctively knows where key votes lie. Since 1994, his strategy has been the same: gain more of the Latino vote. How? Appear on Hispanic television, speak—or try to speak—Spanish, and emphasize the importance of family. Regarding this latter point, Bush had a distinct advantage over his opponents in the 2000 presidential race: his own tightly knit Bush clan, was very much in evidence.

One of the most comprehensive studies done on the Hispanic vote in the 2000 elections—conducted by Adam J. Segal, director of the Hispanic Voter Project at Johns Hopkins University—concluded that Bush and the Republicans spent more than twice what Gore and the Democrats did for airtime on Spanish television. According to the study, entitled "The Hispanic Priority," Bush and his party spent some $2,274,000 on Spanish-language TV ads, whereas Gore's expenditure totaled only $960,000. (Gore's investment was only slightly more than the $909,000 amount that Bill Clinton spent during his re-election campaign of 1996.)

But that's not all. Gore and the Democrats committed a fatal error in deciding to spend absolutely nothing on ads to run on Miami channels 23 (Univision) and 51 (Telemundo). They are the two most watched Spanish channels in south Florida, and their ratings frequently surpass those of the English-language news broadcasts. Bush and the Republicans, on the other hand, spent some $785,000 on paid political ads to be broadcast on Univision and Telemundo's Miami affiliates.[7] Cuban Americans in Miami gave their votes—and thus victory—to Bush in Florida. "In a decision that ultimately may have won Bush the presidency, his campaign and the RNC heavily targeted the Spanish-language television stations in Miami/Ft. Lauderdale, Orlando, and Tampa as part of an aggressive strategy to win the state of Florida and its 25 electoral votes (out of 538 total)," according to Adam Segal.[8]

The critical question, which may sound ironic, is whether Hispanic voters really do watch Spanish-language television. All signs point to "yes," and the numbers are growing. The *New York Times,* using a study conducted by the Pew Hispanic Center, calculated that "about half of Latino voters said they got their news on television in English, 27 percent said they watch English and Spanish news, and 19 percent tune in to Spanish newscasts most of the time."[9] Which is to say, 46 out of every 100 Latinos get at least some of their news in Spanish. This figure is supported by data collected by Hispanic Trends, which puts the figure at 45 percent. But what's really interesting is that, in 1990, only 1 in 4 Hispanics watched Spanish-language news. The figure has nearly doubled. Hispanic viewers of television are multiplying, and quickly.

The impact that Univision and Telemundo had on Hispanic voters is unquestionable. Adam Segal, from Johns Hopkins University, cites Leonard Rodriguez, a former Bush campaign staff member and consultant, who says: "The leader, Univision, draws more than 4 million U.S. viewers to at least one of its national news shows and its credibility was recently proven with an Emmy for reporting. . . . Telemundo is also undergoing phenomenal growth." [10] Pablo Izquierdo, a Hispanic advertising consultant to the Gore campaign, confirms this: "They are crucial. . . . Nielsen has rated the Miami Univision station several times being even more watched during prime time than general market stations." [11]

Both networks' influence is expanding. NBC paid over $2 billion to acquire Telemundo, and Univision—which owns or is affiliated with some 50 Spanish-language television stations—has acquired the Hispanic Broadcasting Corporation (HBC), which encompasses 63 radio stations across the country. The U.S. Department of Justice approved the $3.5 billion transaction in February 2003, thus "paving the way for a behemoth that will dominate Spanish-language television, radio, music publishing and the Internet." [12]

Hispanics are particularly concerned with their children's educations, and with the threats their families face—including drugs, violence, gangs, and divorce—in North American society. It should come as no surprise, then, that both campaigns focused their messages on such themes as how to protect families from high medical bills, school quality, dropout rates, and the problems posed by crime. But differences in presentation were apparent even in the titles the ads used: the Republican commercials were highly personal—"Same as Mine," "How About You?" "The American Dream for Everyone"— while the Democrats' were more direct—"Your Vote," "Issues," and "Faces of North America."

George W. Bush had an advantage over Gore, and he wasn't afraid to use it. His family—his wife Laura; his brother Jeb, governor of Florida, who speaks excellent Spanish; Jeb's wife, Bush's sister-in-law, Columba, who is Mexican; his half-Mexican nephew, Jeb and Columba's son, George P. Bush; and his parents George H. W. Bush and Barbara Bush—participated widely in commercials and interviews throughout Spanish-language media. Gore's family was less influential in this regard: just his wife Tipper and his daughter Karenna—the only one who really spoke Spanish—appeared with any frequency in commercials, news broadcasts, and interviews on Spanish-language television. In the end, not only were viewers presented with a much larger family in the Bushes, but when it came to communicating with voters in Spanish, George P. Bush had a much greater impact than Karenna Gore.

George P. Bush, the half-Mexican son of Jeb and Columba Bush, was a sensation: he appeared on the cover of *People,* more interviews were requested with him than with his father the governor, and I even heard some enthusiastic Republicans remarking that "P" could become the first Hispanic U.S. president. I had the opportunity to speak with him during the 2000 Republican convention in Philadelphia, and it seemed to me that his political interests still had yet to be defined. But his impact on the campaign was considerable: "We spent less than $10,000 on ads and got a couple of million dollars in earned [free] media," said Leonel Sosa, a publicist and producer of the ads.[13] George P. Bush was a more powerful weapon, at least in Spanish.

Bush's 2000 campaign was much more centralized than that of Vice President Al Gore. His adviser, Karl Rove, took the same strategy that Bush used to garner the Texas Hispanic vote and applied it on a national level. And to help him do this, he hired someone who would end up being extremely vital in attracting the attention of Latino voters: Sonia Colín.

It's no exaggeration to say that Sonia Colín was the bridge between candidate Bush and Spanish-speaking Latinos in the United States. Colín, who was born in Mexico City and studied English and psychology at Universidad Iberoamericana, started her professional career as a journalist in Texas. She worked as a producer, reporter, and news anchor for both Univision and Telemundo in San Antonio. And it was there that she got to know Governor Bush; she interviewed him on a number of occasions, and was even twice invited to the Christmas dinner organized for members of the press and held at the governor's mansion.

During his 1998 Texas gubernatorial reelection campaign, Bush found himself fighting to increase his support among Hispanic voters. Once, before a press conference regarding crime prevention in San Antonio, he didn't know how to say a particular phrase in Spanish. He looked around for help, and there was Sonia Colín. Bush asked her how to translate what he wanted to say, and Colín wrote it down on a slip of paper. Bush would never forget this gesture.

After his reelection, Bush got together with Colín for an interview. "What would you do for Hispanics if you ran for president?" she asked. Bush responded with a question of his own: "What would you do?" At the interview's conclusion, Bush asked Colín if she would join with Karen Hughes and Mindy Tucker, his other advisers, and in September 1999, Colín was named spokeswoman and coordinator of the Hispanic leg of George W. Bush's presidential campaign. This was the first time in history that such a position had been created for a Republican campaigning on the national level.

Colín brought things to the table that nobody else in Bush's inner campaign circle could. She had a profound understanding of Spanish-language media in the United States, and the sensitivity to know how to relate to the Hispanics they spoke to. Colín either knew or knew of the main players in TV news, both on the national level and in the smallest towns of Texas, California, Florida, New York, and Illinois. Nobody had ever paid attention to these anchors and journalists— who spoke Spanish, represented tiny media markets, lived highly disconnected from Washington politics, and whose audiences had never voted before in their lives. No one, that is, until Colín began to target them.

"When I started, I honestly didn't have a Spanish strategy for Bush's campaign," Colín told me during an interview for this book. "There was a great need to send information out through Spanish-language media. Everything that came out in English—everything— I wanted to have in Spanish as well. I wanted people to understand what I saw." And what she saw was "a man who would sit down on the sidewalk and eat tacos, who would invite you over to his home as if you were a lifelong friend, and who made an effort to speak Spanish." This simple, familiar, and accessible image of Bush was the one they put out across the Spanish media during the campaign, and it contrasted sharply with Al Gore who, from his position as vice president, seemed cold and distant.

I remember full well how everything that Bush did during his campaign reached us shortly thereafter—in audio, video, photo, or press release format—translated into Spanish and all but ready for the air. For media with few resources and representing smaller markets, the constant bombardment of information in Spanish from the Bush campaign represented a unique opportunity not to be left behind. The only problem lay in getting comparable materials from the Gore camp in order to give our reports a bit of journalistic balance. But all too often, information from the Gore campaign was either unavailable, untranslated, or simply slower in being delivered to us.

Colín worked with a staff of up to eight volunteers and two full-time translators. She had neither an assistant nor a secretary, and her office space was a tiny cubicle. But she could count on the support of over 125 members of the Bush campaign and—most importantly—she had daily contact with Bush's political adviser Karl Rove, his communications director Karen Hughes, his assistant Mindy Tucker, and his financial director Joe Allbaugh. "I spoke with Karl and Karen every day," Colín told me, "several times a day, even." It was always made clear that Rove and Hughes were responsible for drawing up the strategy for targeting the Latino voting community, while her job was to implement that strategy. But Colín opened up channels that Rove and Hughes didn't even know existed.

"My strategies ended up saving the campaign millions of dollars," she told me. "For every dollar we invested in paid publicity, we got three dollars' worth in return. Proper use of the Hispanic media—which gave credibility to our candidate and saved the campaign millions—was very well received by Karen, Joe, and Karl. As a matter of fact, we ended up getting the most extensive coverage in the Hispanic media of any presidential campaign in history."

Even so, Colín soon realized that this wouldn't be enough for Bush, and that the campaign would need to "recruit Latinos who spoke Spanish and agreed with conservative ideas and values." She drew up a list of 60 spokesmen and spokeswomen, including Jeb Bush, Rosarío Marín, Hector Barreto, William de la Peña, Tony Garza, María Ferrer, Abel Maldonado, Henry Bonilla, Al Cardenas, and Mel Martínez, among many others. The idea was that anywhere potential Hispanic voters were, they would have a Spanish-speaking representative of the Bush campaign there as well to convince them to vote in Bush's favor. These spokespersons conducted over 300 interviews in Spanish during the course of the campaign. To Colín, that meant they were reaching "14 million potential Hispanic voters."

Laura Bush was a strong advocate of Colín's efforts. "I'd describe her as being accessible, sensitive, and very receptive to my ideas," Colín told me. "For example, thanks to her help and support, in 1999 the Bushes recorded their first ever Christmas greeting in Spanish, which was then beamed via satellite throughout the Hispanic world." For Colín, this represented another clear example of well-earned publicity.

Colín understood that the majority of U.S. Latinos still have family in Latin America and Europe, and therefore she made sure that media sources in Mexico, Central and South America, and Spain received copies of Bush's speeches in Spanish, and also set up interviews between them and the campaign's Hispanic spokespeople. And when Karl Rove questioned Colín about the need to grant so many interviews to the foreign press, she argued that they represented indirect voters. "Those outside the United States may not be able to vote," she explained, "but a potential voter's grandma or uncle can say to them, 'Hey, Bush speaks Spanish.' " The influence could generate a few extra votes for Bush. And in a race as closely contested as the 2000 campaign was, every vote did prove essential.

Nevertheless, her greatest success was in getting Bush to speak Spanish. They both continued to follow the pattern laid down on that one day in Texas when Bush asked Colín for help: he needed to know how to say something in Spanish, and she jotted the phrase down on a slip of paper and helped Bush practice his pronunciation before the interview. The results weren't always quite what they expected— Bush's Spanish was full of grammatical errors and his pronunciation left much to be desired—but the fact that he was making the effort to communicate in Spanish brought him a great deal of attention. It was particularly surprising that Bush wasn't even worried about his modest command of the language during radio and television interviews in Spanish.

The political instincts of both Bush and Colín led them to suspect that such a strategy would attract more votes. And they were right. Years later, in May 2003, the Tomás Rivera Policy Institute released a study confirming that Bush and Colín's tactics were correct.

"Many bilingual Latino viewers respond to candidates and elected officials who make the effort to speak to them in Spanish," was the study's conclusion, based on the responses of 1,232 viewers surveyed in Los Angeles, Houston, and New York. "Such an effort only matters to about half of respondents, but to those [to whom] it does matter, there is an overwhelmingly positive reaction. Clearly, candidates and office holders need to speak also to the substantive needs of Latinos, but language can offer a tool to make an initial connection." [14]

One of the study's implications was to forever change the way in which politicians attempt to attract Latino voters through their campaigns: "News programming draws bilingual Latino viewers to Spanish-language stations. This finding indicates a strength of Spanish-language broadcasting and a weakness of English-language broadcasting. For policymakers, candidates, elected officials, and others seeking to speak to public issues, Latinos can only be reached through a combination of English and Spanish-language media. English-language media must recognize that they have not been successful in attracting immigrant and other bilingual Latino viewers through their news broadcasts as they have through entertainment programming." [15]

Colín realized this and was worried that Bush would simply learn a few sayings and witty remarks in Spanish. I, for one, was rather surprised when he concluded an interview by informing me that, *"Tengo los ojos de mi padre pero la boca de mi madre."* ("I have my father's eyes but my mother's mouth.") These highly personal comments that combine a sense of humor with knowledge of family are the kind that can bring a candidate closer to a voter. And if they're spoken in someone's native language, the impact is much greater. Plus, few Hispanic viewers expect that a candidate would dare to publicly express the sorts of things that one usually only hears in his or her own home. During that same interview, he also told me, *"No estoy abregado,"* which none of us could decipher save for the possibility that he was attempting to speak Portuguese. Only later, upon reviewing the recording, did we realize that Bush was trying to explain to us that he wasn't a lawyer. (*Abogado* is Spanish for "lawyer," and *obrigado* is Portuguese for "thank you.") Bush would say things like *tarreras* (which doesn't means anything) instead of *barreras,* meaning "barriers," as well as garbled phrases like *"Yo puedo hablar español más bueno que ellos"* (by which he tried to say, in a grammatically confusing way, that his Spanish was better than that of the Democrats). Nevertheless, his responses during Spanish-language interviews usually included effective sound bites directed specifically at Hispanic interests. For example:

> *"El español es un idioma muy grande y muy importante aquí en este país."* ("Spanish is a grand language and very important in this country.")
>
> *"Yo quiero que México y también los otros paises en* Central America, *el sur de América, tienen* economies *que son muy fuertes."* ("I want Mexico and the other countries in Central and South America to have very strong economies.")
>
> *"El sueño es para todos."* ("The dream is for everyone.")
>
> *"Es importante para todos los niños pueden leer."* ("It is important that all children can read.")
>
> *"Tenemos mucho en común."* ("We have a lot in common.")
>
> *"Con ganas."* ("With pleasure"—a phrase he basically used in California, showing his adviser's expertise in Spanish-language regional colloquialism).

Regarding discrimination against Latinos, he told me:

> *"Es una lástima. Es importante que todas las personas que viven en éste país reciban respeto. . . . Sá, ellos han tenido palabras muy feas para las personas hispanas. Y las palabras de Jorge Bush son diferentes. Yo dice que el sueño es para todos."* ("It is a shame. It is important that all the people who live in this country get respect.

Yes, some people have said ugly things about Hispanics. But Jorge Bush's words are different. I say the deam is for everyone.")

And regarding Bill Clinton:

"El presidente es muy preocupado con mí . . . porque él piensa que voy a ganar." ("The President is very concerned about me . . . because he thinks that I'm going to win.")

Bush would usually conclude his interviews by saying, *"Puedo hablar un poquito español pero no quiero destruir un idioma muy bonito y por eso voy a hablar un poquito en español pero mucho en inglés."* ("I can speak a little Spanish, but I don't want to butcher such a lovely language, and so I'm going to speak a little Spanish but mostly in English.") Then he would follow it up with a smile or a good laugh.

The English-language press quickly picked up on Colín's role within the Bush campaign. The *Wall Street Journal* reported that "She was the Bush aid who encouraged him to speak more Spanish in his interviews with the Hispanic press,"[16] while the *Los Angeles Times* described her as "a bilingual spin doctor"[17] and the *Washington Post* reported that "With Colín's help, Bush's campaign runs an almost full service Spanish-language operation."[18]

As anchorman for *Noticiero Univision,* I interviewed Bush twice during his presidential run. I didn't do so more often simply because Al Gore only granted us one interview, and we didn't want our coverage to appear unbalanced. Several of my colleagues—anchors and reporters alike—were faced with the same dilemma: Bush's campaign offered much more access to the candidate—as well as more access to his speeches and presentations via their Spanish translations—than Gore's did, and as objective journalists we couldn't give more attention to one candidate than the other. But I doubt very much that other Spanish-language media outlets, especially those with fewer resources, held quite so tightly to their policies governing journalistic coverage. If they had material about a candidate at their disposal, they used it. It was as simple as that. It's no surprise, then, that Bush's voice was the one that came to dominate the airwaves. Why? Simply because Gore rarely said anything in Spanish.

My interviews with both candidates were never limited to typically Hispanic themes such as immigration and school dropout rates, but rather they included—just as those conducted for English-language media did—everything from the economy to foreign policy. But in Bush's particular case, they were indeed marked by constant jumps back and forth between English and Spanish as well as words in Spanglish, a creative combination of English with Spanish.

During my first interview with the Texas governor and Republican presidential candidate back in November 1999, Bush answered 14 of my questions with a few sentences in Spanish. During my first and only interview with Al Gore in March 2000, the Democratic candiate said only one thing in Spanish to me: *"Me gusta practicar mi español."* As our conversation came to a close I reminded him that in 1998 he had performed something of a Spanish rap—I was hoping that he would give me a small encore performance. But my hopes fell on deaf ears. Gore simply smiled and considered the interview over.

What importance had the Gore campaign given to an interview on the most-watched Spanish news program in the country? It's difficult to know for sure, but Gore did conduct the interview on his own, without the help of any of his core advisers. Bush, on the other hand, was flanked by Karen Hughes and Sonia Colín at all times during both of our interviews.

Nobody should ever vote for a presidential candidate solely on the basis of his ability to rattle off a few words in Spanish. It's important to get to know his message and to consider all the possible ramifications that his policies could have in the life of the voter, his or her family, and their community. But it's also clear that a candidate who can speak a little Spanish, like George W. Bush, has an advantage over someone like Gore whose repertoire includes only a few prepackaged phrases like *sí se puede* ("yes, you can"), *claro que sí* ("of course you can"), *p'alante, siempre p'alante* ("forward, always going forward"), and *comunidad boricua* ("Puerto Rican community") when it comes to elections in which one out of every two Hispanic voters gets their news in Spanish.

Besides the marked differences in their use of Spanish, there were other elements that had a significant impact in the Hispanic press. Access to a candidate and the ability to spend time with him is essential to any journalist. It's the only way to get to know and understand him. The Bush campaign granted access to *Noticiero Univision*—the most important and influential Spanish-language newscast in the United States—almost four months before the Gore camp did. Neither of my interviews with Bush lasted less than half an hour: the first took place in the governor's mansion in Austin, Texas, and the second occurred while on board a train traveling between Oxnard and Ventura, California. Before and after the interviews, there was time to chat with the candidate and for the team to take photos with him. The Gore interview, on the other hand, lasted not 20 minutes and took place in an empty room of a Miami hospital. Gore was tired and hurried, and there wasn't much time for photos after the interview was over. These are, of course, just a journalist's anecdotes, but they do reflect the differences in both parties' dealings with the Hispanic press.

One of Colín's biggest campaign challenges was to get Spanish-language journalists the same access to Bush as those working in English enjoyed. Her daily struggle was to make sure that Bush's schedule included time to meet with Latino correspondants. She calculates that over the course of the 2000 campaign, he gave some 100 interviews to the Hispanic media. Never before had a candidate spoken so much—and in Spanish—with the Hispanic press.

In the end, Bush won 31 percent of the Hispanic vote. Can this be considered a triumph? Yes. In 1996, Bob Dole had won only 21 percent of the Latino vote, so Bush's 10-point increase was significant. And to look at it from another angle, the Bush campaign had cut into Hispanic support for the Democratic candidate, dropping it from the 72 percent who voted for Bill Clinton in 1996 to 67 percent who voted for Gore in 2000.[19]

Sonia Colín had a lot to do with Bush's numbers, and he recognized that. She remembers fondly some of their meetings. *"Ah, ya llegó mi maestra*" ("Ah, here comes my teacher"), Bush would often say when he saw Colín together with her sons José Alberto and Alejandro. "Your mother has made a big difference in my life." "She is a proud mama," he would joke loudly on seeing her arrive at meetings at the governor's mansion in Austin. "Look at her, she is a proud mama."[20]

It's surprising to note that, after the successful presidential campaign, Colín would not be invited to form part of the White House staff. For some reason or another, Colín has decided to keep mum on that issue, even after several proddings from me.

Despite that inexplicable decision by Bush's advisers, Colín says she's happy to have set the stage for a successful political campaign aimed at the Hispanic community. "The most important thing," she told me, "is having set a precedent that future politicians will have to follow: that of giving the Hispanic press the place it deserves."

When the producers of the most popular program on Univision, *Sábado Gigante*—which recently made the *Guiness Book of World Records* as the longest-running show ever—first thought about inviting the two candidates to appear on their show the weekend before the 2000 election, they figured they'd be rejected immediately. But on the contrary, they received a prompt reply from the Bush campaign. "They were very accessible," said Marcelo Amunátegui, the show's executive producer who is of Chilean descent. "They had a key Hispanic member of their campaign, Sonia Colín, and she started looking for potential dates for the interview right away."[21]

It took place at Bush's private ranch in Crawford, Texas. "It's an honor to have you here," Bush said to Mario "Don Francisco" Kreutzberger, the show's host for the past 40 years as well as one of the most famous faces in all the Americas. "I don't usually like to give interviews here at the ranch; besides you, only Barbara Walters has been here." The conversation lasted about 45 minutes; the governor was dressed in jeans, cowboy boots, and a short-sleeved shirt. "Bush always tried to speak Spanish," Amunátegui told me. "He made a great effort to do so, and it seemed to me that he understood a good deal more than he was able to articulate."

The interview with Gore was much more complicated. His campaign was late in accepting the invitation. By which point they couldn't have refused it, as they'd found out by then that Bush had already agreed to do one. Dagoberto Vega, one of Gore's Hispanic assistants, was put in charge of setting it up. At first they proposed an interview in Gore's office in Washington, but the show's producers declined. They wanted a more personal setting. Nor did they like the idea of doing it on Gore's plane. Finally, they decided to do it in New York, but before Don Francisco arrived in the city, the interview was canceled and the camera crews had to return to Miami. The official explanation was "problems with the vice president's agenda." The conflict between the Israelis and the Palestinians had forced Gore back to Washington for an emergency meeting.

The next opportunity was in Cedar Rapids, Iowa, where Gore would be conducting a campaign event. The Univision producers thought it strange that the campaign would have chosen such a site, with very few Hispanics and barely 4,000 people in all coming to see the Democratic candidate. And when everything was set up in a boring government office building and ready to go, Dagoberto Vega came in and informed everyone that Gore had to cancel once again. He was leaving immediately for St. Louis due to the death of Missouri governor Mel Carnahan. Gore, understanding the *Sábado Gigante* team's annoyance at so many changes, came in to apologize personally. "This interview is very important to me," he told Kreutzberger. "I know who you are."

In the end, plans were made for Albuquerque, New Mexico. And there, at one of the airport's gates, the interview finally took place. Gore was dressed in a suit and tie. "There was no way of doing it in Spanish," Amunátegui told me. He also described how surprised he was that Tipper Gore had sent along a videotape for the program to use that didn't place her husband in the most positive light. It showed Tipper recalling their first wedding anniversary and how Gore had forgotten to buy a gift. Instead, he opened up the trunk of his car and produced a box containing a brand new lawn mower. Gore nearly died of laughter at seeing his wife's video, but Amunátegui was surprised that his campaign had released information that made their candidate seem like a workaholic, or even inconsiderate toward his wife.

The difficulties in setting up and actually having the interview between Gore and Kreutzberger reflect clearly the deep-seated problems that the Gore campaign faced: namely, that their candidate had many responsibilities as vice president that prevented him from dedicating 100 percent of his time and energy to the campaign. The constant cancellations with the country's most-watched Spanish-language TV show demonstrated that Gore's participation on *Sábado Gigante* was never a priority for his campaign or the Democratic Party in general, and none of his principal strategists were placed in charge of setting up the interview that was to air on November 4, 2000, three days before the elections. The changes in campaign chairman—first Tony Cohelo and then Bill Daley—also failed to lend any sort of support to Gore's presidential efforts toward Hispanics.

There were many within the Gore campaign who knew that they had to do the interview with *Sábado Gigante,* but I have to ask myself if any of them truly knew why. Bush's campaign always knew that Don Francisco could open the door to the Latino votes that were so vital in such a close race. And this is exactly what happened in Florida.

Janet Murguia, deputy director of congressional affairs in the Clinton White House, was the highest-ranking Latino member of Gore's campaign team. As deputy campaign manager for the vice president, Murguia—the daughter of Mexican immigrants and the current executive director and chief operating officer of the National Council of La Raza—had a responsibility to advise Gore on how best to attract Hispanic voters. But Murguia did not have the authority to redirect the campaign and emphasize the search for the Latino vote.

The Democrats' strategy for winning the Latino vote was never focused in the way the Bush campaign was. The first problem was that the Democrats were split geographically; they were forced to coordinate efforts between the vice president's campaign headquarters in Nashville, Tennessee, and the Democratic National Committee in

Washington. Despite the need to move quickly, decisions involved several meetings and phone calls between these two sites.

The second problem was money. Why did the Gore campaign invest so little money in Spanish-language television—only some $51,000 more than the $909,000 that Clinton spent on commercials during his reelection campaign?[22] "The money that went into courting the Latino community wasn't enough," Murguia analyzed in retrospect. "I certainly felt that it was very important to reach out with Spanish-language advertising but, again, the problem is that they gave us a certain budget and, when it's that limited, you are not able to put together a credible effort to reach the [Hispanic] constituency."[23] Murguia and her assistant couldn't always count on full-time translators and couldn't inundate the Hispanic press with tapes and press releases the way that the Republicans did. Despite an aggresive effort to utilize volunteer surrogates, they did not have the same number of Hispanic spokespersons—60—as the Bush camp did. Murguia recognized that it made a difference between the two campaigns.

The third—and more serious—problem is that the Democrats had a difficult time balancing the needs of their various constituencies. This is an issue in the 2004 election as well, which I will get into later. The Democratic Party encompasses several distinct minority groups, and each one of them clamors within the party for more attention and a bigger slice of the campaign's budget pie. For the Democrats, the Hispanic vote was as important as that of African Americans, Asian Americans, women, or the elderly.

"What we were trying to do was respond not only to the Hispanic community but to African Americans, to women, to nurses, teachers," Murguia told me during that same interview. "We were mobilizing a multiconstituency base, and we didn't have the luxury of the additional resources to invest strictly in the Hispanic community for the wider range of purposes that the Republicans were doing." And to this we have to add the frequent changes in personnel among Gore's campaign directors.

The final problem was that Gore himself had never been obligated during his political career in Tennessee and Washington to develop and implement a strategy dedicated to winning Latino votes. Murguia doesn't feel that Gore's inability to communicate fluently in Spanish was seen as a drawback by Hispanic voters, many of whom are far removed from the days when eating a taco, going to a fiesta, or tossing out a Spanish phrase or two was enough to generate support among the Latino community. "Many people will appreciate the gesture, but I don't think they're going to vote for or against someone simply because he can speak a little Spanish," she told me. "The Latino community is more sophisticated than that. They just want someone who can communicate with them on issues they care about."

This is true. But the question is whether Gore was able to convince Hispanic voters that he understood the so-called Latino experience better than Bush. By virtue of having been the governor of a state that shares a long border with Mexico, trying to speak Spanish, emphasizing family-related themes, and using his nephew George P. Bush in campaign ads, Bush presented himself as understanding the Latino experience better, despite standing on the wrong side of certain other issues important to Hispanics, as his Democratic critics suggest.

A candidate who didn't convey an authentic understanding of the Latino experience, who had difficulty communicating and less money for Spanish-language TV ads, a party divided by its constituent minority groups, the absence of a strategy singling out the Hispanic vote like the Republicans did, an operation that couldn't provide equal information in English and Spanish, and the lack of a greater Hispanic presence and sensibility among the vice president's true inner circle of campaign advisers—all these elements together had negative effects on Gore's campaign.

"We wanted to win," Guillermo Meneses, who worked in the Gore camp attracting Hispanic voters, recently wrote to me. "You have to bear in mind that there was no lack of interest, energy, or enthusiasm among those who worked during the Clinton administration to elect Gore: we gave him 150 percent of our time and energy."[24] But it wasn't enough.

In retrospect, Murguia admits she would change certain things. She sees the need to take crucial, drastic action in certain states so as to reaffirm their dedication to conquering the Latino vote. "Hard choices and strategic decisions must be made in those targeted states. Texas, Florida, California, New York, maybe Nevada, New Mexico, Illinois, Arizona, and Michigan," she concluded. "Political parties must be smarter; campaign resources must be utilized more strategically so they can get the return in terms of the vote that will carry their candidate to victory." But for now, victory for the Democrats will have to wait.

In the year 2000, there were 10 states with Hispanic populations representing 10 percent or more of the total: Illinois (12.3 percent), New Jersey (13.3 percent), New York (15.1 percent), Florida (16.8 percent), Colorado (17.1 percent), Nevada (19.7 percent), Arizona (25.3 percent), Texas (32 percent), California (32.4 percent), and New Mexico (42.1 percent).[25] Any candidate interested in courting the Latino vote will have to focus his efforts on these 10 states.

According to the 2000 census, California—with 10,966,556 Latinos—and Texas—with 6,669,666—contain roughly half of the country's Hispanic population. But the U.S. system, based on each state's electoral votes, removes the emphasis from these totals and places it instead on the percentage of Latinos who vote in every state.

In other words, the importance of the Hispanic vote is defined by its ability to determine an election despite not representing a majority of the voting population. In very close races (such as the one we witnessed in 2000), Latinos can be the ones to decide who our next president will be. They can represent the deciding vote. This is our strength. One hundred and twenty-five years from now—when there are more Latinos than whites in this country—our strength will be one of numbers. But for now, it's the ability to tip the electoral scales in one direction or the other, which forms the basis of Latino power with the broader, electoral base.

In the 2000 presidential election, 5,934,000 Latinos voted out of a potential total of 110,826,000: only 5 percent. In a system based on popular votes, this 5 percent would disappear, drowning in a sea of voters. But the fact that the system is based on electoral votes enables this small number of Hispanic voters to elect presidents. Hispanics are the swing vote, able to determine if a state will go to a Democrat or a Republican.

Bush won five of the states with large Hispanic populations—Arizona, Nevada, Colorado, Texas, and Florida—and lost the other five—California, New Mexico, New Jersey, Illinois, and New York. Yet this was enough to win. How?

Since 1960, California, Texas, and Florida have been key states in presidential elections. Whichever candidate has won at least two of the three states has gone on to win the election. And with a very vocal Latino presence in these ultra important states, Hispanics will surely make their opinions known on a national level.

In 1988, George H. W. Bush won only 23 percent of the Latino vote in Texas, losing the state to the Democratic candidate, Michael Dukakis, who won 76 percent of the Hispanic vote.[26] Of course, it should be noted that the presence of Dukakis's candidate for vice president, Lloyd Bentsen, a Texan himself, had a lot to do with this result.

Arkansas governor Bill Clinton won 58 percent of the Texas Latino vote in 1992, and upped that figure to 75 percent in 1998; Bob Dole garnered barely 17 percent as the Republican candidate.

However, in the 2000 elections, George W. Bush broke with the trend that Dukakis and Clinton had established over the previous 12 years and won 43 percent of the Latino vote in Texas, enough to easily give him the state.[27] This figure is very close to what he received during his successful 1998 bid to be reelected governor.

CHANGES IN LATINO VOTING IN TEXAS

	REPUBLICANS		DEMOCRATS	
1988	GEORGE H. W. BUSH	23%	MICHAEL DUKAKIS	76%
1996	BOB DOLE	17%	BILL CLINTON	75%
2000	GEORGE W. BUSH	43%	AL GORE	54%

This is a clear example of how a swing in the Latino vote can change the course of an election. When Latinos cast their votes in favor of Dukakis and Clinton, both went on to win the state at large, but when George W. Bush convinced 4 out of every 10 Latino voters to side with him, the result was enough to win the state for him. He didn't even need to reach the 50 percent mark.

BUSH IN FLORIDA

The Republicans have always felt a sense of security in Florida. In 1992, George H. W. Bush won two-thirds of the Hispanic votes there, easily taking the state from Clinton. The loss wasn't fatal for Clinton— he would go on to win the election—but nevertheless he felt stung by this defeat and resolved to change things in 1996.

In the 1992 elections, Clinton won only 31 percent of the Latino vote in Florida. The Cuban American community was afraid that he would lift the U.S. embargo on Castro's Cuba and—even worse—that he would accompany that decision with a visit to Havana, similar to the trip that Richard Nixon took a generation before to China. Neither of these things would happen. After a notable increase in the number of Cuban refugees risking their lives on makeshift rafts in the Florida Straits, the U.S. and Cuban governments established a new immigration agreement: all those refugees detained on the high seas would be sent back to Cuba, while those who reached U.S. soil would be allowed to stay permanently. This drastically reduced the influx of Cuban refugees, and it also reduced the already scant support that Clinton had among the Cuban exile community in south Florida.

But in February 1996, Castro's regime committeed a grave mistake when MiG fighter jets shot down two light aircraft operated by the organization Hermanos al Rescate ("Brothers to the Rescue"). All four crew members were killed. The Clinton administration had to do an abrupt about-face and put its purported plans for increased ties with Cuba on hold while it considered various methods of retaliation, including possible strikes against Cuban military bases. Ultimately they decided to endorse the Helms-Burton law, which reinforced the embargo imposed against the island nation. Although many Cuban Americans had wanted a stronger response, Clinton had managed to slightly reverse the negative light in which some sectors of the Cuban exile community perceived him. In the 1996 elections, he garnered 42 percent of Florida's Hispanic vote. He also won the coveted Miami–Dade County, as well as the state at large: something no other Democrat had been able to do since Jimmy Carter in 1976.

Clinton's hands-off attitude toward Cuba didn't change much during the rest of his presidency. During an interview I conducted with him in the White House in May 1997, I asked why China—just as much a dictatorship as Cuba—received such drastically different commercial treatment than the regime in Havana. "We had—just recently—people shot at in the skies and murdered," Clinton replied, referring to the MiG attacks on the Hermanos al Rescate planes. "As far as I know, China has not murdered any Americans recently. If they did I would have a different attitude about our trading relationship." [28] If the Castro dictatorship had not shot down these planes, is it possible that the trade embargo would have been lifted? Perhaps. But all that now lies in the realm of speculation.

The political reality is that by hardening the U.S. policy toward Cuba, Clinton significantly increased his support among Cuban Americans and, with their new votes, he carried the state of Florida in 1996. But this peaceful digression between Clinton and the Cuban community would not last long, and in the end, it was Al Gore who would pay the consequences of the clash between the Cuban community in south Florida and the Clinton administration.

THE ELIÁN SAGA

On November 25, 1999, a 5-year-old boy was rescued off the coast of Florida. He would turn 6 shortly thereafter, and the whole world would come to know his name: Elián González. He was one of only three survivors of a 15-foot aluminum craft that sank in the Florida

Straits, and he spent some 50 hours in shark-infested waters with only a tire for flotation until he was rescued by two fishermen. Eleven others who were on board his boat died, including his mother Elisabet.

Elián's uncle, Lázaro González, and his family temporarily took charge of the boy. But his father, Juan Miguel González, claimed that his son had left Cuba without his authorization—that he had been effectively kidnapped by his mother—and he wanted him returned to the island immediately. What happened next was a drama so intense that it ended up costing Al Gore the presidency.

Lázaro and his family wanted Elián to stay and live in Miami, as were his mother's wishes. But in the first of many judicial decisions, the Immigration and Naturalization Service decided that only the father, Juan Miguel González, could decide what was best for Elián. And the father, still in Cuba, wanted his son back.

Four days after the INS decision, Channel 23 of the Univision network conducted a survey in Miami that showed how sharply divided the city and the country were over the case: 86 percent of Hispanics who responded—mostly Cuban Americans—wanted Elián to stay in Miami, but 70 percent of non-Hispanic whites and 79 percent of blacks agreed with the INS and wanted the boy to be returned to his father in Cuba. Many subsequent surveys would be conducted, and each one invariably reflected the ocean of difference that separated the opinion of south Florida's Cuban exiles from that of the rest of the United States, and even various parts of the world.

The dilemma was whether to leave the child in Miami, separated from his father, or return him to life under a dictatorship. Those who opposed returning Elián to Cuba argued that it would be tantamount to sending a Jew back into Hitler's Germany. Those who wanted him to be reunited with his father—who would eventually come to the United States for him—said that, in the mother's absence, the only legal option was to send him back to Juan Miguel. An endless number of marches, protests, and debates over the child's fate ensued, while the surveys continued to pit the Cuban exiles against the rest of the world.

Faced with the González family's refusal to turn over the child voluntarily, the Clinton administration decided to remove him by force from their home in the Little Havana section of Miami. At 5 A.M. on Saturday, April 22, 2000, Attorney General Janet Reno gave the order to dozens of federal agents—some of whom were heavily armed—to go in after Elián. The agents made their way past the 30-odd protestors who had camped outside the home in the hopes of preventing such a raid, broke into the house at 2319 Northwest Second Street, and carried Elián off. The abuse of force and the terror wrought on the boy's face as he faced the armed agents was evident in the thousands of photographs and video clips that were taken. The commando-style operation lasted no more than five minutes.

Elián was then flown from Miami to Andrews Air Force Base outside Washington, where he could see his father for the first time in five months. At 5:30 A.M., President Clinton was informed that the mission had been a success. Later, justifying his decision, Clinton told the press, "There was no alternative. . . . The law has been upheld, and that was the right thing to do."[29] A few days later, Elián would return to Cuba with his father.

An Internet poll conducted by the *Miami Herald* showed that 79 percent of those who responded disapproved of the manner in which the Clinton administration removed Elián from his relative's house in Miami.[30]

It's interesting to note that the Bush campaign kept rather quiet during the whole Elián crisis. Statements from the Republican candidate were careful and measured, although the Cuban community never considered that Bush would be in favor of returning Elián to Cuba. "We wanted to keep our distance from Elián," Sonia Colín told me. "It was a highly controversial issue; the governor wanted to see how things would play out, and we didn't want to change our entire strategy over one single event."

Al Gore, on the other hand, was thrust into a very uncomfortable situation. He wanted at least a share of the Cuban American vote, perhaps even equal to that which Clinton received in 1996. But he didn't want to publicly question his boss, the president, or stray too far from the party's official stance. On March 13, 2000—nearly six weeks before Elián was forcibly removed from his relatives' house in Miami—I asked Gore what his position was. His response was laden with ambiguity. He told me that an audience ought to be convened to determine custody of the child, and that the final decision shouldn't be made by politicians or immigration officials. "The child's mother lost her life trying to secure Elián's freedom," he told me. "I think that deserves our respect."

Gore never dared to state unequivocally that Elián should remain in the United States, and this linked him inextricably with Clinton's stance in the minds of south Florida's Cuban community. Nor did Gore ever criticize Clinton's decision to remove Elián from his relative's Miami home and allow him to return to Cuba with his father. In the Elián case, Gore didn't distance himself from Clinton at all.

As the Democratic candidate for president, Gore definitely had the freedom to take a different stance on the Elián case than Clinton's. But he didn't do so. And within his own campaign, the issue was debated to exhausting lengths. "It was a big issue," Janet Murguia told me. "Some people argued that since everything had occurred in April, it would become less and less of a factor by the time of the elections in November. But there were some folks who felt that the vice president's position could hurt him in Florida."[31]

"Recuerda a Elián"—"Remember Elián"—was the message broadcast by the most traditional members of the Cuban exile community on Election Day. And Elián was remembered, with a punishing vote against the Clinton administration in general, and Al Gore in particular.

Nevertheless, the Elián case was not what cost Gore Florida. The error was in the campaign's decision not to invest money in Spanish-language television in Miami. That was the fatal mistake. Their decision not to spend money in Florida was based on many factors, including—of course—Elián, and the fact that Cuban Americans tend to vote Republican. For the Gore camp, the more important question was how much money would it take to change this trend, as well as the minds of the Cuban American exile community. The Gore camp decided that this amount of money would be better spent elsewhere—for example, New Mexico—and they stopped battling for Florida. The end result favored Bush.

"I think less money was invested in Florida than should have been," reflected Murguia. "There were definitely split views within the campaign, within the Democratic party. . . . If we had poured more resources into Florida instead of pulling them out, would that have been enough to make a difference in such a close election?"[32] We will never know.

ELECTION NIGHT

At 7:49 and 40 seconds into the evening of Tuesday, November 7, 2000, NBC declared Gore to have won the state of Florida. Shortly thereafter, the result was confirmed by CBS, ABC, CNN, Fox News, Univision, and Telemundo. With Florida, Gore was all but assured the presidency. But his victory would not last long. At 2 A.M. on Wednesday, November 8, the official results from Volusia County came in, and the tables had turned. Six minutes later, Fox News declared that Bush had, in fact, won Florida, and the call was soon confirmed by CBS, NBC, and ABC.[33]

After these developments, Gore—who was staying at the Loews Hotel in Nashville—had a two-minute phone conversation with George W. Bush, conceding his defeat. But, as they spoke, the number of votes separating the two candidates continued to dwindle. An hour later, as Gore was about to make his public concession speech at Nashville's War Memorial Plaza, one of his assistants informed him that Florida was in fact too close to call. Gore then returned to his hotel and called Bush a second time. "Circumstances have changed dramatically since I first called you," Gore told him barely an hour after their previous conversation. "The state of Florida is too close to call." "You do what you have to do," was Bush's reply.[34]

TV news stations—both in Spanish and English—had to admit that they'd spoken too soon, and released a new headline: neither Bush nor Gore could be definitively said to have won Florida. To be fair, the stations had based their calls on exit polls conducted by the well-respected Voters News Service (VNS). Their data was reputed to be next to infallible. Florida proved to be the exception.

The central mistake was that VNS had calculated Cuban Americans as representing 2 percent of the voting population, when in reality the figure was 8 percent. In other words, according to their numbers, there were only 120,000 Cuban voters in the entire state when, in reality, there were over 200,000 in Miami–Dade County alone. Where did their data come from? Why was the percentage of Cuban American voters so wrong?

By underestimating the number of Cuban voters, VNS erroneously concluded that Gore had won the state at large. Its exit polls are what led the various news services to declare Gore the winner shortly before 8 P.M. on November 7, 2000. But the exit polls were not, in fact, representative of the true electorate. Therefore, as the real figures began to flow in, they undermined the original predictions and the whole system began to buckle.

Cuban Americans don't vote the way most Hispanics do. According to analysis conducted by Sergio Bendixen, an expert in Hispanic affairs, 78 percent of Cubans voted for Bush in the 2000 election.[35] This figure is even greater than the number of Hispanics who voted for Bush in all of Florida (61 percent). Florida is a state undergoing rapid diversification, and its Latino community stems from many different Hispanic roots. These subtle differences between the Cuban and non-Cuban electorate also contributed to the VNS's imprecise calculations.

The initial chaos drew out into 36 days of legal battles and electoral affairs. Finally, a little before 10 P.M. on Tuesday, December 12, the U.S. Supreme Court ruled that there would not be a recount of the votes cast in Florida, thus effectively giving the election to Bush by the impossibly thin margin of only 537 votes.

Jeffrey Toobin, a graduate of Harvard Law School and author of the book *Too Close to Call,* concluded that "the wrong man was inaugurated on January 20, 2001" and that we had just witnessed "a Supreme Court opinion that is doomed to infamy."[36] Would a recount of all the Florida ballots have given Gore the victory? We may never know the answer to this. Others, such as Janet Murguia, ask "How many votes were thrown out?" She contends that uncounted votes cast in predominantly African American counties could have produced a significantly different outcome. All this is debatable.

What isn't debatable is that the Bush campaign focused on winning Hispanic votes in several key states, and in particular on winning the Cuban vote in Florida. And in this endeavor, it was successful. The Cuban American community voted overwhelmingly in favor of Bush. The analyst Sergio Bendixen calculated that 50,000 more voted for Bush than had voted for Dole in 1996. This figure represents the "vote of punishment" for the Clinton administration's handling of the Elián case.

Bendixen assures us that we cannot say definitely that it was the Cuban community who put Bush in the White House. "The Cubans have sold the idea that they were the ones who gave Bush the presidency," Bendixen told me once in an interview. "But more sophisticated experts know how things are in reality: of the three million votes cast in Florida, at most only 300,000 were done so by Cubans." Nevertheless, the vast majority of these 300,000 votes went in favor of Bush.

The Supreme Court's decision was out of Bush's hands, just as a recount of Florida's African American votes was beyond Gore's control. What was within the candidates' power was the strategy to go after Hispanic votes where they were needed. This was the Republican strategy. "There's no doubt that the Republican party made the Hispanic vote a priority target," affirmed Bendixen, who has worked closely with the Democratic Party in the past. "They made a much more organized, concerted effort than the Democrats did."

Bush won 61 percent of the Latino vote in Florida, 43 percent in Texas, 33 percent in Colorado, 34 percent in Arizona, and 33 percent in Nevada.[37] These figures are no coincidence, nor were they dependent upon a Supreme Court ruling.

Bush's math was correct. Since 1970 (when the statistical category of "Hispanic" was first counted in the U.S. census), no candidate has won the presidency without winning at least 30 percent of the Latino vote. Jimmy Carter defeated Gerald Ford in 1976 with 76 percent of the Hispanic vote; Reagan won 33 percent and 37 percent in 1980 and 1984, respectively, to defeat Carter and Walter Mondale; Bill Clinton won 61 percent and 71 percent in 1992 and 1996, respectively, to defeat George H. W. Bush and Bob Dole; and finally, George W. Bush won 31 percent of the Hispanic vote in his dramatic race against Al Gore.

The facts are quite simple: Bush won the 2000 presidential election thanks to the Hispanic vote in Texas, Colorado, Arizona, and Nevada, and to the Cuban American vote in Florida. He courted these voters with fervor. The 537 votes that gave Florida to Bush were cast by Cubans. And Bush agrees with this conclusion.

On Friday, February 16, 2001, during the first bilingual television interview he gave as president—from President Vicente Fox's private ranch in Mexico—I asked him: "Do you think that you won the election because of the Cuban vote in Florida?"

"Yes," he replied. "I think they had a lot to do with it. And I'm most proud and very thankful and very grateful for the strong support I received *de los cubanos en el estado de la Florida. Y por eso no voy a olvidarlos*" ("from the Cubans in Florida. And that's why I'll never forget them").

Bush said these last 16 words in Spanish, of course. His thank-you, in the language preferred.

CHAPTER TWO

THE NEW NEIGHBORS NEXT DOOR

IN THE UNITED STATES, new Hispanic neighbors aren't anything like the stereotypical characters portrayed on *Latino USA, I Love Lucy,* or *The George Lopez Show.* New Hispanic neighbors are so hard to classify that oftentimes we don't even know how to identify each other.

The problem is that the term "Hispanic"—or *Hispano*—can refer to a girl from Michoacán, Mexico, who illegally crossed the Río Bravo (or Grande, as it is referred to in the United States) just as easily as it can refer to a U.S. passport–carrying Puerto Rican whose family has lived in New York City for years. Nor is it a question of race: the U.S. Census Bureau reminds us that the word "Hispanic" does not fall under the same category as "Caucasian" or "African American." Hispanics can be members of any race. New Latino neighbors could be anything from black Dominicans to white Chileans. "Latinos are not on a straight track to becoming whites, but they are not indelibly marked as nonwhite outsiders, either," writes Robert Suro, director of the Pew Hispanic Center, in his book, *Strangers Among Us.* "They challenge the schematic of racial identity that Americans use for a wealth of activities."[1]

Nor is it a question of social class. Within the Latino community, we find everything from members of Spanish royalty to former dwellers of *favelas,* the poorest and most dangerous neighborhoods in Brazil. And it's not a question of money, either, for just as many Colombian multimillionaires as Salvadoran *campesinos* have fled the violence in their own countries to settle here.

The extremely wide net cast by the terms "Latino" or "Hispanic" includes the descendants of Mexican families who lived in modern-day Texas and California before these lands were taken over by the

United States in the middle of the nineteenth century—and the young Honduran man who just yesterday may have decided to stay here after his student visa expired. The Hispanic community also includes Cubans who've fled Castro's dictatorship, as well as Nicaraguans and Venezuelans who could no longer stand life under the Sandinista or Hugo Chavez regimes.

Bill Richardson, who became the governor of New Mexico in 2002, is just as Hispanic as a Nuyorican or the newest member of an East L.A. gang. The Chilean writer Isabel Allende—who lives in San Francisco—is no more or less Hispanic than the thousands of young Latinos who drop out of high school each year. There are Hispanics who only speak Spanish, and those who only speak English. There are very Latin Americanized Latinos, and there are those who are very North Americanized. In the 1991 war against Iraq, one out of every two Latinos supported U.S. military intervention while the other one questioned it. Many Latinos are proud of their Mexican, Cuban, or Puerto Rican roots; others are ashamed of them. Some can trill their Rs with force, others do so more softly, and still others can't correctly pronounce such words as *perro,* the Spanish word for dog.

To be Hispanic is to be many things at once—and to cease to be others.

The majority of Hispanics in the United States don't wear sombreros, have beards, or sing like famous Mexican crooners Pedro Infante or Luis Miguel. We don't joke around like comedians Cantinflas or Alvarez Guedes, we don't dance when we walk, we don't cook pork and lamb on our patios, or have a carpentry or paint shop at home. We don't wear guayaberas to the opera, we're not all undocumented immigrants, and we don't all quit school before finishing the twelfth grade.

You won't usually find workshops set up on our patios or exotic flora and fauna in our bathrooms, and it's even less likely that you'll find us digging pits in our backyards to cook meat in. We're just as likely to be astronauts or investors as we are to be farmers or restauranteurs. We keep our money in banks, not under our mattresses. We invest in securities and have 401K plans so that we can retire when we reach our sixties, just like everybody else. A good number of us speak both English and Spanish. We enjoy basketball, baseball, and football, just like any other "American." We watch more TV than we should, including the Super Bowl (a.k.a. the *Super Tazón*), the Oscars and Grammys (in Spanish), the news (also in Spanish), and soap operas from Mexico, Colombia, Venezuela, and Brazil. And we support our troops, wherever they may be. We may have doubts about the true reasons for starting a war, but once committed, we respect the bravery of a soldier in the battlefield more than the thought given to the decision that got him there.

We're not all unskilled laborers or curio dealers. There are over 1.2 million businesses with Hispanic owners, a figure that rose by 30 percent between 1992 and 1997.[2] In the year 2000, over 573,000 Hispanics were lawyers or doctors, or had masters or doctorate degrees.[3]

It's absurd to categorize us according to television and movie stereotypes, especially because we aren't even sure ourselves of the category we fit into. Are we Hispanics or Latinos? Hispanic Americans or Americans of Hispanic origin? Mexican Americans? Portocubanoamerianos? Latin Americans living in the United States or immigrants? A U.S. resident or a U.S. citizen born in Havana? An illegal Dominican, a Venezuelan tourist with an expired visa, or a potential resident? About to be deported or about to be granted documents? American, North American, or U.S. citizen? Born here but a citizen elsewhere, or vice versa? A Mexican in the United States, or a Mexicanized American? White or Hispanic? White and Hispanic? Black or Latino? How about an African American Latino? A mestizo with a green card, a Guaraní Indian with a work permit, or an exiled Guatemalan politician with temporary protection? First-generation or third? Chicano or Pachuco? A New Mexican Mexican, or simply a New Mexican? *Salvatrucha* (from El Salvador), *pana* (from Venezuela), *o cuate* (from Mexico)? Nuyorican (Puerto Rican New Yorker), Nudominican, Nuecuadorean, or Numexican? Gringo or Americanized? Born in Juárez and living in Arizona, or from Mexicali and living across the border? From the South or from the North? A southern Northerner or a northern Southerner? From this side of the Río

Grande or across the Río Bravo? Soaked in the Bravogrande and dried in the California Desert? Come on rafts, on the Mariel boat lift, in a yawl or a speedboat? Political prisoner or economic refugee? What the hell are we?

WHO ARE THESE PEOPLE?

The twin towers had fallen two days ago. The feelings of disbelief and vulnerability were beginning to show themselves in stammering speech, unfinished sentences, nervous tics, crying, and trembling legs that could barely support our weight.

On the night of September 13, 2001, after a 22-hour drive from Miami to New York, I sought refuge in a little Italian restaurant in lower Manhattan. We had just finished *Noticiero Univision*'s usual 6:30 live evening broadcast, and joining me for dinner was our New York correspondent, Blanca Rosa Vilchez, and *Noticiero Univision*'s weekend anchor, María Antonieta Collins. We were devastated. We couldn't believe what had happened. Blanca Rosa sipped her glass of merlot and—still trembling with fear—told us how she had nearly been crushed when one of the twin towers fell.

The restaurant had a smallish patio that overlooked the street, and the waiters had done an extraordinary job of giving the place some semblance of normalcy: there was bread and butter on the table, Pellegrino in the glasses, and our orders were exactly right. Seated at a table along one edge of the patio, in plain view of everyone, was the actress Sarah Jessica Parker from the HBO series *Sex and the City*. She has one of those faces that makes viewers think instantly of New York City. Soon she was joined by a friend, and the two of them chatted away without concern. Nobody bothered them.

In the distance, the rubble from the twin towers continued to smolder. People came and went with their eyes lost in the memory of an urban landscape that no longer existed. But to our surprise, life had not stopped in New York. I doubt it ever could.

As they brought out our dessert—a tiramisu with three forks—

a few Latinos and immigrants walking past the site recognized us—
"Hey, you're from Channel 41, right?"—and thus ended our chance
to enjoy the rich cake in peace. They cheerfully asked for our autographs and if they could take a few photos with us, and we agreed
with pleasure. Channel 41, Univision's New York affiliate, is one of
the most-watched stations, and it competes regularly with English-
language channels like ABC, NBC, and CBS for the top spot in the
ratings war. We weren't surprised, then, that someone would know
who we were.

What was odd about the situation was that this ritual of pictures
and autographs went on for several minutes without ever including
the truly famous person—the real celebrity—in the restaurant: Sarah
Jessica Parker. Before we got up to go, we noticed that the actress
asked the waiter something, and the two of them turned to look at us.
One would expect the protagonist of a popular TV series in English
to attract more attention than a group of Spanish-speaking reporters,
but this wasn't the case here. Something was changing. New York was
changing, and it wasn't just because of terrorism.

"Who are these people?" That's the question I'm hearing more
and more often during my travels across the United States.

During the book tour to promote my autobiography *No Borders:
A Journalist's Search for Home,* I was able to visit the country's major
Hispanic cities, including Dallas, where I gave a presentation at the
city's main library. Unfortunately, the library hadn't been set up to
handle such a large crowd, and the police had to be called in to preserve order. "Who are these people?" I heard one surprised Anglo-
Saxon officer exclaim.

The same phenomenon repeated itself at a Borders bookstore in
Denver and at a Barnes and Noble in Houston, which was inundated
with some 3,000 people. Nobody had expected that so many Latinos
would be interested in reading a Spanish-language book. The important thing here was not the book, but rather the incredible presence
that Hispanics have in this country's cities and suburbs. I heard "Who
are these people?" again in bookstores in Texas and Colorado, where a
couple of disoriented Americans struggled to understand what was

going on. "Who are they?" they wanted to know, looking concerned. "Where did they come from?"

We are, in short, the New Americans. We are the new next-door neighbors.

WHAT ALEXIS DE TOCQUEVILLE DIDN'T SEE

When the young Frenchman Alexis de Tocqueville visited the United States in 1831, one of the things that most stuck him was the relative similarity in rights, obligations, and privileges of its inhabitants. "In the United States, nothing struck me more forcibly than the general equality of condition among the people," he wrote in his book *Democracy in America*. "The more I advanced in the study of the American society, the more I perceived that this equality of condition is the fundamental fact from which all others seem to be derived."[4]

This sense of equality that made such an impression on the noble French traveler was maintained despite the constant influx of immigrants. "Every citizen being assimilated to all the rest, is lost in the crowd, and nothing stands conspicuous but the great and imposing image of the people at large,"[5] he described in the two volumes of his observations, published in 1835 and 1840.

But this process of assimilation was possible because of two factors that new immigrants had in common with previous U.S. inhabitants: language and a tradition of respect for free and independent institutions. "The emigrants who came at different periods to occupy the territory now covered by the American Union differed from each other in many respects. . . . These men had, however, certain features in common, and they were placed in an analogous situation. The tie of language is, perhaps, the strongest and the most durable that can unite mankind. The emigrants spoke the same tongue; they were all offsets from the same people." The second unifying element that Tocqueville commented on was, "At the period of the first emigrations, the township system, that fruitful germ of free institutions, was deeply rooted in the habits of the English."[6]

The contrast with the current situation couldn't be more striking. Immigrants continue to arrive, just as they did at the beginning of the nineteenth century. And many certainly do become assimilated, Americanized, and lost in the multitudes, as Tocqueville observed. But today's new immigrants—contrary to the case of the English and, later, the Irish—come neither from places where English is the predominant language, nor from countries where, in contrast with today's Latin America, free, independent, and democratic institutions typically govern public life. And in a display of cultural defiance, they maintain certain aspects of their countries of origin in their adoptive home, especially the Spanish language and Latino values and cultural norms.

The Mexican writer Carlos Fuentes—himself a fine example of a modern Tocqueville, through his tireless travels, his powers of observation, and his unparalleled critical eye—sees the United States today as a multiethnic, multicultural country, marked by *mestizaje,* a mixture of races and languages. "Los Angeles is now the second largest Spanish-speaking city in the world, after Mexico City, before Madrid and Barcelona," he wrote in his book *The Buried Mirror.* "You can prosper in southern Florida even if you speak only Spanish, as the population is predominantly Cuban. San Antonio, integrated by Mexicans, has been a bilingual city for 150 years. By the middle of the coming century, almost half the population of the United States will be Spanish-speaking."[7] Where Tocqueville found homogeneity, Fuentes now sees heterogeneity.

It is premature, however, to declare the idea of the melting pot to be dead. Our new immigrants continue to be assimilated, especially after two or three generations. This is Americanization of Latinos. But the Latino wave is fundamentally changing life in this country. In record numbers, immigrants from Latin America and the Caribbean are becoming—through weddings, jobs, visa lotteries, or drawn-out, painful, and often fraudulent bureaucratic processes—new Americans. The last wave moved from east to west. This wave is sweeping in from south to north.

In his writings, Tocqueville debunked the myth that European immigrants of the time were settling in the frontier wilderness. Of course they weren't. Those newly arrived established themselves primarily along the eastern seaboard, where industries already existed that required their work. Populating the West was a rich man's adventure, declared Tocqueville, who was only 26 at the time of his arrival. But he did notice something related and interesting: The Europeans, after a long transatlantic voyage, made their new homes in New York, Boston, or Philadelphia, while established Americans moved ever westward to seek their fortune. "This double emigration is incessant," he wrote. "Millions of men are marching. . . . Fortune has been promised to them somewhere in the West, and in the West they go to find it."[8]

If Tocqueville were to visit the United States at the start of this new millennium, he would find a plurality and diversity that did not exist in 1831. He would see hundreds—thousands—of brown tracks leading from the equator, passing through Central America and Mexico, and heading north from there. He would observe the crisscross blue-and-white stripes on a yawl heading from the Dominican Republic to Puerto Rico, and on a raft floating from Cuba to Florida. He would see "millions of men" marching northeast, coming not from Europe but from the South. He would meet Latin American and Caribbean men preceding their families, their compasses pointing north, embarking on a quest in search of a better life in the United States. He would note how, without intending to, they have Mexicanized states like California, Texas, and Illinois, Cubanized Florida, Puerto Ricanized and Dominicanized New York City, the capital of the world, and culturally reconquered lands that belonged to Mexico before 1848.

To be fair, Tocqueville had no strange astigmatism that prevented him from seeing the shades of brown among the country's inhabitants. It's just that his travels didn't include the millions of square kilometers that in those days formed northern Mexico. He arrived several years before the bloody border wars that ended with U.S. annexation of large swathes of Mexico in the 1848 Treaty of Guadalupe Hidalgo. But in 1831, the time of Toqueville's visit, the city of Los Angeles, as well as those that would later bear such names as San Francisco, San Diego, and San Bernadino, still had to report to the government in Mexico City.

If Tocqueville were to tour the country today, he would see more brown and mestizo faces and fewer white ones. He would note that instead of settling in the cities, new immigrants are beginning to collect and gather in the suburbs.

"Clearly, the growth of the Latino population is no longer limited to just a few regions,"[9] the Brookings Institution concluded irrefutably. The majority of Hispanics are concentrated in California, Texas, Florida, Illinois, and New York. The top five cities in terms of Latino population (Los Angeles, New York, Chicago, Miami, and Houston) haven't changed much in recent decades,[10] but the new demographic tendency points toward an expansion throughout the nation.

It should come as no surprise that many of the cities with extremely high percentages of Hispanic populations—such as McAllen with 88 percent or El Paso with 78 percent—are located near the border with Mexico. But the really interesting thing is that Latinos are starting to settle in large numbers in places that have never before been thought of as being very attractive to Hispanics or even tolerant of immigrants. Between 1980 and 2000, truly staggering increases in Hispanic populations have occurred in places like Raleigh, North Carolina (a 1,180 percent increase), Atlanta (995 percent), Greensboro (962 percent), Charlotte (932 percent), Orlando (859 percent), Las Vegas (630 percent), and even in the capital, Washington, D.C. (346 percent).

These facts belie the extremely difficult emotional process that precedes the decision to move and live elsewhere—generally in search of better economic opportunities. What if there aren't any others like us? And if they discriminate against my children in school? And if I don't like the jobs they have for me there? What if my working conditions are unbearable? These are some of the questions frequently asked by someone thinking about moving to a new city, but they take on added relevance among minorities who are rightly afraid of encountering resentful attitudes and behavior.

The first people to seek their fortunes in these places were men—especially young men. In those U.S. cities in which there has been an explosion in the Latino population—over 300 percent growth in some cases—there are roughly 117 men for every 100 women. And if there's an excess of young Latin American men in U.S. cities, then it follows that there must be a shortage of them in Latin America. I can't help imagine towns and villages absent of men. There is nothing quite so devastating as seeing the virtual ghost towns in the Mexican states of Michoacán, Puebla, or Aguascalientes, populated now only by women, children, and the elderly. The same thing is occurring in the Dominican Republic and Ecuador as well.

A study conducted by Princeton University between 1982 and 1997 concluded that young, single, Mexican men who have friends, families, or other contacts in the United States have twice as many opportunities as those who don't know anybody. Demographers Sara Curran and Estela Rivero-Fuentes analyzed some 6,000 Mexicans between 17 and 25 years of age in 52 different cities and towns, and they found that almost 60 percent of those who came to the United States already knew someone there.[11]

In early 2003, I attended a conference on migration in Quito, Ecuador, where I listened to the president-elect, Colonel Lucio Gutierrez, say that he wanted to reverse the tide of Ecuadorans leaving the country. Gutierrez, who had participated in the 2000 military coup, said that during the campaign children would come up to him in droves and beg for the return of their mothers or fathers, who had gone off to live in the United States or Spain. Heartrending, of course, and these sorts of anecdotes generate votes. But these are only populist promises.

I played the spoilsport at the conference—maybe that's why I was invited to attend. Far from supporting the presidential theory that it would be possible to stop the 400,000-plus Ecuadorans who annually leave the country, I suggested that the number of emigrants could increase by a factor of 10 by the time Gutierrez relinquishes his power in 2007. I don't think this contention was well-received by the military, who proposed the creation of a special agency designed to attend to the interests of Ecuadoran emigrants. Later I visited some Ecuadoran towns and was greeted by the sad sight of enormous homes, built with euros or U.S. dollars and equipped with luxurious refrigerators and televisions, standing totally empty. Just as in Mexico, Ecuador's main export isn't oil, but migrant workers.

The year 1831 must have been an extraordinary time: adventure and curiosity reigned supreme. While Tocqueville was heading for the United States, Charles Darwin, himself only 21 years old, was weighing anchor in England and setting sail aboard the HMS *Beagle* for Ecuador and the Galapagos Islands. Ecuador entered the European consciousness on account of its tortoises, the biodiversity of its islands, and the theory of evolution that Darwin would propose three decades after realizing his voyage. It had nothing to do with the people of Ecuador. Now, however, its main interest is the immigrants who attempt to make themselves Americans.

Tocqueville could not have imagined the current migratory wave; today there are more Ecuadorans in New York than in any city other than Quito or Guayaquil. Nevertheless, he did notice something that has held true in this country even until today: "Everyone is in motion," he wrote, "some in quest of power, others of gain." [12] This mobility, this idea of seeking one's fortune, is not lost on Hispanics— which is why so many have exchanged their city homes for more suburban ones. Already by the year 2000, 54 percent of Latinos were living outside urban areas. This represents a 71 percent increase from the previous decade.

A study conducted by the Center on Urban and Metropolitan Policy in conjunction with the Pew Hispanic Center established that "many Hispanics, by choosing the suburbs, are following the familiar path from city neighborhood to the urban periphery. . . . The survey reveals not only the vast and widespread growth of America's Hispanic population but also the emergence of new forms of growth and new areas of settlement across the nation's metropolitan landscape . . . in sum, the Latino population is on the move and spreading out as it grows."[13]

This fact forces us to look at Hispanics from a new perspective. It is constantly growing more and more difficult to put them into a single, fixed category. There is just so much diversity even within the Hispanic minority. Myths continue to implode, one after the other. Latinos are not a homogenous bloc, nor do we live only in big cities, nor are we all unskilled laborers, nor are we mainly undocumented immigrants. We are everywhere, and there is no occupation or activity in this country that escapes our influence. This century is ours.

To end our discussion of Tocqueville, we should note that, even in his day, he was able to identify the two problems with Latin America that, 150 years later, have provoked a migratory stampede. "South America has been unable to maintain democratic institutions. . . . There are no nations upon the face of the earth more miserable than those of South America."[14]

Poverty and the lack of democracy are the two things that have forced so many Latin Americans out of their countries of origin. "The happy and the powerful do not go into exile,"[15] he concluded. And in this, he proved correct.

UNSTOPPABLE: IMMIGRANTS AND THE INVISIBLE BORDER

Not much science is required to understand the impressive growth of Hispanics in the United States. The two primary factors that explain this phenomenon are immigration and the high birth rate of Latinos: thousands and thousands of Latin Americans enter the country each year, while those who already live in the United States have, on average, more children than the general population.

Few people were taken by surprise when the *New York Times* reported, on January 22, 2003, that the number of Hispanics had surpassed the number of African Americans in this country. But what is surprising is that this occurred so rapidly, and that the numerical distance between blacks and Hispanics will continue to grow swiftly from this date forward.

Why? First the obvious: the poor and others of little means in Latin America often leave to seek better lives in the United States. Immigration, both legal and illegal, will not stop because it is intrinsically linked to the workforce. As long as there are unemployed workers in Latin America and jobs for them in the United States, there will continue to be a strong and constant migration flowing toward the north, and as long as workers in Ecuador, El Salvador, or Mexico earn $5 a day, but can earn that same amount in under an hour in the United States, new immigrants will continue to arrive. Ultimately, it's a simple matter of supply and demand.

There exists the false notion that the terrorist attacks of September 11 significantly reduced the number of people emigrating to the United States. This has not been the case. While it is true that the number of arrests made along our borders declined in the weeks and months following the attacks, nearly 1 million undocumented immigrants from Latin America were detained in 2002, and we'll never know just how many more were able to evade the border patrols. Nevertheless, what is clear is that it's much harder to be an immigrant to enter the United States today than it was before the fall of the twin towers. Undocumented immigrants who come here for economic reasons have been made into scapegoats because of the acts committed by 19 terrorists with political motivations. The consequences range from a heightened vigilance at points of entry to the impossibility of getting a driver's license or other form of identification.

The irony is that Mexicans who cross the border illegally have absolutely nothing to do with the terrorists who struck on September 11. Thirteen of the 19 attackers were living in the United States with some type of visa—which is to say, they entered legally. There is no proof of how the other six entered, nor is there any indication that they did so illegally across the Mexican border. Anyone who wanted to sneak in did it from Canada. Not Mexico. Canada's official position is that none of the September 11 terrorists entered the United States illegally through their country.

So the question becomes, how can we protect the United States from a new terrorist attack and avoid discriminating against immigrants in general—without taking into account their jobs, financial contributions to this country, and the prevailing trends of immigration?

The possibility of amnesty for all undocumented immigrants fell along with the World Trade Center. The irony here, as Illinois Congressional Democrat Luis Gutierrez points out, is that a victory against terrorism cannot be achieved without first identifying the roughly 10 million undocumented immigrants living in the United States. And still the number of immigrants continues to increase, despite any and all new difficulties and prejudices.

Even organizations that oppose current levels of immigration have had to recognize that hunger is more powerful than fear. "There is no evidence that the economic slowdown that began in 2000 or the terrorist attacks in 2001 has significantly slowed the rate of immigration," the Center for Immigration Studies (CIS) announced. "Immigration has become the determinate factor in U.S. population growth. The arrival of over 3 million legal and illegal immigrants, coupled with 1.5 million births to immigrant women over the last two years, accounts for nearly 90 percent of U.S. population growth since the 2000 census."[16] The report veritably begs for an alarmist interpretation. But according to the Census Bureau itself, Hispanics accounted for only 40 percent of the population growth between 1990 and 2000, not the 90 percent that the CIS report suggests.[17] In either case, however, nobody can deny that the United States is subject to extraordinary growth.

These figures, particularly those regarding undocumented immigrants, can also be questioned. Nobody knows how many illegal immigrants there are in this country, nor how many cross over the border every day. All figures are based on estimates and calculations. "The level of legal immigration can be changed, as can the amount of resources devoted to reducing illegal immigration," Steven Camarota, director of research for the CIS, said in a press release.[18] Perhaps. But the one thing that remains clear is that the flow of immigrants is unstoppable, and is the future lifeblood of a New America, like it or not.

THE LEGAL ONES

Facts and figures fail to give us an idea of this phenomenon's true dimensions. According to the Immigration and Naturalization Service, 1,064,318 people received green cards (permanent resident status) in 2001. This represents a significant increase from the year before, when only 849,807 people received green cards.

The interesting thing about the 2001 statistics is that the majority of people—653,259 of them—who received their green cards were already in the country when they began the paperwork, preferring to pay the $1,000 fine under Law 245-i. The 411,059 others completed the long and complicated bureaucratic process from their home countries. In other words, the feet beat out the papers. Even among those who legally enter the United States, there are laws—in this case 245-i—that apply to their extraordinary situation, and not vice versa. When it comes to immigration, the pressures of reality are what matter, not laws.

Every year, the largest percentage of legal immigrants comes from Mexico. In 2001, 206,426 Mexican citizens received green cards, representing 19.4 percent of the total issued.[19] This figure is three times greater than the number of people admitted from India, and four times the number of those coming from China. That same year 31,272 people arrived from El Salvador, 27,703 from Cuba, 21,313 from the Dominican Republic, 19,896 from Nicaragua, 16,730 from Colombia, and 13,567 from Guatemala. The predominance of Hispanics among legal immigrants is indisputable, and this isn't going to change because of short-term political and economic crises reverberating from the United States down into Latin America.

WHY DO THEY COME?

The economic problems that the United States has experienced during the first few years of the new millenium have had very negative consequences in Latin America. The United States is Latin America's main business partner. For example, around 90 percent of the products Mexico exports go north of the border—and if Americans and Canadians find themselves unable to buy Latin America's exports, then the southern continent will find its economic situation doubly aggravated.

Along with this, we need to consider the frequent political crises that, over the last few years, have kept Latin American democracies in a precarious situation: Ecuador had five presidents in as many years before voters chose one of the country's coup orchestrators, Colonel Lucio Gutierrez, as their head of state. The legitimately elected president of Argentina was forced from office by popular pressure. A coup d'état removed Venezuelan president Hugo Chavez for a 47-hour period, and later a lengthy general strike sought to peacefully remove him from power. Relative peace has not meant the end of criminal violence in El Salvador or Guatemala. The former Nicaraguan president Arnoldo Alemán was placed under house arrest after being accused of corruption. The list goes on and on. Political instability simply doesn't create jobs or promote foreign investment.

Neoliberal politicians have sown the seeds for more healthy and responsible governments in Latin America. Populism has been beaten back by fiscal reforms, manageable budgets, and the reorganization of foreign deficits. But the sad result of two decades of free markets, privatization, and globalization is an alarming increase in poverty in many Latin American countries. With the exception of Chile—whose economic strategy has been to combine exports with a rising tax on the most needed items—many of these countries produce poor people who subsequently become immigrants.

If poverty is one of the region's most deeply rooted problems, the levels of inequality among its citizens is another unmistakable and discouraging sign of backwardness. Latin America has the most unequal earnings distribution in the world. The most privileged there commanded nearly half of the country's income in 2002.[20]

Mexico occupies a unique spot in the world of social inequality. According to *Forbes,* in the country that boasts 12 citizens whose per-

sonal fortunes exceed $31 million, 40 percent of its citizens live below
the poverty line. Mexico has more multimillionaires than Brazil (7),
Spain (7), Turkey (6), India (2), South Korea (2), or Ireland (2).

When faced with the age-old problems of poverty and wage inequality, migrating north is the only real opportunity for millions
of Latin American citizens. If a family has lived under the crushing
weight of poverty for generations, it may well feel the need to do
something drastic to break the cycle of hunger and despair.

Latin America's main export is its most resolute, disciplined workers. They are voting with their feet as they leave their countries of origin and go to seek their fortune elsewhere; it is a flight of hands and
minds and talent and youth and energy.

Over half of Latin America's population is under 25 years of age,
and this migration is a story whose protagonists are mainly young
men. It is these adventurous youths with nothing left to lose who
abandon towns like Azuay, Ecuador, and Aguascalientes, Mexico, in
search of better luck in the United States.

When Vicente Fox won Mexico's presidential election on July 2,
2000, he knew only too well that the one way to stem the flow of immigrants moving north was to create new jobs. The huge disparity in
salaries was something that, at the time, was impossible to confront.
But creating new jobs was a manageable task. I spoke with President
Fox a day after his victory, and he told me that his goals of 7 percent
annual growth and 1,300,000 new jobs in his first year were attainable.
But the demographics in Mexico present imposing problems: every
year, 1 million new young men and women enter the workforce. *Every
year.* And unless the government is in turn able to implement policies
to employ these new workers, then unemployment, poverty, crime,
and immigration are inevitable.

Fox's promises remained just that: promises. Though it's not all his
fault: the downward turn in the U.S. economy, the uncertainty caused
by the terrorist attacks, the Bush administration's refusal to negotiate a
new immigration agreement (Bush's unilateral temporary workers
proposal notwithstanding), and the general international climate of

apprehension brought about by the conflicts in Iraq and Afghanistan have made it difficult for the Mexican economy to recover and grow. Fox hasn't been able to meet his predicted number of new jobs, and is still faced with the very real problems posed by unemployment. Moving north has been the contingency of choice for one out of every six Mexicans, and everything seems to indicate that this trend will continue. Fox wanted to be president to 125 million Mexicans: the 100 million who live in Mexico, and the 25 million who live in the United States. And in a way he is: the Mexican economy depends heavily upon the millions and millions of dollars that workers in the United States send back home to their families in Mexico.

But Mexico's condition is not the exception in Latin America. The region as a whole has soaring poverty rates, sometimes as high as 50 percent, and the highest levels of earnings inequality in the world. These trends have changed very little throughout history. What is a young, unemployed man going to do when he has no money to continue his studies? What about a father whose salary is scarcely able to put food on his family's table? Or a woman, a secretary, who knows that her boss earns 10, 20, or even 100 times what she does, and that there is no possibility of closing this gap? Inevitably, these people are going to look to the north. To the United States.

According to a report issued by the United Nations Economic Commission for Latin American and the Caribbean, of the 20 million Latin Americans and Caribbeans who live outside of their countries of origin, 14 million do so in the United States.[21] And in 2000, these immigrants sent some $17 million back to their countries of origin—a much greater amount than the economic aid United States contributed to the region. The study doesn't indicate how many of these immigrants are living in the United States illegally, but there are ways of calculating this.

HOW MANY UNDOCUMENTED IMMIGRANTS
REALLY LIVE IN THE UNITED STATES?

The U.S. Census Bureau calculated that in the year 2000, there were roughly 7 million undocumented immigrants in the United States.[22] This same office reported that there were some 3.5 million in 1990 and 5.8 million in October of 1996. In other words, the complicated official method of calculation—because it's nothing more than that, a calculation—indicates that during the 1990s, 350,000 immigrants were entering the country illegally each year.[23]

These figures roughly coincide with the results of a joint study conducted by Mexico and the United States. The Binational Study on Migration calculated that, between 1990 and 1996, 105,000 undocumented immigrants entered the country from Mexico each year.[24] A far cry from "a million who each year walk from Mexico towards the United States," as Pat Buchanan suggested in a 1993 *Washington Times* editorial.[25]

The study found that the cyclical path traveled by many immigrants between Mexico and the United States is starting to slow. In other words, fewer and fewer are returning to Mexico once they arrived in the United States. Interestingly, one of the study's conclusions was that "The most important direct result of the migration is the money that migrants send home to Mexico."[26]

The border between Mexico and the United States is a border between a superpower and an underdeveloped country with a fledgling democracy. The overwhelming majority of undocumented immigrants in the United States are Mexican, and this isn't going to change. In the year 2000, 69 percent of all undocumented immigrants (4.8 million) were from Mexico, and 32 percent of them (2.2 million) settled in California.[27] And these numbers do not include immigrants coming from other countries. It is not a stretch to say that the border between the United States and Mexico is open to whoever wishes to cross it.

The Bureau of Customs and Border Protection, created under the

recently formed Department of Homeland Security (DHS), assures us
that it is getting increasingly difficult to enter the United States illegally, and as evidence they show us the declining number of arrests
being made at the border over the past few years:[28]

1999	1,579,010
2000	1,676,438
2001	1,266,213
2002	955,000

These figures are indisputable. They could mean that fewer people are attempting to cross. The DHS doesn't tell us how many do, in
fact, manage to cross. After all, the reduction in arrests could also mean
that more and more immigrants are able to evade the border patrols. In
fact, nobody has precise figures on this matter. But the census shows us
that tens of thousands, and perhaps hundreds of thousands, of immigrants manage to enter the country illegally each year, despite some
10,000 federal agents posted along the U.S.-Mexican border.

Here I should clarify that not all illegal immigrants enter the country by swimming across the Río Bravo/Grande or by risking their lives
in the mountains and deserts that separate the two countries. The majority of them arrive by plane. According to the National Immigration
Forum, "six out of every ten" enter the United States with a tourist,
business, or student visa, and eventually violate the terms of that visa
when they decide to remain in the country after it has expired. The
forum also calculates that around 300,000 immigrants do this every
year in the United States.[29]

President Bush knows perfectly well why immigrants take such
pains to come to the United States. He told me so in an interview, and
repeated his statement nearly verbatim a few days before the terrorist
attacks in Washington and New York: "There are people in Mexico
who have got children who are worried about where they are going
to get their next meal from," he said in an August 24 speech. "And

they are going to come to the United States, if they think they can make money here. That's a simple fact."[30] As long as they can earn in an hour here what might take them days to earn in their countries of origin, they will continue to come. And no act of terrorism is going to change this.

WHAT CHANGED (AND WHAT DIDN'T)
AFTER SEPTEMBER 11

After September 11, 2001, I traveled along the border between Mexico and the United States to see how the terrorist attacks had affected the passage of undocumented immigrants. I swam the Río Bravo/Grande in Texas, walked across part of the California desert where temperatures soared over 100 degrees and ran into dozens of immigrants ready to risk everything for the chance to make it in the United States. Crossing over is supremely difficult, but not impossible. The "coyote" business—that of smuggling undocumented and falsely documented immigrants across the border—is booming.

And it will continue to do so. Near the town of Reynosa, in the Mexican state of Tamaulipas, a coyote who called himself Abraham offered to take me across the river for $200. He never realized that he was speaking with a reporter.

Each year around 350 immigrants die from drowning, asphyxiation, or dehydration. A few days before my conversation with Abraham, a 16-year-old boy named Fabián Gonzalez watched as his father Miguel died after spending three days in the Arizona desert without water. The coyote who was smuggling them had left them on their own, and they had gotten lost in the middle of a desert that boils during the day and freezes at night.

Those who are successful in crossing have a large network of counterfeiters and forgers at their disposal to help them find work. While I was undercover and gathering information for a story with a hidden camera, a young Mexican boy nicknamed "the Hulk" tried to sell me a Social Security card and a green card for $90. The surprising thing is that this took place out in the open on Roosevelt Avenue in Queens, New York, only a few minutes from where the World Trade Center once stood.

In other words, the terrorist attacks have done very little to dissuade Latin Americans from entering the United States illegally. It continues to be relatively easy to cross the border and obtain false documents once inside the country. Nothing—not the National Guard, not higher walls, or stricter laws, or greater vigilence, not even the worst terrorist attack in the history of the United States—will stop the thousands who each year come in search of a better life in the United States. Nothing.

It's important to point out that not all the immigrants who enter the country illegally or who violate the conditions of their visas elect to stay here permanently. A good part of them are contract laborers who come to the fields of California, North Carolina, and Florida during harvest season, and then return to Mexico or Central America once their work is done. These cyclical immigrants (for lack of a better term) have also been affected by the terrorist attacks. Crossing the border is getting ever more difficult, as surveillance efforts and the number of border patrol agents have increased. Since September 11, many of these cyclical immigrants have broken with their established routines and stopped returning to their homes south of the border for Christmas and New Year celebrations. So the terrorist attacks on New York and Washington have actually reinforced a trend that has been going on for the past two decades and shows signs of becoming only more common in the years to come: immigrants deciding to stay in the United States permanently. And in many cases, this fosters resentment.

LAND OF IMMIGRANTS

The resentment and rejection of immigrants is nothing new. The United States has a contradictory history of immigration: everyone who lives here—save for the indigenous peoples who populated the continent some 12,000 years before the arrival of the first Europeans—is either an immigrant (forced or unforced) or descended from immigrants. Yet there is also a constant sense of resistance—at times fierce and racist—toward recent arrivals.

The first great wave of immigrants took place between 1840 and 1860, when nearly 3 million Irish and Germans came to the United States. As often happens today with Latin Americans, the Germans were derided for not speaking English, and the Irish were accused of stealing Americans' jobs. The posters that hung in the windows of northeastern businesses—"No Irish Need Apply," or simply "NINA"—presage the signs that appeared in the parks of Colorado in the 1930s: "No Mexicans, No Indians, No Dogs."

After the wave of Irish and German immigrants—who were slowly but surely assimilated—a new wave of some 4 million Italians, Poles, Hungarians, Russians, Lithuanians, and other Eastern European peoples arrived between 1880 and 1920.[31] Journalists Peter Jennings and Todd Brewster contend that "The last great immigration wave changed American society dramatically."[32] They compared that wave with the current one in a number of important ways: for example, "The Mexican has discovered Utah . . . famously white [and] famously Mormon." The last migratory wave—like today's—was led "by people who were ready to do the jobs that old-line Americans didn't want to do."

The new Italian manpower replaced the Irish, but the surprisingly strong xenophobic reaction was reflected in the tightest immigration laws in U.S. history. The governmentally imposed Emergency Quota Act of 1921 reduced the number of legal immigrants by half, and the Immigration Quota Act of 1924 reestablished set limits: no more than 200 percent of the total number of immigrants who lived in the country in 1890 could enter in any given year. This cut the influx to only 164,667 immigrants per year.[33] In the years leading up to the enactment of this law, some 800,000 immigrants entered the United States annually.

At best, new laws can be interpreted as providing a respite from the massive waves of immigration. At worst, it amounts to state-mandated ethnic prejudice. But in either case, these restrictions were successful in stemming the tide of new European immigrants. The limits were modified in 1952, but it wasn't until the amendments adopted in 1965 that the system of quotas based on race or country of origin was eliminated.[34] Around that same time (1964), the highly controversial "migrant worker," or bracero, program—which brought a total of 4.8 million Mexican workers to the United States legally over a period of 22 years—also came to an end.

What nobody could foresee in those days was that the new great wave of immigrants would come not from Europe but from Latin America. In 1951, 89 percent of new immigrants came from Europe and places other than Latin America, Asia, and Africa.[35] Half a century later, things have changed drastically: 79 percent of legal immigrants are either Latin American, Asian, or African. And the single largest country represented is Mexico (14.5 percent).

What happened? By the late 1960s Europe had completely recovered from World War II and was again powerful, thanks to the reforms and investments that had been realized since the end of the war. Latin America, on the other hand, was unable to deal effectively with the challenges it was facing in this period. The change in U.S. immigration laws coincided with the population explosion in Latin America of the 1960s and 1970s and the resulting rise in poverty, the patent inability of governments to employ their citizens, the establishment of authoritarian and military regimes. In general, there was much political instability. All of these factors drove people north.

In 1968, the Mexican government, headed by Gustavo Díaz Ordaz, played host to the Olympic Games. Díaz Ordaz represented the Institutional Revolutionary Party, or PRI, which had held sway over Mexico since 1929 and which in some ways was a result of the Mexican Revolution of 1910. But nearly 60 years after the revolution began, the country was caught in the throes of the worst political crisis of its modern history. On October 2, 1968, the Mexican army, acting on orders from President Díaz Ordaz and his secretary of government, Luis Echeverría, killed and wounded hundreds of students who had gathered in the Plaza de las Tres Culturas in Tlatelolco to demand democratic reforms. The changes these martyred students demanded would not come until 32 years later, when Vicente Fox defeated the PRI in Mexico's first democratic elections in almost a century. The Tlatelolco massacre was but one example of what Mexican life was like in those days, with a murderous, antidemocratic, authoritarian government and a people pushed to the brink.

It should not seem strange, then, that the significant growth in numbers of Latinos started in the late 1960s and early 1970s. The 1970 census indicated that only 5 percent of the population was Latino; this figure would triple over the next three decades. The lifting of immigration quotas coincided with the generally poor economic conditions in Latin America, and these two factors combined to form a veritable tsunami sweeping to the north, which—at least today— seems unstoppable.

WHEN HUNGER OVERPOWERS THE FEAR OF DEATH

Marco Antonio Villaseñor, a boy of only 5 years of age, was already pale and weak. His father, José Antonio, tried to lift up his head so that he might breathe through a tiny hole in the upper part of the trailer, but it had little effect. If they didn't open up the doors of the truck soon, all the people inside—at least 80 of them—were going to die. Finally, someone opened the trailer doors. What he found inside was horrible: 17 corpses and people on the brink of death.

Marco Antonio and his father were among those who died inside that trailer on Wednesday, May 14, 2003. Two other immigrants would die hours later in a hospital. The incident, which occurred outside Victoria, Texas, is one of the worst on record. But the saddest thing of all is that such tragedies continue to happen much more often than they should.

What is it that drives a person to overcome fear and risk his life and the life of his 5-year-old son in an attempt to enter the United States? Why risk drowning, dehydration, and asphyxiation? Because of hunger: the hunger brought on by not having enough to eat, as well as the hunger for a better life for oneself and one's family. Marco Antonio's grandmother told the *Washington Post* that José Antonio took his son from Mexico City to the United States "to give him a better education." [36]

The death of 19 Mexican, Salvadoran, Honduran, and Dominican immigrants in Texas became news because it was unprecedented. But this tragedy is a constant one. On average, one immigrant dies every day while trying to cross the border.

For every one that dies, roughly a thousand manage to cross the border or stay on past the duration of their visas. But border crossing is getting more and more dangerous. Since September 11, the border patrols have been stepped up, forcing potential immigrants to attempt crossings in more and more dangerous places, most notably in the desert.

According to the Mexican government, 371 people died crossing the border in 2002. The figure for 2001 was nearly identical, 370 deaths recorded. These figures are notably higher than those given by the U.S. government. In 2001 the United States recorded only 322 immigrant deaths along the border. Why the difference? Because the Mexican government includes those potential immigrants who die before ever reaching U.S. soil. But whichever figure is considered, the real tragedy is that each and every one of these deaths could have been avoided with an immigration agreement between the two countries. The current U.S. policy fosters loss of life and still fails to stop the flow of immigrants. It is, in no uncertain terms, a failure. Unless, of course, the true policy is to silently permit a certain level of illegal immigration so that certain segments of the American workforce can continue to operate. Perhaps—and this is both sad and hypocritical—the true immigration policy is the status quo: leaving things exactly as they are.

Two days after the deaths in Victoria, another trailer with 18 immigrants inside was stopped in the same exact place. Sadly, the tragedy in Texas seems doomed to happen again and again, because hunger is more powerful than the fear of death. And the body of young Marco Antonio Villaseñor is there to prove it.

THE WAVE FROM THE WEST

Clearly, the constant migration from Latin America is a fundamental part of the enormous rise in this country's Hispanic population. But there is another, even more powerful component that doesn't carry the stigma of illegality, and which has an enormous influence on American society from within its own ranks: in families and schools.

Traditionally, Hispanics have more children than other segments of the population. Mothers of Mexican origin have, on average, 3.3 children, and Puerto Rican mothers average 2.2, while African Americans and non-Hispanic whites have just over 2.[37] This is a cultural phenomenon linked, in part, to the high birth rates still prevalent across Latin America. The idea of having large families does not stem—as some have absurdly implied—from a certain genetic tendency to be more sensitive and sexual, from having the spirit of the salsa and the samba ingrained in one's blood, from a heightened libido, or from enjoying more free time than other ethnic groups.

In preindustrial and predigital Latin America, every able-bodied boy could work in the field, and every girl was an extraordinary asset in running a home and in taking care of infants and elders. In other words, having a large family provided some measure of insurance for the physical and emotional survival of the group against disease, days of work under the sun, and low life expectancies. A large family could mean the difference between eating and starving to death. Today children represent a significant expense (universities, health care, etc.) to their parents, while only a few decades ago they were seen as an investment in the future.

With industrialization came the migration from the fields into the cities. The number of farmers has been drastically reduced throughout Latin America. In some cases, as in Mexico, it's no longer a prerequisite to be a farmhand. Ironically, Mexico now imports corn from the United States in order to produce the millions of tortillas that make up a significant part of the Mexican diet. Such minor positive aspects aside, the North America Free Trade Agreement (NAFTA) between

Mexico, the United States, and Canada has left field workers unpro-
tected since January 2003.

After NAFTA went into effect in 1994, Mexican farmers were to
have a decade of governmental incentives to improve their production
techniques so as to be able to compete on a "level playing field" with
U.S. farmers. This has not happened. In January 2003 Mexican farmers—who work an average of only 5 hectares of land—simply could
not compete with European and U.S. farmers, who enjoy government
subsidies; modern irrigation equipment; the latest tractors, combines,
and technical information required for producing larger, stronger
crops; cheap manual labor (yes, from Mexico); and 150-hectare harvests.

How can a Mexican *campesino* compete with a U.S. farmer who
receives a portion of the $180 million in agricultural subsidies that
President Bush authorized from 2002 through 2012? According to a
calculation published by the Mexican daily *Reforma,* U.S. farmers can
sell their products at prices 20 percent below the cost of production.
And like the United States, Europe also subsidizes its farmers.[38]

The Mexican *campesino* is an endangered species. And if he wants
to continue to live off the land, the best thing he can do—ironically—
is go to the United States, the very country whose subsidies undermined his own harvests. Yet when the *campesinos* migrate, their
cultural practices—like having large families—don't disappear as they
cross the border.

If we consider that 16 million out of the 31 million foreigners living in the United States in 2000 came from Latin America, and that 68
percent of the Hispanic population was either born in another country or to at least one foreign-born parent,[39] it's easy to understand how
certain cultural practices continue on here.

The differences in growth rates is impressive. From April 2000
to July 2001, the Hispanic population grew 4.7 percent while Asian
Americans grew only 3.7 percent, Native Americans grew 2.3 percent, African Americans grew 1.5 percent, and non-Hispanic whites
grew 0.3 percent.[40] This includes new immigrants in addition to new
births. By 2001, 13 percent of the country's population was Latino,

whereas blacks made up 12.7 percent, or 36.2 million inhabitants. And even if we focus exclusively on birth rates, the figures are just as impressive. One out of every five new babies born in this country is Hispanic. Of the 4 million births in 2000, 20 percent were Latinos: 815,868 to be precise.[41] If we subtract the 107,254 deaths among the Latino community, we are still left with a very high figure.[42]

The wave comes from the west. In 2003, Texas no longer had a white majority. This was the first time this occurred in two centuries. In 2003, non-Hispanic whites became 49.5 percent of Texas' total population. The same happened in California previously. California is where we can gauge the consequences of this enormous growth with the highest degree of accuracy. There, the majority of new babies are born to Latino mothers. Between July and September 2001, the figure was 50.2 percent, whereas non-Hispanic whites represented only 31.4 percent, Asian Americans made up 11.3 percent, and African Americans made up 6.1 percent.[43]

Commenting on this impressive growth, David Hayes-Bautista, the director of UCLA's Center for the Study of Latino Health and Culture, said, "The long-anticipated Latino majority has arrived. For the next 40 years, each new phase of human development will be experienced in this state by a Latino majority."[44] The reverberations that this majority will have in California are striking: in 2006, the majority of children entering kindergarden will be Latinos; in 2014, the majority of teenagers entering high school will be Latinos; in 2017, the majority of people entering the workforce will be Latinos; and by 2019, the majority of young adults of voting age—18—will be Latinos. It is therefore only a matter of time until Hispanics begin to occupy California's highest public offices, from the governor's mansion on down. Just as Cuban Americans have come to dominate the Miami political scene, so will Mexican Americans come to control the political processes in California in a couple of decades.

But remember: we're not talking about immigrants here. We're talking about U.S. citizens of Latino origin, with all the rights and privileges enjoyed by any other person born in this country.

A measurable, undeniable Latino majority already exists in California, but the true change is still several years in the offing. Provincially minded people may foolishly try to change this trend. Congressman Buck McKeon, for example, proposed amending the U.S. Constitution after learning that some 96,000 babies had been born to undocumented mothers in 1992 in California alone. McKeon actually had the xenophobic audacity to propose to deny U.S. citizenship to the American-born children of undocumented mothers. The proposal splattered like an egg in a frying pan. It was patent ethnic prejudice along the same lines as Proposition 187. Approved by California voters on November 8, 1994, Prop 187 would have denied education and medical attention to hundreds of thousands of children and undocumented immigrants had it not been struck down by a higher court.

Despite xenophobic and racist initiatives by former California governor and proponent of Prop 187 Pete Wilson and congressmen like Buck McKeon, the Latino community continues to grow and prosper. But not at the expense of state and national budgets—a point I will address in a later chapter.

For now, the important thing is to establish that the Latino population is growing by roughly 1.5 million people per year. This figure takes into account births, deaths, and new immigrants—both legal and illegal—and represents the basis for the Latino wave.

At the moment, migration is the dominant force behind the growth of the country's Hispanic population. Very soon, however, a second generation of Hispanics—those born in the United States—will comprise the majority of the Latino population. "Births in the United States are outpacing immigration as the key source of growth," concluded a study done by the Pew Hispanic Center.[45] "Over the next twenty years this will produce an important shift in the makeup of the Hispanic population with second-generation Latinos—the U.S.-born children of immigrants—emerging as the largest component of that population."

From 1970 through 2000, first-generation immigrants from Latin America made up 45 percent of the total Hispanic population, while their children—the second generation, born on U.S. soil—represented barely 28 percent of the population. But, according to the calculations done by the Pew Hispanic Center, first-generation Latin American immigrants will—by the year 2020—have dropped to a mere 25 percent of the total, while their second-generation children will have swelled to 47 percent of the U.S. Hispanic population. This is the Americanization of the Latinos.

THE ROAD TO PUEBLA YORK

We enjoy "fitting in" and following the same path as others. Los Angeles has more Mexicans, Guatemalans, and Salvadorans than any other place on Earth outside Mexico City, Guatemala City, and San Salvador. There are as many Puerto Ricans outside of Puerto Rico as on the island. Miami absorbs people flowing in from this or that Latin American nation in crisis: now they may be Venezuelans and Colombians, whereas before they were Argentines and Nicaraguans. If the current trend continues, within a few short decades over half the population of Ecuador will be living in the United States or Spain.

When an old friend of mine named Amanda decided to leave the Mexican state of Michoacán and move to the United States—after her husband stopped sending her child support payments and murdered her own father—she didn't have to think much about where to go. Her sister's family lived in southern California, and that's where she went. She left her mother in charge of her son, took a bus to Tijuana, and with the help of a coyote, she and her 11-year-old daughter crossed over into the United States illegally. A few years later, her mother and son made the same trip. Amanda's sister had opened the door, and all she had to do was follow her lead. There are thousands of stories just like this one, especially in California and Texas, where half of all U.S. Hispanics live.[46]

José Pablo Fernández Cueto, president of the Mexican Institute of Greater Houston, told me in a letter that "the Mexican immigrant community in Houston totals over 500,000 people . . . which is more or less the same size of the entire city of Xalapa, Veracruz."[47] The institute was established in 1991 with the goal of helping parents better educate their children and thus put the brakes on very high dropout rates plaguing the Hispanic community. They're a group of Mexicans helping other Mexicans inside the United States.

Eight out of every ten Latinos living in Houston is of Mexican origin (the Latino population as a whole surpassed 1 million in 2000), with the majority of Mexicans from four states: Guanajuato (14 percent), San Luis Potosí (15 percent), Nuevo León (16 percent), and Tamaulipas (8 percent). How do we know? It's easy: the majority of immigrants who apply for their *matrícula consular* (a form of official identification issued by the Mexican government) at the Mexican consulate in Houston are from those four states. The path couldn't be clearer. In northeastern Mexico, Guanajuato borders San Luis Potosí, which, in turn, neighbors the states of Nuevo León and Tamaulipas, which share a border of their own with Texas. It's a geographical domino effect, with Texas the last falling domino.

"How can you stand it here when it's so cold?" I find myself constantly asking the Mexican immigrants I run into in Chicago. *"Pos no hay d'otra"*—"there's no other choice," they usually reply. *"Venimos a chambear"*—"We come to work." The Pilsen neighborhood is no longer German; now it's mostly Mexican. On 18th Street between Western and Halspead you can find markets, butcher shops, record stores, innumerable money-sending and travel agencies, restaurants and old barber shops, where you can still get a haircut and a shave *a navaja*—with a straight razor—just like in any little Mexican town. In the Girón bookstore, one of the best in the city, it's often tough to find a title in English, but rarely will the best-sellers in Spanish be missing. At the Nuevo León restaurant—which is now run by Daniel Gutierrez since his mother, María Gutierrez, left the kitchen for a life of semi-retirement in her apartment upstairs—I had a breakfast of eggs and chorizo that reminded me of . . . Mexico. It's that flavor—how to describe it?—that I grew up with, and which makes sure that the Nuevo León staff do not rest on Saturday and Sunday mornings.

At first it might seem hard to explain the presence of so many Mexicans in a place as intemperate as Illinois. But this phenomenon can be explained with two words: trains and beets. That's how Mexicans get to Chicago. The first ones to arrive were fleeing the violence of the Mexican Revolution and the subsequent *cristero* war. But the truly massive wave of Mexicans migrated because of the need for people to build and maintain the country's fledgling railroad system and work the beet fields.

U.S. companies began building railroads in northern Mexico toward the end of the nineteenth century, and thus thousands of Mexicans had a way to get to the beet fields of Illinois, Michigan, Ohio, Minnesota, Nebraska, and the Dakotas.[48] Similarly, Mexican farmhands who worked in the southern United States were shipped north on trains to where their work was in demand. Sugar was scarce, importing it had become expensive after a new tax established in 1897, and beets—or *remolachas,* as they're called in Mexico—became the only source of relatively cheap sugar that could meet the growing demand in the United States. Beets have a large, fleshy root that is rich in sucrose and can also be used as livestock feed. And so the road to Chicago was painted red with beet juice. It's not hard to imagine those field hands, working for $2 a day, their hands stained blood-red with beet juice. But we don't have to imagine it; we can look at the photographs in the revealing book by Rita Arias Jirasek and Carlos Tortolero entitled *Mexican Chicago.*

Chicago has the highest Zacatecano population of any U.S. city with the exception of L.A. There are even more Zacatecanos in Chicago than there are in the capital of Zacatecas, one of the poorest states in Mexico. Chiapas arguably suffers from greater poverty, but the arid climate and unforgiving land of Zacatecas give it one of the highest exodus rates in the country. But the Zacatecan character, once removed from the land, is very sociable indeed. There are over 200 Zacatecano clubs in the United States, several of which are in

Chicago. And there are regional federations that group individual clubs together. These organizations serve as something of a compass—a magnet—for immigrants and offer a support structure for the newly arrived. It's almost impossible for a Zacatecano to get lost in Chicago or Los Angeles—the road is well-marked.

Speaking about the presence of Mexicans in Chicago no longer surprises people. But what if we now bring up the Mexicans in Vail, Colorado? In any given winter there—if it weren't for the snow, the mountains, the damn cold, the skis, the Rolex watches, mink coats, and Maui Jim sunglasses—you might just think you've landed somewhere in Mexico. I close my eyes and listen to the typical Mexican sing-song all around me: "Paaaty, wwwe'll sssee yyyou up at the tttop, OK?" *"Oye güey,* wwwe're going to dddo a ffffew mmmore little rrruns; it's nnnot sssnowing tttoo mmmuch," *"Buenooo . . ."*—answering with his new Nokia cellphone—*"quihúúúbole* my brother, ¿on'tas?" "Paaapi, but I dddon't wwwant to ski, I wwwant to snowboard. It's wwwhat all the gggringos are dddoing, cccan't you sssee?"

You can certainly find more rich Mexicans in Vail than in *Forbes* magazine. On a recent visit there, I was waiting for one of the chairlifts when I met a Mexican family buying four 2-week lift tickets. At $71 per day, this amounted to $3,976, which is over half the average Mexican's annual salary. And this didn't even include equipment rental ($40 a day), gloves, fleece jackets, ski pants, long-johns, scarves, and hats to guard against the wind and cold. The father—a man in his forties—took out his credit card and signed away a small fortune without hesitation. "I've gggot the tttickets, *mi viiida,"* he called to his wife as he walked away, not concerned in the least.

These upper-class Mexicans, who wouldn't ever think of setting foot in a communal tractor trailer in Mexico City, Monterrey, or Chihuahua, are happy to join Americans in the free shuttle buses that take skiers from their hotels to the base of the mountain. *"Híííjole,* this is just like the truck in a Refooorma or the meeetro in Constituy-eeentes," I heard a young mother tell her child who wouldn't take his seat, referring to the crowded bus routes in Mexico City. The shuttles are where you learn that "The ssskiing in Ssswitzerland is mmmore awesome than in Canada" but that "the vvvibe in Aspen is the bbbest."

Aprés-ski Vail Village was a tough place to get a table, especially since most of the good restaurants required reservations weeks in advance, although one Mexican guest tried a furtive bribe to get in. "We're booked," the host at Sweet Basil—which was quite fashionable—told the solemn woman with dyed-white hair who looked as if she had never heard the word "no" before in her life. This would never happen in Mexico City restaurants like El Izote, Hacienda de los Morales, or El Estoril. She insisted, forcefully and confidently, certain that she would get her table. "We're sorry," they said again, and the woman sulked off like an angry dog, surely thinking to herself, *"piiinche güera,* ssshe's got nnno idea wwwho mmmy husband wwworks wwwith." Her long coat swept at the snow collecting on the pedestrian walkways. She'd try her luck later at Campo di Fiori or the Game Creek Club.

When faced with scenes like this, it's easy to forget that poverty, unemployment, and general hopelessness are getting worse every day in Mexico. Vail is visited by many of the privileged 10 percent of Mexicans who control 40 percent of the country's income. But what's much more interesting is that many of Mexico's 60-odd million poor are also coming to Vail. The way lies in the snow.

The cooks are Mexican. The hotel maids are Mexican. The day-care workers are Mexican. The trash collectors are Mexican. Mexicans are doing the jobs that nobody else wants to do.

Verónica from Zacatecas and Elvia from Veracruz earn $8.50 an hour to turn down beds in a four-star hotel. *"Pos sí,* it's hard work, but it's not as hard as it is back there," one of them told me. "And wwwe're already used to the cold," the other added, laughing. Lorena, from Chihuahua was more fortunate. She earns $10 an hour—more than the average Mexican earns in a day. But it comes at a high cost: "My whole family is back in Chihuahua," she told me the day after Christmas.

Without Mexicans, Vail would grind to a halt. There just wouldn't be enough labor power to keep the town running. And there wouldn't be enough pesos (changed into dollars) to maintain the mighty tourist business.

The strange—and sad—thing is that the same structures, classes, and attitudes (pedantic, submissive, vertical authority) that exist in Mexico find themselves repeated in Vail . . . only with a lot more cold to go along with them. But the low temperatures exaggerate the enormous differences between those Mexicans who are well-off and those who have little more than their jobs. Some sport warm fur coats and stylish Rossignol skis. Others are shivering inside their polyester fleece jackets and plastic boots, hustling, in subzero temperatures so they can send money back to their families in Mexico. These are the two Mexicos that ski and collide on the slopes of Vail.

It's cold, but the way is well marked.

New York is full of people from Puebla. You can get the best *mole poblano* outside Mexico there. And you'd be hard-pressed to find a single restaurant in Manhattan that doesn't have at least one poblano either in the kitchen or waiting tables. They prepare sushi, wash frying pans caked in pasta or the grease from a T-bone steak, and—to be quite honest—make it possible for millions of New Yorkers to live a flavorful life. Welcome to Puebla York.

During a recent visit to Lectorum Books, which has the city's best collection of books in Spanish, I randomly asked three people where they were from, and each of the three gave me the same answer: "From Puebla." "From Puebla." "From Puebla."

Poblanos come to New York for the same reason that thousands of inhabitants of the Marshall Islands go to Tennessee to work for Tyson Foods: there are jobs to be filled and a network of support for recently arrived immigrants.

The 2000 census didn't specify the number of *Poblorquinos*—only that there are a little over than 260,000 people of Mexican origin in New York State. We also know that they continue to come for three reasons: one, there is already an extensive network of friends and relatives to take them in; two, New York has jobs for them; and three, there are so many foreigners in New York that it's next to impossible to tell who is undocumented and who isn't. In other words, Poblanos are less fearful of being deported than they might be in California, Texas, or Illinois.

Of course, these factors don't make for an easy life. After September 11, many immigrants have become scapegoats for the frustration of a government that has not been able to capture Osama bin Laden and which lives under the constant threat of new terrorist attacks. But despite all this, Poblanos continue to come to New York.

Although Mexicans remain the third largest Latino group in New York—after Puerto Ricans and Dominicans—their influence is impossible to miss. *"Pero Sigo Siendo el rey"* ("But I go on being king") can be heard pouring from the Mariachi Academy of New York. That's a line from "El Rey," one of Mexico's most popular *rancheros,* which 50 young Hispanics—the children of immigrants—are now learning at the East Harlem academy.

Mariachi music in New York? Of course! And *mole* as well. The road to Puebla-Nueva York is marked by sounds and smells, the latest coming from Mexico.

CHAPTER THREE

WHY LATINOS ARE DIFFERENT:

THE MELTING POT MYTH

IN 1751, BENJAMIN FRANKLIN was afraid that parts of the United States were in danger of becoming "Germanized" in the same way that, today, many people fear this country is becoming "Mexicanized" or—more generally—"Latinized." It seems incredible that someone as open-minded as Franklin could have expressed his discontent with new immigrants so brutally. Intelligence, it seems, does not always defend against prejudice.

Immigration levels in Franklin's day were insignificant when compared with those of today; before 1840, annual numbers never surpassed 60,000.[1] Still, to Franklin, it was a huge number. "why should the *Palatine Boors* [Germans] be suffered to swarm into our Settlements, and by herding together establish their Language and Manners to the Exclusion of ours?" he asked. "Why should *Pennsylvania,* founded by the *English,* become a Colony of *Aliens,* who will shortly be so numerous as to Germanize us instead of our Anglifying them, and will never adopt our Language or Customs, any more than they can acquire our Complexion."[2]

It's interesting that the word Franklin used over 250 years ago—"aliens"—is the same one that appears on the green cards of today and is used disparagingly by anti-immigrant groups. Until I read his "Observations" I never thought of Franklin as a man laden with anti-immigrant sentiments. But his suggestion that new immigrants wouldn't be physically similar to him has forced me to wonder just how racist this founding father might have been.

But that's for another study. Here we're dealing with similar prejudices that exist today—though I ask myself if Don Benjamin—inventor of the lightning rod and promoter of colonial independence—would be as scandalized by the Latinization of today's United States as he was by the Germanization of yesterday's Pennsylvania.

Everything begins with language. The defining characteristic of the Latino community is that the majority of us speak a language other than English. And language is inextricably linked to change: the process of American Latinization begins with the Spanish language.

I'm not one of those people who thinks that the central common bond that unites those of us who live in the United States is the English language. No. I believe that this country's two main characteristics are its acceptance of immigrants and its tolerance for diversity. These things are what bind us together; we're here thanks to these unifying principles. That's what it means to be American. Not your ability to speak English.

TALK TO ME IN SPANISH . . . OR AT LEAST TRY

I sometimes go entire days without having to speak a single word of English, eat hamburgers or pizza, or even watch TV in a language other than Spanish. My e-mails will also sometimes come entirely in Spanish, with greetings such as *hola* or *aló* instead of hello. Such things could be considered normal in Bogotá, Santiago, or San Salvador. But it's also becoming more and more common in cities like New York, Los Angeles, Houston, Miami, and Chicago.

Some like to call this process *la reconquista,* the reconquest. The same lands that Mexico lost to the United States in 1848—Arizona, Texas, California, New Mexico—and many others that didn't form part of the Mexican Republic—like Florida and Illinois—are experiencing a true cultural invasion. Surnames like Rodríguez, Martínez, and Estefan dominate the music and sports worlds, and Spanish is spoken in every corner of this country, even the White House.

According to the U.S. Census Bureau, in 2000 there were around 28 million Spanish speakers over the age of 5 in the country. In other words, nearly 11 percent of the population speaks Spanish at home. In certain states, of course, the figure is much higher—28 percent in New Mexico, 25 percent in California, and 27 percent in Texas—but even Alaska (2.9 percent), Montana (1.5 percent) and North Dakota (1.4 percent) are becoming more Hispanophonic.[3]

Spanish is, of course, one of the major common threads that bind different groups of Latinos together. A nationwide poll conducted by the Pew Hispanic Center and the Kaiser Family Foundation concluded, "One of the key traits that defines the Hispanic population and distinguishes it from other racial and ethnic groups in the United States is the large number of individuals who predominantly speak Spanish."[4]

Spanish is one of the things that fosters communication and the passing of cultural values and references. I've always been intrigued by the fact that even those Hispanics who aren't fluent in Spanish will toss out a few words—*hola, cómo estás, que tal*—to let other Latinos know that we're members of the same group. Speaking, understanding, or being otherwise connected to Spanish is a powerful form of cultural identification. It's the first sign of auto-affirmation that we give to the rest of society: we're different. Though these differences go far beyond our ability to be bilingual.

Census data must be interpreted carefully. It is common sense that new immigrants from Latin America will speak Spanish. It's true that 90 percent of Latinos speak Spanish at home, but that figure can be broken down. Some Latinos (21.6 percent) speak only Spanish, especially if they are new immigrants. Others simply prefer to speak Spanish (29.9 percent) or can speak both languages (12.9 percent). Even so, one out of every four Latinos (24.2 percent) prefers English to Spanish, while others (11.4 percent) can't hold a conversation in Spanish at all, according to the Nielsen company.[5]

Many Latino parents make a concerted effort to teach their children Spanish, especially if they are born here. But more than an effort, it's a concern: how else could they communicate with their relatives in Latin America? There is a good deal of pressure on immigrants to maintain their language skills and to make sure their children speak proper Spanish as well. Common jokes like "Hey, your kid speaks Spanish like a gringo" or "Your daughter's already starting to forget where she's from" form part of the network of family alliances and friendly pressure that supports the preservation of Spanish in the home.

Interestingly enough, this is something that the majority of Latinos don't even question. Our education and social manners are well-ingrained. We take it for granted that it's good to speak both languages and preserve Spanish in the home, even though we live here in the United States. This act of faith regarding the boons and benefits of speaking Spanish—and with the language comes a whole set of cultural norms—is our main point of departure from mainstream America.

Spanish will continue to exist here as long as there is a constant in-flux of Spanish-speaking immigrants and an extensive network of Spanish-language media. Several studies have been done that show that second-generation Latinos (born in the United States) prefer to speak English and cannot communicate properly in Spanish. When we look at the third and fourth generations, it's next to impossible to find a Latino with a flawless command of Spanish. This is all part of the process of assimilation. Yet, the majority of Latinos are familiar with the Spanish language. It's part of their roots, their identity, and it will never disappear entirely.

Immigration isn't the only reason for the persistence—and even propagation—of Spanish in the United States. Spanish-language media continues to grow, thus reinforcing the use of Spanish. Every major city in this country has radio, television, newspapers, and maga-zines in Spanish. We can find Spanish programming and information in even the smallest and most remote places. This media must not be underestimated. It's thanks to them that the Spanish language and Latin American culture live on as energetically as they do here in the United States.

According to the Latino Print Network, "The number of Spanish language newspapers in the United States has increased from 14 in 1990 (with a total circulation of 440,000 copies) to 40 in 2003 (with a much larger circulation of 1,800,000 copies)." Some examples: in 2003, the *Fort Worth Star-Telegram* turned its weekly paper *La Estrella* into a daily newspaper; *The Dallas Morning News* launched its paper *Al Día*. And, in 2004, the following were launched: *Rumbo* and *Conexión* in San Antonio; *La Frontera* in McAllen; *El Nuevo Heraldo* in San Benito and Harlingen, Texas; *La Vibra* in Houston; *Hoy* (already established in Chicago and New York) reaches Los Angeles; and the two most prestigious Spanish-language daily papers in the United States, *La Opinión* of Los Angeles and *El Diario/La Prensa* in New York, joined editorial forces.

Spanish-language media is revitalizing the language and culture on a daily, and even hourly, basis. It's the engine that drives Latino cultural reinforcement. No other immigrant group in history has had such an extensive system for recycling and securing the values and customs brought over from their countries of origin. The effect is such that, for many Latinos, the United States isn't even a true foreign country. After all, their friends and families are here, and can help them maintain the language of their birth.

The question is whether Spanish-language media has the strength and influence to keep Spanish alive and well in the United States, even if the waves of immigrants were to dry up or be significantly reduced. It's tough to say. Still, it's an important hypothetical question to ask in both short- and mid-range time frames. For now, immigrants continue to come from the south, Spanish-language media continues to grow at an impressive rate, and the United States continues its process of Latinization.

But despite all this, Spanish does not remain solitary. What happens is that most Latinos end up becoming bilingual.

"The most important linguistic characteristic of Latino infants in the United States setting is their potential for becoming bilingual," concluded Barbara Zurer Pearson of the University of Massachusetts at Amherst. "With two languages as their 'first language,' Latino infants may participate as insiders in two language communities—and even perhaps in a third, the community of bilinguals." But the most important thing, according to the study, is that "babies don't decide to be or not to be bilingual: their parents (and educational institutions) make these decisions for them."[6]

Again, it's the parents and older family members who impress upon their children a world vision in which Spanish is important and—in some instances—vital to understanding who you are and where you're from. It's not an exaggeration to say that in some families, the concept of being Hispanic depends exclusively upon being able to speak Spanish or be bilingual. But this attitude isn't always well-received by those who aren't bilingual themselves.

The United States is the only country I know of where people seem to think that speaking one language is better than learning two or three. Why can't we follow Switzerland's example, where nearly every child grows up speaking three languages? From Germany to Latin America, most children in public and private schools have the opportunity to learn English and one other language, usually French. There, the belief that "more is better"—at least as it refers to language—is unquestioned. In the United States it is not.

Speaking Spanish in the United States is seen by some as being divisive and by others as being a threat. The former presidential candidate Pat Buchanan complains in his book *The Death of the West* that "Mexicans not only come from another culture, but millions are of another race. . . . Millions of Mexicans are here illegally. . . . Millions have no desire to learn English."[7]

But the reality of the situation is something very different: four out of five Latinos can express themselves in English. In other words, they have achieved at least some degree of bilingualism. It's the Americanization of Hispanics. As the statistics have shown, only one out of five Latinos speaks only Spanish. And even this segment of the community eventually learns English at some point. Most understand that being successful in this country means being bilingual as well. Immigrants don't come here intending to fail and starve. And English is essential to our success.

"Bilingualism is a reality out there in America today," said Harry Pachón, president of the Tomás Rivera Policy Institute, while announcing the results of a survey on Latinos' TV viewing choices.[8] One of his most important conclusions is that "Latinos have a wider palette of television programming options than does the population as a whole. Fully three-quarters of Latinos routinely watch television in English and Spanish."[9] And here's the reason:

LANGUAGE OF VIEWERSHIP AMONG LATINOS[10]	
EXCLUSIVELY SPANISH	11%
PRIMARILY SPANISH	13%
BOTH EQUALLY	50%
PRIMARILY ENGLISH	12%
EXCLUSIVELY ENGLISH	13%
DON'T WATCH TELEVISION	1%

According to a study conducted by the University of Southern California, Latino children learn English relatively quickly. Dr. Dowell Myers demonstrated that 7 out of 10 children from 5 to 14 years of age who came to the United States during the 1970s spoke English "very well" by 1990,[11] thus debunking the myths and alarmist concerns that some people have about immigrants not being interested in learning English.

Other studies have confirmed these results. "Over half (58%) of Latinos with children say our children usually speak English with their friends," agrees the Pew Hispanic Center.[12] Fully 45 percent of children of foreign-born parents speak Spanish with their friends as well. This is due in part to the belief among parents that English is essential to getting ahead in this country: "About nine in ten (89%) Latinos indicate that they believe immigrants need to learn to speak English to succeed in the United States."[13]

This is not isolated data. A Public Agenda report supports the results of the USC and Pew Hispanic Center studies by confirming that "eighty-seven percent [of immigrants] say it is extremely important for immigrants to be able to speak and understand English." Sixty-five percent even agree that "the U.S. should expect all immigrants who don't speak English to learn it." Relatedly, Latin Americans scorn the false stereotype that all recent immigrants are lacking in education: "Thirty-seven percent of immigrants say they already had a good command of English when they came to the U.S."[14]

Can one out of three "average Americans" claim to speak a language other than English? The December 2002 issue of Condé Nast *Traveler* printed the following joke regarding the typically "American" attitude toward language in their Letters section:

Q: What do you call a person who speaks three languages?
A: Trilingual.
Q: What do you call a person who speaks two languages?
A: Bilingual.
Q: What do you call a person who speaks only one language?
A: An American!

The Mexican writer Carlos Fuentes enjoyed seeing bumper stickers in Texas that read "Monolinguism Is a Curable Disease."[15] They prompted him to ask himself, "Is monolinguism unifying and bilinguism disruptive? Or is monolinguism sterile and bilinguism fertile? The California state law decreeing that English is the official language of the state proves only one thing: that English is no longer the official language of California."[16]

Fuentes's conclusion—that multilingualism is the precursor or omen of a multicultural world—is exemplified in many ways in today's United States. Los Angeles is, without a doubt, one of the world's most multicultural cities, with over two dozen languages being spoken there. It's a marvelous mix of Latin American, Asian, African American, and Anglo-Saxon. There is even a growing Arab population, which manages to live there in relative peace with Israelis and Jews.

But California is also the source of a movement—albeit destined for failure—that aims to put an end to the state's linguistic and cultural diversity. Like the innumerable forking branches of a tree, the people and culture of California are constantly searching for new methods of expression, while others—seeking to ban the Spanish language and bilingual classes, among other things—are like gardeners attempting the impossible task of pruning back all but a scant few of that tree's leaves. For every leaf that is stripped from its branch, others flourish and the tree grows stronger. Rather than being suppressed, our culture is reinforced.

It's not surprising that resistance to cultural diversity in this country—and, therefore, resistance to Latinos—focuses on things related to the Spanish language. Language is the first thing that distinguishes us from the rest of society, and that makes it a prime target for often vehement attacks.

The movement to make English the official language of the United States, and the proposals in certain states to eliminate bilingual education, are poor disguises for those who fear or reject the fact of this country's overwhelming cultural diversity. They fight against the use of Spanish because it sounds less racist than to say they are fighting against Hispanics because they are simply a different ethnic group. These movements lace their educational agendas with goals of standardization and—even worse—nationalist reduction. They claim that being a patriot—being a so-called American—means speaking English. They can't conceive of any other way of going about it and seek to impose their beliefs on the rest of society through the implementation of new laws. "You're different," they tell us, "and so you've got to become more like me." Being an American is far more than language-deep.

In 1998, the millionaire Ron Unz threw his considerable economic and marketing support behind California's Proposition 227, affecting in the process some 400,000 students whose native language was something other than English. In official terms, Prop 227 ordered that "all children in California public schools shall be taught English as rapidly and effectively as possible."

And so voters tried to once and for all do away with bilingual education in California. But the key word here is "tried." In reality, teaching bilingual classes in places like (for example) Los Angeles was much tougher than people realized, given the fact that in 1988 the school district there was made up of some 160,000 students who spoke 81 different languages.[17] That would have been an impossible task. But a core of seven languages—Spanish, Cantonese, Korean, Japanese, Armenian, Vietnamese, and Filipino—would be manageable, according to the Los Angeles Unified School District.

The basic idea of bilingual education—that students be able to take classes in their native languages while at the same time learning English as their second language—reflects the best traditions of tolerance and diversity in a multicultural society like Los Angeles. But the sudden cries of a well-financed group who fear diversity can be enough to send shivers of xenophobia down the electorate's spine. Bilingual education was always merely an option—never an imposition—of students and their families. Why would anyone want to deny children this option? It was designed simply to help prevent students from falling behind in their progress, and thus discourage them from dropping out of the system altogether.

The supporters of Prop 227 argue that the measure was a success, citing the fact that the number of students who went from having deficiencies in English (classified as "limited-English-proficiency," or LEP) to having near-native skills ("fluent-English-proficiency," or FEP) increased by six-tenths of a percent—from 7 to 7.6—in the year after the measures were implemented.[18] But as Patricia Gándara of the University of California at Davis points out, the irony here is this increase was made possible thanks to the bilingual teachers who helped students with gaps in their English to come out ahead during the year-long transitional phase—called "structured immersion" into English or "sheltered English"—which Prop 227 allowed.

The efforts to end bilingual education in schools soon spread to Arizona, where similar methods were approved by voters in 2000. But in 2002, the millions of dollars Ron Unz had earmarked for shutting down bilingual education in Colorado were met by a sum three times as great that Pat Stryker invested in hopes of defeating Amendment 31. Stryker is the granddaughter of the owner of the Stryker Corporation—the company that develops, manufactures, and markets specialty surgical and medical products—but more importantly, her daughter attends a school in Fort Collins where classes are offered in two languages.

That same year, Massachussetts voters also decided to do away with bilingual education in their public schools. But more interesting than that is that a state as conservative as Colorado had seen the advantages of this type of education. Despite having representatives like Tom Tancredo—who launched a crusade against a young undocumented immigrant who wanted to attend college and, eventually, asked the INS to deport his entire family—Colorado is an increasingly diverse state. Its Latino population has grown by almost 25 percent over the last decade, and now totals some 735,000 members, mostly of Mexican origin.

Proposition 227 exudes fear—fear of difference, fear of things that come from other places and aren't like me or mine—as does any proposition that seeks to bring an end to bilingual education. If domestic flights give safety instructions in both English and Spanish, and if Spanish is used by politicians and companies to attract new voters and business, then why not use both languages in schools as well? If bilingual messages are already so common in the United States, then what motive can one really have for wanting to push Spanish aside in the classroom?

Such attitudes also reflect the hypocrisy that underlies much of U.S. society. As Amherst College professor Ilan Stavans points out, "Curiously, in the United States, to be a member of the upper class and a polyglot is a ticket to success. But multilingualism among the poor is unacceptable and, thus, immediately condemned."[19] In other words, it's alright for the children of investors, lawyers, doctors, and bankers to be bilingual, but it's not alright for those children who have to attend this country's public schools.

Things have certainly changed in the public schools of California, Arizona, and Massachusetts. But if the ultimate objective is the elimination of Spanish—and any other language that doesn't happen to be English—from the United States, then they can look forward to a resounding defeat. Spanish starts at home, not in the schools. Schools can reinforce it, of course. But the home is where it lives and grows. Plus, the Spanish-language media gives it legitimacy and keeps it alive. What will they do next? Ban the speaking of Spanish in U.S. homes?

Arrest immigrants for speaking together in their native tongues? It's ridiculous. Worse still, it's futile.

For parents of Latino families, Spanish holds one of the most important pieces of their cultural identity. But young Hispanics tend to speak English among themselves at the earliest opportunity. It's virtually impossible for the parents' influence to compete linguistically with the constant bombardment (in English) of the TV, radio, school, and friends. My son Nicolás and my daughter Paola speak English to each other without the slightest hint of an accent, and then turn around and speak Spanish to me. There can be no doubt that Latino children—even those newly arrived from Latin America—end up with a very good command of the English language. They, like the majority of Hispanics, are bilingual. Already 93 percent of second-generation Latinos—those born in the United States—are bilingual or speak English predominantly.[20]

Bilingual education isn't about promoting another language above English. Sooner or later, immigrant and Latino children do learn English. What this is about is giving the children help when they most need it—before they master English—so that they don't end up dropping out of high school.

The efforts to end bilingual education in this country's public schools and designate English as the official language of the United States are two areas—in addition to affirmative action programs—where the country's cultural diversity is called into play. Since 1981, several different organizations have attempted to declare English as the country's official language. But this is a futile, unnecessary, and divisive struggle, and frankly one soaked in racism.

For such a resolution to be passed, two-thirds of both the Senate and the House of Representatives would have to approve it, after which it would move to the state legislature, three-fourths of which would also have to approve the measure. The idea is so without merit that no congressional committee has dared to call it to a vote, much less the Senate or the House at large.

When the selectmen of Brown County in Green Bay, Wisconsin, declared English as the official language there, the consequences were

barely perceptible: documents continued to be translated and inter-
preters provided whenever they were required by federal law. One
board member called the resolution the "least significant document"
to cross his desk in a decade.[21] And yet on July 17, 2002, they approved
the measure by a vote of 17 to 8, and the only real effect it had
was to alienate the 4 percent of Brown County that represented its
foreign-born population and prompt protests and demonstrations that
compared the country's new linguistic mandate with that of Hitler's
Germany.

By mid-2002, 27 states have declared English as their sole official
language, though Hawaii is officially bilingual and the courts in Alaska
and Arizona have struck down the prospect as unconstitutional.[22]
The fundamental problem with this "English only" movement isn't
the practical consequences of such an act; rather, it has to do with the
unequivocal and disturbing message of resistance propagated by those
who refuse to acknowledge that this country is changing before their
very eyes.

ASSIMILATION OR CHANGE

Back in January 1983, during my first English class in this country—
which was part of UCLA's extended course program—the professor
had us discuss the term "melting pot." In those days I hadn't the slightest idea what it meant, but my classmates—French, Arabs, Asians,
Latin Americans, etc.—gave me a clue. No matter how hard we tried,
we would never sound like native English speakers. But the thing is,
we didn't want to sound like them. Sure, we wanted to become comfortable with the new language, but we also wanted to maintain certain customs and memories that linked us with our countries of origin.
Maybe our class was particularly taken with nostalgia; I don't know.
But after an hour's worth of discussion in broken, accented, English, it
was clear that we were never going to form part of the melting pot's
liquor. It was a sad realization on my first day of English class. My first
in the United States.

Assimilation and change are two very powerful forces. What we're seeing is a two-way process: the Latino community is indeed being assimilated in certain ways—for example, their adaptation to the democratic process and a market economy—but in other areas—like language, culture, and the adoption of certain values—they have resisted assimilation and are instead prompting change.

Centuries of assimilation aren't undone by a single migratory wave or because of high birth rates. Nevertheless, the force of the Hispanic current is so strong that the face of the United States can't help but be changed. And this change is what's important: both for its fundamental depth and for its pervasive reach into every corner of this country.

The Peruvian writer Mario Vargas Llosa informs us that "this is the first time in history where a community originating outside the United States has not been subject to the homogenizing processes of the cultural melting pot in order to be recognized as 'Americans.' "[23] This is true. Latinos have managed to maintain their own identity; they haven't diluted their culture in order to enter the stew of the majority. There has been integration, especially when it comes to economics and even politics. But not the widespread assimilation that other immigrant groups experienced before them.

Latinos have not changed the essence of the rules of democracy and capitalism in this country, but they are changing the way in which these fundamental elements are applied to their particular reality. When a Latino buys groceries at the store or votes in an election, he or she isn't changing the system. On the contrary, he or she is reinforcing it through participation. It's the process; one wholly built for change.

Anyone who wants to open a business on Eighth Street in Miami or on 18th Street in Chicago's Pilsen neighborhood had better understand the particular habits of Latino consumers or face the risk of quickly going bankrupt. Here in Illinois and south Florida, Hispanics aren't changing the nature of business transactions; rather, they're changing the way in which those transactions are realized. Without getting too far off the topic, traditional Latin American business requires that you get to know your associate (and even his or her family) personally before signing a contract or completing a transaction. And while that tradition is changing rapidly, we still cannot underestimate the importance of personal contact in the business world. On the other hand, a previous personal rapprochment with someone is not a prerequisite for doing business with them here in the United States. That generally happens later.

The same principle applies to the world of politics as well. Hispanics tend to vote for people rather than political parties (this will be examined further toward the end of the next chapter). After all, the presence of Hispanic voters is not changing the essence of U.S. democracy, but because candidates are making greater and greater efforts to attract Hispanic votes, it is changing the way in which campaigns are run. There are certain electoral districts in Texas and California where it's very difficult to get elected if you don't speak Spanish or at least speak to the issues that directly affect the Hispanic communities there, such as poverty, lack of affordable housing, and high dropout rates. And there are cities like Miami and Houston where exposure in the Spanish-language media is vital to winning an election.

We are marking this country with a unique and pervasive stamp: from the *mestizaje* inherent in our faces to U.S. foreign policy. Integration means forming part of a whole, but it doesn't imply the disappearance of the individual parts. This is what's happened with Latinos: they have become integrated, but not completely assimilated. Better than a melting pot that simmers and distills everything put into it, the comparison that may best describe Latinos in the United States is that of a salad, where all the ingredients can be distinguished even though they form part of the whole. "The process of assimilation is one that entails the gradual erosion of social and cultural heterogeneity,"[24] affirms sociologist Peter Kivisto. In this respect, Latinos will never fully cooperate.

Assimilation doesn't depend on an individual's desire to form part of a group. The process is much more complicated. Up until the 1980s, for example, the migratory currents flowing out of Mexico didn't foster it. Many immigrants—usually young men—come to the United States to work for a time and then returned home. There was never any intention of staying permanently. The attitude was, if I'm not going to live here permanently, then why go through the trouble of adapting myself to new customs? But bit by bit these patterns have changed.

As this cyclical path slowed down, the process of incorporating into the various walks of life in the United States began to increase. After comparing dozens of studies conducted over the past 100 years, the economist James P. Smith of the Rand Corporation concluded that "the children and grandchildren of Hispanic immigrants progress up the educational and income ladder in the same way as immigrants who came here from European countries."[25] If we look at the processes of assimilation over the long term, we get a more realistic, less pessimistic picture of Hispanics' educational and economic advances.

The same study found that "third-generation Hispanic descendants [are] only about 10 percent behind their white counterparts (third-generation descendants of European immigrants) in relative incomes."[26] Results relating to education are also heartening "Mexican immigrants born in the early 20th century had an average four years of schooling. Their American-born sons double that schooling, with the third-generation descendents graduating from high school."[27] But to what is this success due? "A lot of success we have seen from immigrant groups is because of the strong American school system," contends Smith. "If the schools fail to deliver, then we have a problem."[28]

Latinos have an extraordinary confidence in the U.S. system. In its chapter on U.S. assimilation, the Pew Hispanic Center's 2002 National Survey of Latinos emphasized that "a large majority (89%) of Hispanics feel that the United States provides more opportunities to get ahead, and that the poor are treated better in the United States than they are in their country of origin (68%)."[29] Similarly, 80 percent of Hispanics are convinced that their children will have a better education than they have, and 76 percent believe their children will have better jobs and earn more money than they do.[30] This is a demonstration of the faith Latinos have in the United States.

Hispanics turn a blind eye to certain aspects of the U.S. system.

But the reservations they do harbor are much more personal, and here is where assimilation breaks down. Nearly three-quarters (72 percent) consider the moral values and beliefs in their home countries to be superior to those found in U.S. society, and four out of five (79 percent) feel that Latin American families are generally stronger than U.S. ones. It's not surprising, then, that 78 percent of Latinos also believe that it's better for children to live at home until they marry, and that a similar percentage (73 percent) think that grandparents should live with the rest of their family instead of in a retirement home.[31] All this points toward an undeniable conclusion: while Hispanics do accept the values prevalent in their schools and places of work, when it comes to matters of the family, they have a distinctly negative opinion of U.S. society and are afraid that it could affect or even destroy their homes.

As we discussed earlier, the majority of Hispanics consider themselves Democrats, but many of their tenets and beliefs still coincide with those of more conservative Republicans. Large numbers of Hispanics oppose abortion (77 percent) and homosexuality (72 percent), numbers which contrast sharply with non-Hispanic whites, whose numbers are 45 percent and 59 percent, respectively. It's the same with divorce: 40 percent of Hispanics consider it to be unacceptable, whereas only 24 percent of Anglo-Americans feel the same way.

When considering such fundamental differences of opinion as these, it's impossible to accept the theory of assimilation for U.S. Latinos. The proverbial melting pot—which served so well for generations—is in many ways today just a myth. It exists in politics, the workforce, and with greater frequency in schools. But the winds of change are strong, not only because most Latinos can speak Spanish and identify with their countries of origin—how many people do you know who say "I'm from Germany," "I'm from Ireland," or "I'm from Italy" the way Latinos say "I'm from Mexico," "I'm from Puerto Rico," "I'm from the Dominican Republic"?—but also because they have morals and family values that differ distinctly from the rest of the American population.

It's their way of life—shopping, reading, writing, raising a family, communicating with each other, watching the news, choosing candidates, protecting their children and elders, making important decisions, reacting to abortion and divorce—that makes Hispanics different. We have a unique outlook on life. And we have the ability to leap from one world to another in a single bound, sentence, or breath. It's the ability to be two or more things at once.

I can almost hear the recriminations now: "If Hispanics are so different—if there are so many things you don't like about this country—then why come?" It's simple: to reinvent ourselves.

"In America . . . you get to write the script of your own life," Dinesh D'Souza suggested in his book *What's So Great about America?* which could only have been written by a foreigner who's fallen in love with the ideals of this country. Here, you can determine the direction of your own life, he argues, not your tribe, caste, sex, or birth order. It's this sense of self-determination, of the possibility of starting from zero, of forging your own destiny, that attracts Hispanics. Latinos agree with the foreign-born journalist Fareed Zakaria when he wrote in *Newsweek:* "The belief that anyone can aspire to anything is one of America's greatest gifts to the world."[32] Both D'Souza and Zakaria were born in India. It's interesting to note that thinkers whose families have lived outside the country for generations have come to understand full well the attraction that the United States holds for the rest of the world.

The question now is this: Who is changing whom? Is U.S. society changing Latinos, or vice versa?

I believe that the force of change in this country rests with Latinos. A nation that emphasizes Latinos' morals and family values while maintaining the prevailing U.S. political and economic processes would, without a doubt, be a healthier and more humane society.

WHEN SPANISH (AND SPANGLISH) INFILTRATE ENGLISH

The Latino wave sounds different. And there's no better way to understand this difference than to watch and listen to Spanish-language news programs. When I first came to the United States over two de-

cades ago, a producer predicted that I'd never be able to work in television. "You have too much of an accent in English," he told me. "It'll
never work." "What about working in Spanish?" I argued. "Spanish-
language news programs are on the verge of extinction. Hispanics
are all about assimilating." Of course, in reality, the opposite occurred.
Spanish-language media grew by leaps and bounds, I got a job as a
reporter working for a local Spanish-language station in L.A., and
the producer who foresaw my failure—well, he fell off the face of the
earth.

The difference between Latinos and other immigrant groups is
clear. Italians don't have three broadcast stations and dozens more on
cable featuring programming in their own language. Hispanics do, in
Spanish. Germans don't control a network of literally hundreds of
radio stations across the country. Latinos do. Poles and Russians don't
have thousands of newspapers and magazines in their native languages
all across the country. We do.

As the Latino population grows, it makes sense that some of the
Spanish-language news services would begin to top the English programs in the ratings wars. On September 27, 2002, the *San Jose Mer-
cury News* ran the following headline: "Spanish-Language Newscast
Most-Watched in Bay Area." To the paper's surprise, *Noticias 14*—
Univision's San Francisco affiliate—had topped the latest ratings list
for the important 18-to-49 age demographic, which included English-language news programs as well. This was a direct result of much
hard work on the part of the station manager, Marcela Medina; the
news director, Sandra Thomas; and the entire team of reporters, producers, technicians, and writers.

But to those of us journalists who work in Spanish, this news came
as no surprise. It represented just the latest indicator in the long
progression to the top of the ratings charts. As the same article recognized, "Spanish-language newscasts in Miami and Los Angeles in the
past few years have outranked all stations in their respective markets."
And in New York, as well.

A few days after this news from San Francisco, Channel 41—
another Univision affiliate—made a similar report from New York.

The news program anchored by Rafael Pineda and Denisse Oller had, for the first time, beaten out the other five players competing for the 6 P.M. time slot. As *Pareja Media Match* observed, "Never before has a Spanish-language TV station's local newscast won the hotly competitive household ratings race against stiff competition from major English-language network-owned stations.[33]

What is indeed surprising is that this happened in cities like New York and Los Angeles, which are intrinsically identified with this country's news and entertainment industries. Upon hearing these results, some English-language stations complained to the Nielsen Corporation, which calculates the ratings. But they were checked and reconfirmed, though the pressure continued and several petitions were even filed to change the way in which ratings were calculated.

"How is it possible that a Spanish-language station—with far fewer resources than us—can win out?" Such was the daily lament of English-language TV executives. Univision is the fifth largest station in the country—behind ABC, CBS, NBC, and Fox—and its news audience frequently outnumbers those who watch CNN or Fox News. More teenagers watch Univision than MTV, and more women watch it than the Lifetime Channel. But we're not talking about just one channel here: in Los Angeles, six separate stations are currently competing for the Hispanic and bilingual market.

Nor are we dealing with a strictly quantitative phenomenon here; it's a qualitative one as well. If we compare *Noticiero Univision* with ABC's *World News Tonight with Peter Jennings,* we see huge differences in programming choices. Social scientist América Rodríguez conducted one of the most comprehensive studies on this topic, and concluded that "the largest difference between the two networks [ABC and Univision] is found in those sound bites categorized 'Latino': just over 1 percent of ABC sources (6 out of 466) were U.S. Latinos; 35 percent of Univision sound bites were of U.S. Latinos. . . . Nearly half, 45 percent, of each *Noticiero Univision* is about Latin America while just under 2 percent of ABC's *World News Tonight with Peter Jennings* is taken up with news of Latin America; an enormous disparity in story selection, and the most direct evidence of the distinct world views of these two U.S. television networks.[34] In other words, Spanish-language programming tends to be much more international in scope—more open to the world—and this has the direct result of increasing its audience, especially among Hispanics.

All of the above was confirmed in a study done by the Tomás Rivera Policy Institute, which in 2003 found that 57 percent of bilingual Latinos prefer to watch their news in Spanish, whereas 16.3 percent prefer English and 26.7 percent watch both English and Spanish reports. Why do they do this? Because 63.6 percent believe that there are significant differences in coverage between Spanish- and English-language news programming. An example: among Hispanics who watched the TV coverage following the terrorist attacks of September 11, 30.3 percent preferred to stick with their Spanish-language news, whereas only 12.5 percent watched the broadcasts in English; 56.2 percent flipped back and forth between the two languages.

The emergence of Spanish-language television programming has its parallel in radio as well. In New York, *El Vacilón de la Mañana* often tops *Howard Stern* in the ratings war. And before a controversial switch from a morning to an afternoon time slot, *El Cucuy de la Mañana*— hosted by the Honduran Renán Almendarez Coello—drew more listeners than any other morning show in all of Los Angeles, English and Spanish.

Clearly Latinos listen to a lot of radio and watch a lot of TV in Spanish. If those who argue that Latinos are assimilating completely into U.S. society were correct, then we would expect the number of Hispanics who watch Spanish-language TV to be in decline. In fact, the opposite is happening. Let's look again to the example offered by news programming: in 1990, only 25 percent of Latinos who were registered to vote watched news in Spanish. But by 2000, this figure had increased by 45 percent.[35] And if this is happening among registered voters—who have above-average educations and are most often bilingual—then we can only imagine what the figures must be like for that portion of the Latino community that prefers to communicate mainly in Spanish.

This is explained not only by the dramatic growth in the Hispanic population but also because programming executives for Spanish-language stations are more in touch with Latinos' sensibilities than their English-language counterparts. *Telenovelas*—Spanish soap operas—are an old Latin American tradition that has been transplanted and adapted to the tastes of American Latinos, and the highest-rated prime-time shows are often *telenovelas* from Mexico, Venezuela, Colombia, and Brazil. But that's not all.

To get up-to-date news and in-depth analysis of the candidacy of the pro-union leftist Lula da Silva in Brazil; of the leader of the military coup who was elected president of Ecuador; of how CIA-laundered drug money goes to finance narcoguerrillas in Colombia; of the Salvadoran gangs or *maras;* of the arrest of former Nicaraguan president Arnoldo Alemán; of how former New York mayor Rudolph Giuliani was paid $4 million by the Mexican government to act as an outside consultant on reducing crime in Mexico City; of attacks against affirmative action; of the recall of California governor Gray Davis (which among other things would prevent thousands of immigrants from obtaining driver's licenses); of how drugs and immigrants seep across the porous U.S.-Mexico border; of a possible amnesty being granted to millions of illegal aliens in the United States—for many of these things, you have to turn to Spanish-language news programs.

While the United States was consumed with the possibility of war in late 2002 and early 2003, there was another headline that had seized the attention of the Latino community: a national strike was threatening to bring down President Hugo Chavez. Only the Spanish-language news stations provided constant coverage of the standoff, while their English-language counterparts all but ignored this developing crisis. This is why Hispanics are looking more and more often to Spanish-language news sources. It's through them that they remain connected to their countries of origin and reinforce their cultural references.

The Hispanic community has grown so much that it now seems impossible that it could ever fully assimilate into the Anglo-Saxon culture at large. Hispanic culture is unique—and reinvigorated by each new immigrant, each new Spanish-language television show, every long-distance phone call, every package sent to Latin America, and every book written in or translated into Spanish.

The world of Spanish-language books in the United States is currently undergoing a bit of a revolution. Less than a decade ago, few publishers would have dared to bring out Spanish-language editions, and none would have expected a best-seller. But things are changing at a dizzying speed. Two of the world's largest publishing companies opened new divisions to compete for the giant's share of the U.S. market for books in Spanish: HarperCollins/Rayo and Random House Mondadori. And there are dozens of other presses and distributors—both U.S. and Latin American—fighting word for word for Latino dollars.

At first glance, the U.S. market for books in Spanish has yet to bloom: in 1999, 48 million of the 905 million total books sold were in Spanish.[36] But those 48 million volumes—representing 5 percent of total sales—are priced in dollars and thus generate earnings far beyond similar sales figures in Spain or Latin America. There, it would be practically impossible to charge more than $15 or $20 for a book. Here, it's commonplace. The purchasing power of a Hispanic family in the United States is, on average, four or five times greater than a comparable family in Latin America. In other words, U.S. sales of books in Spanish could potentially surpass earnings from the entire publishing industry in any other country.

Yet there is much room for growth. Latinos buy only one book for every three that non-Hispanic whites do.[37] Even so, book clubs are flourishing—like Bookspan's Mosaico and one started by New York's *El Diario La Prensa*—and more and more space is being given to book promotions on the radio, on the Internet (www.baquiana.com), and on television (Univision's *Despierta Leyendo*).

The first volume of Gabriel Gárcia Márquez's autobiography sold tens of thousands of copies—in Spanish—here in the United States. Sadly, papers like the *New York Times,* the *Washington Post,* and *USA Today* didn't include it on their best-seller lists, simply because it wasn't written in English. But the *Los Angeles Times* did, and did so in an inventive, jazzy way. "Without benefit of reviews or publicity, *Vivir para*

Contarla found its way onto the *Times*'s bestseller list,"[38] explained the book review editor; García Márquez's memoir had found itself at number 14 on the list for February 16, 2003. But the *Los Angeles Times* went even further, publishing a review of the book written in Spanish by the Nicaraguan poet and writer Gioconda Belli and paired with an English translation by the venerable U.S. scholar and translator Gregory Rabassa.

The example set in L.A. did not, however, reach the northeast. The *New York Times* started running a new bestseller list for children's books when the Harry Potter craze was sweeping the nation. But sadly, and perhaps ironically, no similar move was made on behalf of García Márquez's book.

García Márquez's Spanish is without equal. Nobody else writes like him, and nobody in the United States speaks in the way that he writes. The Spanish spoken here has nothing to do with Macondo, Madrid, or Monterrey; our Spanish is more Miami, Manhattan, and Modesto. It's often said that only Castilian Spanish—or the Spanish spoken in Colombia or Mexico—is proper. "If it's not in the Royal Academy Dictionary of the Spanish Language, then it's incorrect," is the argument offered by writers who refuse to accept neologisms, Anglicisms, and words in Spanglish. But soon—if it hasn't happened already—there will be more Spanish speakers in the United States than in all of Spain. In fact, it's only a matter of a few years before U.S. Latinos become the world's largest Hispanic population outside of Mexico. When this happens, who will be influencing whom?

The way we speak reflects who we are. We can't speak an Iberian or Mexican form of Spanish because we don't live there. We live here in the United States, and we live using our own hybridized language derived from native Spanish speakers who, for various reasons, ended up living in a country dominated by English speakers. The way we communicate with each other is intrinsically linked to the way we live.

We can't speak pure Spanish or pure English because we live in a world defined by mixture. Ana Celia Zentella—an expert in the field and professor at the University of California at San Diego—puts it thus: "Anthropological linguistics assumes that the ways in which Latinos in the United States speak English and Spanish cannot be divorced from socioeconomic and political realities."[39] Our vocabulary is rife with words in Spanglish—*grincar* (green card), *troca* (truck), *aseguranza* (insurance), *parqueadero* (parking lot), *bipiar* (to beep), *Emilio, bloque, cel, te hablo p'atrás, soshal*—as well as terms that denote our countries of origin: *ándale* (Mexico), *órale* (Mexico), *qué vaina* (Venezuela), *qué berraquera* (Colombia), *chula, está bien nice, chévere* (all from Puerto Rico), and so on. And each of these expressions says something about who we are and how we see each other.

In the editing room where I work, debates often spring up about which words should be used to describe the simplest things. What a Mexican would call an *engrapadora* (stapler) is a *corchetera* to a Chilean. A *guagua* is a bus to a Cuban, a baby to some South Americans, and the sound a dog makes (think "bow wow") to the rest of Latin America. In Mexico we use the word *gubernatura* (government), whereas in Colombia or the Caribbean, *gobernación* is the preferred term. And the *secretarios* of the Mexican government become *ministros* further to the south. Qualifying Spanish as being Colombian, Dominican, Puerto Rican, Mexican, or Cuban is simply a way of underlining our enormous differences—though, of course, there are common rules. Without these rules—mainly imposed by Spain—we'd never be able to understand each other.

Since the majority of Latinos are of Mexican origin, the outcomes of these debates in Univision's Miami offices tend to favor Mexican usage. But ultimately we've adopted a "neutral Spanish" that can be understood throughout the United States, the 13 Latin American nations, and the Caribbean where our programs air. It's this neutral Spanish that is heard every day by millions of people and, according to our critics in Latin America, "is a very poorly spoken Spanish." Maybe so, but our viewers understand us.

And in addition to our neutral Spanish, we've adopted a "neutral accent" so as not to offend any of our many different viewer constituencies. The toughest Spanish accents to hide are Castilian and Argentine, but whichever accent one might use, it's always peppered with a mix of English and Spanglish expressions.

Those who constantly conflate English, Spanish, and Spanglish are often looked down upon, not only by those who only speak English but also by Latinos who have a better command of one language than the other. Our speech—and other people's response to it—has put us in a unique position in society. As Zentella explains, "Of particular importance is the dominant language ideology that equates working-class Spanish-speaking Latinos with poverty and academic failure and defines their Spanish-English bilingual children as linguistically deficient and cognitively confused."[40]

Zentella points out that second-generation Latinos—or, as in my case, those of us who have lived here for a generation's worth of time—are often accused of not having a solid grasp of either English or Spanish, of corrupting both, of being academically lackadaisical, and of being baffled on an intellectual level. But of course these accusations are unjust and unwarranted, especially since they don't take into account the fact that our particular means of communication reflects a world that is linguistically very complex. We speak the way we live, and—far from denoting a lack of depth or dedication—our language simultaneously expresses conflict and an expansive wealth of culture.

Of course, these debates and recriminations are never levied against English-language programming. The larger stations—desperate to avoid losing their market shares—are constantly struggling to attract new, bilingual Hispanic viewers. It's not some sort of heavenly blessing or humane gesture; rather, it's a simple matter of economics and going after the bread of our future. Toward the end of 2002, for example, ABC began airing *The George Lopez Show*. According to the *Wall Street Journal,* the comedy—which is based on the vicissitudes of a Hispanic family living in the Los Angeles suburbs—reflects "Latinos' growing hunger to see themselves portrayed as part of the American mainstream."[41] The same article quotes Linda Navarrete of the National Council of La Raza as saying that "Latinos like it because it's an extraordinary thing to turn on the TV and see somebody that is just like your dad, just like your uncle; and for once the portrayal is positive."

Ironically, ABC promoted the show—which features only a few Spanish words here and there—in Spanish-language media. The results were bittersweet: only 11 percent of Hispanics ages 18 to 49 tuned in, compared with 18 percent of African Americans and 63 percent of Anglo-Saxons.[42] But there's little doubt that *The George Lopez Show,* like the others that preceded it, is a sign of the networks' interest in and attention to the growing Latino market and the positive integration of Latinos into greater U.S. society. Every day you turn on the TV, you can see Hispanics—from multimillion-dollar baseball players to Latina divas—on English-language television.

On Wednesday, November 13, 2002, Diane Sawyer interviewed the Puerto Rican singer and actress Jennifer Lopez for a full hour on the ABC program *Prime Time Live.* Sawyer pressed her repeatedly about the diamond ring given to her by actor Ben Affleck, treating her as if she were the new Liz Taylor. According to social commentator Liz Smith, "Jenny from the Block" (as she has referred to herself) has become "La Lopez." But it's precisely this sort of treatment and dialogue—superficial, chatty, removed from any real Latino issues, and "for entertainment purposes only"—that proves the extent to which Latinos have penetrated the U.S. mainstream. Lopez was never asked to comment on bilingual education, affirmative action programs, or discrimination in Hollywood. All Sawyer wanted to know about was that pink diamond ring. And as if following suit, *USA Today* ran an article entitled "Lopez Following Liz Taylor's Script as She Prepares for Husband No. 3."[43]

All things Latino or Hispanic in the United States are felt, in all areas: two of the best pitchers from the 2002 World Series—Ramón Ortiz of the Anaheim Angels and Liván Hernández of the San Francisco Giants—were born in Cuba and the Dominican Republic, respectively; among the few singers George W. Bush has invited to the White House are the Mexican Americans Jaci Velásquez and Jennifer Peña and the Peruvian Gian Marco; Paquito de Rivera—author of *Mi Vida Saxual*—is one of the most beloved saxophonists on Earth, and the rhythms of Celia Cruz are danced the entire world over; one of the most renowned painters in the United States—and whose works fetch some of the highest prices—is the Colombian Fernando Botero; the murdered singer Selena has reached mythical proportions in Texas; the Cuban Oscar Hijuelos, the Chilean Isabel Allende, and Sandra Cisneros have written more best-selling novels than most U.S. authors; Salma Hayek, from the Mexican state of Veracruz, recently became the first Latina actress to be nominated for an Academy Award for her portrayal of the Mexican painter Frida Kahlo; during the 2003 Grammy Awards on CBS, Procter & Gamble aired "the first Spanish-language ad to be featured on a national broadcast geared to a general English-speaking audience;"[44] and the woman who once signed her name to all legal tender in this country when she was secretary of the Treasury is called Rosario Marín. All of a sudden, being Latino is *muy en la onda.* It's cool. But what really is a Latino? And what's a Hispanic?

HISPANICS, LATINOS, OR WHAT?

Richard Nixon baptized us Hispanics.

Up until the 1970 census, there was no way to categorize all people of Iberian American origin. Nixon, whose presidency began in 1969, was by then well aware of the federal government's shortcomings in its dealings with Mexican Americans, Cubans, and Central Americans. The U.S. government did not have a representative number of Iberian Americans among its employees. It was a political embarrassment, and would later result in the establishment of the Sixteen Point Program for the Spanish Speaking.[45] The program's goal was simple: recruit more Latinos. Nixon was therefore under a lot of pressure to espouse the ideal of equal and just treatment of all minorities, not just blacks. And he had the opportunity to prove this with the 1970 census.

In his book *Counting on the Census,* Peter Skerry relates just how the census category of "Hispanic" came to be: "The finalized questionnaires for the 1970 census were already at the printers when a Mexican American member of the U.S. Interagency Committee on Mexican American affairs demanded that a specific Hispanic-origin

question be included. . . . Over the opposition of Census Bureau officials who argued against inclusion of an untested question so late in the
process, [President] Nixon ordered the Secretary of Commerce and
the Census director to add the question."[46]

The very existence of a committee representing several federal
agencies and dedicated to analyzing the interests and concerns of
Mexican Americans is a clear sign of the growing importance of this
segment of the population. Why did Nixon ultimately make the call
and add the question to the census? For purely political reasons.

As you've seen, I use the terms "Hispanic" and "Latino" in-
terchangeably. In California and Chicago, people generally prefer
"Latino." In Florida and Texas, "Hispanic" usually takes priority. But
when it comes down to it, most of the people I know don't use either
of these terms to describe themselves. They say, "I'm Mexican," "I'm
Cuban," "I'm Puerto Rican," "I'm Colombian," or "Mexican American." What they don't say is "I'm Latino" or "I'm Hispanic." To use
those terms is to group us together, whereas specifying one's place of
origin has a more personalizing effect. It breaks down one large
generic group into multiple individualized ones.

According to the Pew Hispanic Center, "More than half (54%) indicate that they primarily identify themselves in terms of their or their
parent's country of origin; about one in four (24%) chooses 'Latino' or
'Hispanic,' and about one in five (21%) chooses 'American.' "[47] But
while a small percentage of the population does prefer to define themselves as such, the terms "Hispanic" or "Latino" have been invaluable
in their ability to quantify a growing segment of the population and
give it a single categorization. By grouping together under one name
(or two), we can present a united front, on both political and economic matters as well as in defense of our civil rights and education. If
an official, unifying category did not exist, our incipient political
power would be much more diluted.

Officially, however, we were Hispanics until the 2000 election,
not Latinos. The writer Earl Shorris tells how this came about: "In ac-
cordance with the will of the people who took part in the decision [to
choose the word used in the 1970 census], the term 'Latino' won. But

at the last minute someone said that 'Latino' was too close to 'Ladino,' which was an ancient Spanish dialect spoken by only a handful of Spanish Jews. And so instead, 'Hispanic' was chosen."[48] Shorris, who authored one of the most comprehensive books on this ethnic group, *Latinos: A Biography of the People,* prefers the term "Latino" because "language defines the group, provides it with history and home; language should also determine its name—Latino."[49]

Strictly speaking, "Latino" is a reference to the language that was spoken in the region of Latium, which lies in modern-day Italy and includes the province Latina (previously known as Littoria) to the southeast of Rome. Two millennia ago, Roman conquerors imposed their language on the Iberian Peninsula, and in 1492, "Spanish"— with its roots in both vulgar and classical Latin—crossed the Atlantic with Christopher Columbus and entered our hemisphere. "Latino" is intrinsically linked to the Spanish language as well as to the culture and history that is transmitted through that language. Those who reject the term "Latino" generally do so by arguing that they don't speak Latin but rather Spanish, and that to emphasize a bond within Latin America excludes Spain and the Spanish-speaking islands of the Caribbean.

"Hispanic," on the other hand, bears a direct reference to power, geography, and a history of imperial domination. As Shorris explains, it is the term preferred by the king of Spain himself, Juan Carlos de Borbón. According to the Royal Academy Dictionary of the Spanish Language, "Hispanic" is "that which pertains or relates to Hispania," or the Iberian Peninsula's territory. This term provokes much debate, owing to its connotations of imperialism and domination by Spanish conquistadors. Also, it's not very precise: the portion of the U.S. population with roots in Spain barely registered on the 2000 census (0.3 percent, or 100,000 respondents). But "Hispanic" was the official designation used in the census, although elsewhere on the same questionnaire the category was expanded to read "Spanish/Hispanic/Latino."

Nor should it seem strange that the term "Hispanic" has been the official term for the past 30 years, and that—as is so often the case with bureaucracy—it will continue to be so. "Hispanic" is easier to pronounce in English, and its neutral gender eliminates any potential "Latino/Latina" confusion. In a society that strives to be politically correct, there are already people who have started to write the word in a more gender-neutral form—"Latin@." Clearly, Latin@ is gender-neutral, but how does one pronounce it?

The fascinating thing about both terms is that they each emphasize aspects of the group's culture—its geographic origin, in the case of "Hispanic," and its language, in the case of "Latino"—without any racial elements. This represents a significant moment in the history of the United States, which, since its earliest beginnings, has demarcated its people along racial lines, especially black and white. Hispanics/Latinos have sidestepped this standard. Race becomes less relevant in the presence of Latinos, since it can't be used by itself to define us. When talking with Hispanics, race is not as important as their cultural antecedents. Hispanics exemplify what the 2000 census instructions underlined: they can be of any race.

The terms "Hispanic" or "Latino" force people to think in new and different ways. All of a sudden, the racially polarized view of the world—a world of black and white—is being supplanted by a vision of a truly multiethnic, multicultural society. No longer can everything be explained along racial lines; the population can now be divided along ethnic lines into Hispanic and non-Hispanic. The United States has been redefined, in a fundamental way, by the Hispanic presence. In the 2000 census, under the section "Race and Hispanic Origin" question 5 splits the country in two.

5. Is this person Spanish/Hispanic/Latino? Mark the "No" box if not Spanish/Hispanic/Latino.

☐ No, not Spanish/Hispanic/Latino
☐ Yes, Mexican, Mexican Am, Chicano
☐ Yes, Puerto Rican
☐ Yes, Cuban
☐ Yes, other Spanish/Hispanic/Latino (print group)

The triple definition of "Spanish/Hispanic/Latino" that the Census Bureau now uses shows just how difficult it is to define us—even for ourselves. When I had to fill out the survey for my son Nicolás, I had to check off almost every category so as not to lie. It ended up saying that he was "White" like his paternal grandparents, "Cuban" like his maternal grandparents, "Puerto Rican" like his mother, and "Mexican" like his father. I didn't know how to explain that he also surely has some indigenous blood in him, as I do. Maybe the next census will have a space for clarifying that. But before any other single definition, the Hispanic identity is a mixture. And there is my son Nicolás—a white Puertocubanomexicanoamerican with indigenous traces and born in Miami—to prove it all.

THEIR OWN WAY:
THE DILEMMAS OF HISPANIC IDENTITY

How does one unite those who are different?

When the Mexican poet Octavio Paz visited Los Angeles during the middle part of the last century, he was struck by the patently Mexican character of the city: "At first glance, the traveler is surprised by not only the purity of the sky and the ugliness of the scattered, ostentatious buildings but also by the city's vaguely Mexican ambiance, impossible to suppress with words or concepts," Paz wrote in his masterpiece, *The Labyrinth of Solitude*.[50] "This Mexican character—affinity for adornments, heedlessness and opulence, negligence, passion, and discretion—floats through the air."

Los Angeles—*el Pueblo de Nuestra Señora la Reina de los Angeles de Porciúncula*—has always been a town marked by things Hispanic. It was founded in 1769 by the Spanish explorer Caspar de Portolá and a few years later—in 1781—it became an agricultural center. Los Angeles was a Spanish city first, and then a Mexican one, and finally a U.S. one. But it has never lost that "vaguely Mexican ambiance."

Paz also noted that the same dilemma many Latinos face today—whether to adapt completely to U.S. society—was already being confronted by the Pachuco population—"bands of youths, usually of Mexican origins, who lived in the cities of the U.S. south, and who distinguish themselves as much by their dress as by their conduct and language. . . . The Pachucos don't want to return to their Mexican roots; neither, apparently, do they wish to meld into U.S. life."[51]

Paz didn't see this resistance among the blacks, who, "persecuted by racial intolerance, resolved to 'walk the line' and integrate with society." But with the Mexicans he saw that "far from attempting a problematic adaptation to prevailing norms, they affirmed their differences, underlined them, tried to make them notable . . . they espoused neither injustice nor the shortcomings of a society that had not succeeded in assimilating them, but rather their personal desire to continue being different." It is this same desire that continues to mark the Latino population today.

The problem consists in how to balance both desires: that of forming part of U.S. society without being smothered and swept away by it. "So the cultural dilemma of the American of Mexican, Cuban or Puerto Rican descent is suddenly universalized: to integrate or not? To maintain a personality and add to the diversity of North American society, or to fade away into anonymity in the name of the after all nonexistent 'melting pot.' "[52]

The problem with identity is always present among the Hispanic community. In March of 2003, over 30,000 U.S. citizens who had renounced their Mexican nationality got it back thanks to a temporary change in the Mexican constitution. These Mexicans, who had opted for U.S. citizenship, didn't want to stop being Mexican altogether and chose to undertake a long, complicated, bureaucratic process to formally get their Mexican status back. It was an act heavily laden with symbolism—and difficulties—with few practical benefits.

The interminable lines that formed outside the Mexican consulates in the United States before the March 20, 2003, deadline, are proof that identity is a supremely complicated issue for many Hispanics. The majority of those who recovered their Mexican nationality had no intentions of returning to live in Mexico. But it was important for them to continue to be Mexican, even if they did keep their U.S. passports safely guarded at home. They felt comfortable in two countries, and after all, they could legally belong to two countries as well.

Hispanics feel a double pull—wanting to live in the United States while wanting to remain distinct. And they reaffirm these desires constantly. Some may see these as opposite, irreconcilable forces, but they're not. It is possible to be different and be a proud part of the United States at the same time. A Latino is not afraid of mixtures—of races, beliefs, or history—because ultimately he is himself the product of *mestizaje*. He has roots in indigenous and Spanish, native and European cultures. This unique mixture is our essence and the reason we are not afraid of compounds, of browns and grays. If we can be Spaniards and Indians at the same time, why can't we be Americans too?

Every nation, no matter how pure and unpolluted it thinks itself, is "a relationship of solidarity between race, language, culture, religion, and general ambiance," as Mexico's former secretary of foreign relations, Emilio O. Rabasa, once wrote. "Nevertheless, the two transcendental elements are a shared common history and a desire to participate in a future, also shared."[53] These two elements are clearly exemplified by the Latino community in the United States.

When Mexican philosopher José Vasconcelos wrote *The Cosmic Race* in 1925, one of the prevailing worldviews was that of Charles Darwin's natural selection, where favorable traits would survive to be passed on to the next generation while unfavorable ones would be phased out. Perversions of this theory gave rise to Social Darwinism and ideas of racial purity, such as the Nazis espoused, and even today serves as the basis for nationalist movements that spout off theories of white supremacy. But amid all the rhetoric on the division of races and cultures, Vasconcelos proposed bringing differences together and attracting opposites.

Even if, at the end of his life, Vasconcelos himself recognized the impossibility of a cosmic race "fashioned out of the treasures of all the previous ones," his work still emphasized the importance of mixture and synthesis. "The ulterior goal of history," he wrote, "is to attain the fusion of peoples and cultures." After noting that the American continent has been home to the greatest races in contemporary history—"the white, the red, the black, and the yellow"—he concluded, with a certain amount of idealism, that "the so-called Latin peoples . . . are the ones called upon to consummate this mission."[54] According to Vasconcelos, the union of races and cultures would define the future. And he wasn't alone in his beliefs.

As we've seen in Paz, Fuentes, and Vasconcelos, every time the issue of the uniting of differences is raised, conflicts arise. Living amid diversity is complicated. And that's what life in the United States is all about.

HISPANICS AND THEIR OBSESSION
WITH THE STORY OF ME

The autobiographies of Latino writers who live in the United States are an excellent resource for better understanding the conflicts of the Hispanic identity, and they show how powerfully the desire to assimilate and insistence on individuality can collide. A Hispanic person's life story is almost always a voyage through a world filled with conflicting opposites. Three Latinos in particular provide good examples of this: Marie Arana, Ilan Stavans, and Richard Rodriguez.

Marie Arana is an "American" girl. Born to a Peruvian father and a U.S. mother, Arana learned from an early age how to take advantage of her double identity. When she first learned that her full name was Marie Elverine Arana Campbell, she came to the conclusion—in the presence of her Aunt Chaba and her grandmother in Peru—that would forever change the way she looked at herself. "I am not Peruvian. . . . I'm not like them. . . . I'm an American. Un Yanqui. My name is Campbell."[55]

Sometime after Arana emigrated to the United States with her parents, she read a theory that made her question her biculturalism. It suggested that being bilingual could have negative consequences, because "in operating as two distinct personalities with two distinct tongues, a bicultural person will be highly suspect to those who have only one culture. . . . Only an imposter would hide that other half so well. A liar." [56]

The problem wasn't that others looked at her in such a light; rather, that she herself—Marie Elverine Arana Campbell—did. "I had been fooling people for years. Slip into my American skin, and the playground would never know I was really Peruvian. Slip into the Latina, and Peruvians wouldn't suspect I was a Yank. . . . It was a new kind of independence." [57]

In the end, Arana didn't resolve her contradictions, but she learned to live with them: "I, a Latina, who—to this day—burns incense, prays on her knees to the Virgin, feels auras, listens for spirits of the dead. I, an Anglo, who snaps her out of it, snuffs candles, faces reality, sweeps ash into the ash can, works at a newspaper every day. I a north-south collision, a New World fusion. An American *chica*. A bridge." [58]

When Ilan Stavans—a Mexican Jew—went to the ceremony that would finally convert him into a U.S. citizen, he knew that he'd have to hand over his Mexican passport. After an INS agent called his name—Ilan Stavchansky—she asked him, "Mexican?" to which Ilan jokingly replied, "I'm about to give up the vice." But when he went to surrender his Mexican passport, the agent stopped him. "Don't bother," she said. "You may keep it. What use is it to me?" "But don't I have to give up my Mexican citizenship?" Ilan asked. "Well . . ." she mused, after a silence. [59]

Ilan tried symbolically to renounce his Mexicanness. But he couldn't. Nor will he be able to. "What does it mean to be an American?" he asked himself. Ilan had dedicated himself to an academic life and the study of languages, and he himself spoke Spanish, Yiddish, Hebrew, and English. But, "English was not . . . the great equalizer, at least not at the moment when a citizen is sworn in." [60]

Ilan's triple identity—Mexican, Jewish, and (relatively recently) U.S.—coupled with his polyglot status didn't necessarily facilitate his integration into this country. As an immigrant, "one gets the impression of ceasing to be—in Spanish, the feeling of *no estar del todo*," he reflected of his own experience. "The immigrant feels trapped in the space in between words and in the intricacies of the journey. . . . But sooner or later, loss is transformed into gain: the immigrant is born again—rejuvenated, enriched by the voyage." [61]

Ilan considers that "Latinos needed to recognize, and reconcile, their forking self, part Hispanic, part American." [62] He, like Marie Arana, has learned to handle the forces pulling at him from many different directions. But more than living (in his particular case) in three different worlds, he lives between them: "My Mexican self is not altogether gone, nor is my American self so prevalent as to erase everything else. In between the two stands my Jewishness, moderating the tension, becoming an arbitrator—and perhaps a censor."

Richard Rodriguez resists the temptation to define himself as Hispanic, but he can't help writing—and thinking—like one. If one phrase had to be chosen to define all three of his autobiographical works, it would have to be his question: "Do Hispanics exist?" [63] And with his own particular brand of irony, he writes, "For a larger fee, I will add that there is no such thing as a Hispanic." [64]

Beyond his controversial opposition to bilingual education and affirmative action, Rodriguez (there is no accent over the "i") contends that the term "Hispanic" was invented by Richard Nixon—"the dark father of Hispanicity" [65]—and that such categories are unnecessary in a country as defined by mixtures as the United States is. At times, one has to think that Rodriguez would prefer a bipolar nation—one seen in black and white—than one that includes Hispanics in general and himself in particular. Why else would he choose to base his definitions on race and not the history, language, and culture of different ethnic groups?

Nevertheless, Rodriguez cannot—nor does he want to—deny Hispanic influence. "Thanks to Hispanics, Americans have come to see the United States . . . in north-south or hot-cold terms," he writes in his book *Brown*. "It's a new way of situating ourselves in the 21st century."

Again, we see that the Latinization of Americans and the Americanization of Hispanics are parallel phenomena. But Rodriguez notes with irony, "What Hispanic immigrants learn within the United States is to view themselves in a new way, as belonging to Latin America entire—precisely at the moment they no longer do." [66]

The color of coffee, the mixture, the encounter between worlds, histories and identities, have marked Rodriguez's life. "In Latin America, what makes me brown is that I'm formed by both conquistador and Indian. My brownness is a memory of conflict. And of reconciliation. In my mind, what makes me brown in the United States is that I'm Richard Rodriguez. My given name and my last name wed the English with the Spanish, rivals of rebirth."

Distinctly reserved in his own space yet always ready to fight off any attempt at classifying him, Rodriguez tries to offer the preemptive definition of mestizo: "My mestizo boast: As a queer Catholic Indian Spaniard at home in a temperate Chinese city in a fading blond state in a post-Protestant nation . . ." [67] Perhaps. But ultimately the important thing is his prophecy about the United States: "The future is brown, is my thesis; is as brown as the tarnished past." [68] In other words, the future belongs to the Hispanics—even if, in his opinion, they don't exist.

Rodriguez, Stavans, and Arana describe for us a world of different currents, a space where identity is formed by forces colliding. There is yet another immigrant's autobiography where these collisions are perfectly rendered, but this time we're not talking about a Hispanic writer. The writer and thinker Edward Said was born in Palestine and raised and educated in the United States. Said writes of the same roiling waves that form his identity as Rodriguez, Stavans, and Arana do.

"I occasionally experience myself as a cluster of flowing currents. I prefer this to the idea of a solid self. . . . These currents, like the themes of one's life, flow along during the waking hours, and at their best, they require no reconciling, no harmonizing. They are 'off' and may be out of place, but at least they are always in motion, in time, in place, in the form of all kinds of strange combinations moving about, not necessarily forward, sometimes against each other, contrapuntally yet without one central theme. A form a freedom, I'd like to think." [69]

This description is applicable to Hispanics in the United States. These confrontations—these conflicts that occasionally have no resolution—are the defining structure of Hispanics, and of the very nature of the United States itself.

Whichever way you look at it, the Latino presence in the United States is a definitive, expansive one. This is no longer a country in black and white; it's a mestizo one. And its strength radiates from the tolerance of that very diversity. But, as Octavio Paz said, the challenge is for the United States to recognize itself: a multi-ethnic, multiracial, multicultural nation. The many in the one.

Will America have the courage to look itself in the mirror?

CHAPTER FOUR

HOW TO WOO LATINOS: A GUIDE

WHILE IT IS TRUE that the majority of Latino voters are registered with the Democratic Party, on certain issues—like abortion, homosexuality, divorce, and the use of contraceptives—they often identify more closely with the Republican Party's position.

When the results of the Pew Hispanic Center study were released in October 2002, the fact that Hispanics tended to identify with Democrats over Republicans by more than 2 to 1 was a great relief to Democratic leaders.

According to a statement made by Democratic National Committee chairman Terry McAuliffe, "Despite the sleek marketing gimmicks and Republican mariachi-style efforts to pander to Latinos, the bonds that unite the Hispanic community and the Democratic Party are stronger than ever."[1] Other Democrats were singing the same tune: "Republicans are desperately trying to play catch-up to the Democrats' successful outreach efforts," commented Democratic press secretary Guillermo Menéses. "They can't achieve in a two-year period what we have achieved over a 20- to 30-year period."[2]

Nevertheless, things changed dramatically after the 2004 presidential election, when President Bush and Republicans almost tied the number of Latino votes obtained by John Kerry and the Democrats. Since November 2, 2004, neither party could say it controlled the Latino vote. Why? Roberto Suro, director of the Pew Hispanic Center, has an explanation: "Despite strong democratic leanings, Latinos show significant partisan ambivalence. At a time of very sharp partisan divisions, they're not ideologically committed to either of the major parties." The only notable exception is that of Cuban Americans, who have consistently voted for the Republican Party.

The aversion that Cuban Americans feel toward the Democratic Party goes far beyond the Elián González incident in 2000. We can look to the Kennedy administration's failure to provide air support during the attempted Bay of Pigs invasion. On April 17, 1961, some 1,500 Cuban refugees disembarked either in the Bay or at Girón Beach with the objective of removing Castro from power. The operation was coordinated by the CIA and was supported by the 2506 Brigade and exiled Cubans, but the air support on which they were counting never arrived, and the invasion was repulsed.

Since then, Cuban exiles have never forgiven Kennedy and, by extension, his party for what they consider an act of betrayal. More recently, it's been the Republicans who have most staunchly defended the U.S. embargo against the island. While it may be true that the embargo hasn't been a success (at least in terms of forcing the Castro regime from power), many Cuban Americans consider it to be a question of morality and principles: they don't want to do business with a dictator.

Cubans know how to play the political game in this country. Despite being a minority among the Latino community, by 2002 they had managed to put four Cuban American representatives in Congress to help them defend their particular interests. And, in 2004, they elected the first Cuban American senator in history: Mel Martínez.

It would be ignorant to claim that all Cuban Americans vote as one. Studies show that there are clear divisions even among the exile community. But what is certain is that they have had great success in controlling the two major political positions in southern Florida. If other Hispanic groups—particularly Mexican Americans and Puerto Ricans—were to similarly develop their political potential, we may well see Latino mayors in Los Angeles, New York, and Houston.

THE 2002 LATINO VOTE: CANDIDATES, NOT PARTIES

The 2002 elections resulted in two concrete gains for the Hispanic community: the first Latino governor since 1986 (Bill Richardson of

New Mexico) and an increase in the number of representatives in Congress from 19 to 22. Mario Díaz-Balart (R-Fla.), Linda Sanchez (D-Calif.), and Raul Grijalva (D-Ariz.) joined the 19 Hispanic incumbents, all of whom won reelection.[3] For the first time in history, there were two pairs of Latino siblings in Congress: Linda and Loretta Sanchez of California, and Mario and Lincoln Díaz-Balart in Florida.

Still, 22 congressional representatives aren't a lot. African Americans—whose numbers were almost identical to those of Hispanics in 2002—managed to raise their number to 37 representatives. To accurately reflect their percentage of the population (13 percent), there would need to be 13 senators, 56 House members, and 6 governors.

In 2002, there was not a single Hispanic senator. Historically there have only been three: Octaviano Larrazolo (R-N.M.) in 1928, Dennis Chavez (D-N.M.) in 1936, and Joseph Manuel Montoya (D-N.M.) in 1964. Regarding governors, there is a similar disparity.

Bill Richardson became the eighth Latino governor in U.S. history. He defeated the Republican candidate John Sanchez in a contest that, more than any other thing, emphasized the political maturity of New Mexico's voters. Richardson is the fifth Hispanic governor they have elected. And 2002 marked the second time in New Mexico history (the first was 1918) that two Latinos ran against each other for the office.

Richardson, who served several terms as a congressman from New Mexico, as well as the U.S. ambassador to the UN and Energy Secretary under the Clinton administration, used his impressive experience and image to easily defeat Sanchez. "The experience I have with national and international issues, for example, can bring more jobs from Mexico and Latin America to New Mexico, which is a very poor state," Richardson said in an interview before the November 2002, election. "The Hispanic vote will be decisive and thank God that the Hispanic vote is with me."[4]

He was right: the Hispanic vote was with him. Fully 70 percent of Latinos voted for him, compared with the 20 percent who favored Sanchez.[5] Richardson would now have to concern himself with such things as school budgets in Santa Fe and the foundering economy in Albuquerque; gone were his globe-trotting days, hopping from Iraq to North Korea, calming dictators and resolving international crises. His election to the governorship made him the most influential Hispanic politician in the country. How did he do it? In part by not exaggerating his ethnicity.

When the August 2000 issue of *George* magazine asked Richardson how he felt about being labeled Hispanic—his mother is Mexican—he answered, "I'm very proud [of being Hispanic], but try not to wear it on my sleeve, don't overemphasize it. I am not a professional Hispanic. To get ahead you must deal with mainstream issues, not just Hispanic ones."[6]

One might also ask how much influence a Hispanic governor has over the issues affecting the Latino community? The answer is, a lot, and here's an example: On March 18, 2003, Governor Richardson signed a new law that made New Mexico the first state ever to permit undocumented immigrants to obtain driver's licenses. Instead of giving them a Social Security number, they were assigned an IRS identification number with which they could apply for a driver's license. Within months of his election, Governor Richardson was already having a positive effect on the Latino community, immigrants included. I have to wonder whether a non-Latino governor would have done such a thing so rapidly.

The 2002 gubernatorial campaigns in Florida, Texas, California, and New York also clearly reflect both the importance of the Hispanic vote and the enormous differences that exist in that same electorate.

The most Americanized Latinos live in Texas and New Mexico, while the most Latin American live in California and Florida. In Texas, there are three Latinos with U.S. citizenship for every one without, whereas in California the ratio is one to one. In other words, Texas and New Mexico Latinos have a greater impact on elections than those in California do.

One of the most important conclusions that the National Council of La Raza has drawn is that "Latino voter behavior in the 2002 election provided further evidence that Latinos judge candidates by their record and issue positions, not party affiliation."[7] Jeb Bush, the governor of Florida, is a good example.

Governor Bush sought to attract not only the Cuban American vote but also the votes of those non-Cuban Latinos who were more often affiliated with the Democratic Party. "It's important to not only speak Spanish but also to understand something about the aspirations of the Hispanic communities in Florida," he said—in Spanish—in an interview. Note that he used "Hispanic communities" in the plural. "The fact that I'm married to a Mexican woman and that my daughters are Hispanic helps."[8] It certainly does.

During his reelection campaign, Bush placed a lot of emphasis on the fact that during his term, literacy rates rose among Hispanic children, that there was a 150 percent growth in the number of Hispanics employed by the state government, and that he named the first Latino to Florida's supreme court. Jeb then went on to defeat his Democratic challenger Bill McBride in several Florida counties with high Latino populations with Democratic tendencies.[9]

A similar phenomenon took place in New York, where Republican governor George Pataki made an enormous effort to attract Latino support. After the terrorist attacks of September 11, I had the chance to interview him, and was surprised to learn that his Spanish classes had served him well. We didn't have a very complicated conversation, but he was able to communicate some of his messages in Spanish effectively. But it was more than that; when it comes to issues important to New York Latinos—for example, the temporary protection of Colombian immigrants—Pataki has assumed a distinctly pro-Hispanic position. But his most valiant decision was the one he made to oppose the U.S. Navy in Vieques.

This severely undermined the Democratic base of his opponent H. Carl McCall, who made a number of personal slipups during the campaign. In the end, Pataki won 38 percent of the Latino vote, which represented a significant increase over the 25 percent he got in 1998.[10] As a headline from the *New York Times* put it, Pataki broke from the traditional mold that is expected to fit most Republican candidates. And in doing so, he also won 39 percent of the vote in New York City, which is characterized by its high percentage of Democrats.

Looking to the Democratic gubernatorial campaign in Texas, the Hispanic vote served as an indicator of some very serious problems within the Tony Sanchez camp.[11]

The $59 million that, according to the Associated Press, Democratic candidate Tony Sanchez spent during his campaign wasn't enough to win him the governorship. A significant part of this sum came out of his own personal fortune. In the end, he found himself far behind the Republican candidate, Rick Perry, who had inherited the position from George W. Bush in December 2000. Perry spent half as much as Sanchez, but won 58 percent of the vote to Sanchez's 40 percent, thus bringing to a close an election rife with personal attacks.

Pre-election statistics showed that 2 out of every 10 Texas voters were Hispanic and 7 of 10 were white. Sanchez was the first Hispanic candidate in the state's history. In order to win, he would have to dominate the Latino vote while still commanding a significant percentage of the non-Latino vote.

Sanchez did just about everything he could to win the Latino vote. As many journalists have corroborated, he speaks Spanish with only the slightest accent, he supports affirmative action programs—"it helps those people who have suffered from discrimination"—he understands (as many Hispanics do) that "a good education is the basis for getting a good job with a good salary," and tried to orchestrate a Spanish-language debate against his challenger for the Democratic nomination, Dan Morales. Morales ended up declining to debate in Spanish, and Sanchez won the nomination. But it is possible that some non-Hispanic whites found Sanchez to be too Latino for their taste. Bill Richardson, on the other hand, chose not to overemphasize his Latino roots because he knew that white voters represented the majority of his electorate. Just as they do in Texas.

The serious personal accusations that Perry levied against Sanchez and his financial practices didn't help him either. So on November 5,

2002, the majority of whites voted for Perry and the majority of His-panics voted for Sanchez. Perry won.

The question is, how do we break down the Latino vote? According to Republican Party pollster Mike Baselice, Perry won 35 percent of the Hispanic vote, whereas the Southwest Voter Registration Education Project (SVREP) puts the figure at only 12 percent.[12] That's quite a difference. But what this proves is that Texas—which has historically been a very Democratic state—has been turned into a political battlefield through elevated Republican efforts to attract more Latino voters.

If we accept the 35 percent figure, it is still less than what George W. Bush commanded when he was reelected as governor. If Sanchez did in fact lose 35 out of every 100 Hispanic voters, then something went wrong with his campaign. Could he have done something else to have swung the Latino vote even more decisively in his favor? Perhaps yes. As one influential Spanish-language TV executive told me, Sanchez took it for granted that the Hispanic community would vote for him and didn't invest enough effort or money into Spanish-language publicity. What he did spend totaled $1.8 million dollars.[13] But the lesson is that the mere fact of being a Latino candidate doesn't guarantee that the Latino community will throw its full support behind you.

When Perry found out that he would be facing a Hispanic opponent, it forced him to make decisions that would be looked upon favorably by the Latino community. "As soon as they announced my candidacy, [Governor Perry] started naming Hispanics left and right," Sanchez said in an interview. "Before that he didn't know that we were here, that we've been here for 300 years. All of a sudden he finds us, and to me that's an insult."[14] Perhaps. But it worked.

Another, albeit less publicized, triumph was the designation of Cuban American Bob Menendez as vice chairman of the Democratic Party in the House of Representatives. He won his post—the second highest in the House Democratic hierarchy—in a closed vote of 104 to 103. Interestingly enough, Menendez decided not to emphasize his

Hispanic roots in his acceptance speech, opting instead to speak to issues that concern all citizens, such as education, the economy, and
health care.

This is not to say, however, that Menendez considers Hispanics to
be no different from other immigrant groups. "We recognize the
enormous power that lies in being able to speak another language, in
this case Spanish," he told me during an interview. "We represent
something different in this country's history of immigration."[15]

Different how? Well, on November 13, 2002, Congressman Ciro
Rodríguez became the new chairman of the Congressional Hispanic Caucus, replacing Silvestre Reyes in the important position.
And what makes this different? The fact that Ciro Rodríguez—one of
the country's most influential Hispanic congressmen—was born in
Piedras Negras, Mexico. In other words, an immigrant has become
one of this nation's most important Hispanic leaders.

In the 2002 elections, there were more Latino congressional candidates than ever before, including 11 Democratic candidates running
in Arizona, California, Florida, Kansas, New Mexico, Nevada, and
Texas.

According to Adam Segal of Johns Hopkins University's Hispanic
Voter Project, over $16 million was spent on Spanish-language public-
ity. Twenty candidates running for governor, six for the Senate, and
dozens more for the House made use of Spanish-language ads. The
figure is still dwarfed, however, by the some $1 billion spent on all the
publicity in English.

When I mentioned these statistics to an executive well-connected
to the Spanish-language television industry, he replied, "There's a lot
of rhetoric and hypocrisy with respect to the importance of the Hispanic vote when you compare it with the amount of money actually
spent on Spanish-language publicity." Very true. The amount spent
didn't even come to 2 percent of the total expenditure during the 2002
elections.

THE LATINO WAVE   155

THE 2003 CALIFORNIA RECALL ELECTION

On Tuesday, October 7, 2003, Californians made a decision unprecedented in their state's history. By 55 percent in favor versus 45 percent against, they voted to recall Governor Gray Davis and replace him with an Austrian-born actor. Arnold Schwarzenegger took over the post with 49 percent of the vote, followed by Gray's lieutenant governor, Cruz Bustamante, who garnered 32 percent.

The Latino vote found itself in a clash of currents. The majority was against the recall (55 percent) and in favor of Bustamante (also 55 percent), and only 31 percent voted for Schwarzenegger.[16] That was all he needed, however.

Why did Arnold win? He made a calculated bet and won. He knew that if he took an anti-immigrant position, he would indeed lose the Latino vote. But at the same time, this would allow him to win the support of voters who were upset with undocumented immigrants, feminists, and affirmative action programs. And he was right.

On an electoral level, these blocs of voters were much larger than the Latino voting community, which makes up only 20 percent of the California electorate. And to woo them, Arnold hired former California governor Pete Wilson—who is often accused of being anti-immigrant—as his campaign chief. He revealed that he'd been in favor of Proposition 187, which would have denied some 3 million immigrants access to hospitals and public schools. Later during the campaign, he said that one of his first decisions as governor would be to eliminate driver's licenses for undocumented immigrants, a program that then-governor Davis had signed into law shortly before the recall as a means of increasing his support among Hispanic voters.

Schwarzenegger's strategy worked. He made it his goal to appeal to the majority's interests, and he proved correct. In California, it still pays—and pays well—to be anti-immigrant. And thus Schwarzenegger—an immigrant himself, born in Austria but a U.S. citizen for several decades—won California's gubernatorial race, by turning his back on immigrants.

But Schwarzenegger won for other reasons too. Millions of

women decided to vote for him despite the accusations that he had sexually harassed at least 16 women. "How can you have voted for a candidate accused of treating women in this way?" I asked a female voter who lives near San Francisco. "His wife Maria supports him," she replied, "which means that many of the accusations may be false." Having his wife, Maria Shriver, at his side was sufficient to counteract the accusations that sprung from an exhaustive investigation by the *Los Angeles Times.*

Another factor that helps explain Schwarzenegger's overwhelming victory is his money. When someone has a bank account of $56 million—$1 million for each year of his life—then spending a few million to win the governor's mansion doesn't represent much of a risk. His children and grandchildren have their futures secured.

During one particular interview, Cruz Bustamante complained bitterly that he couldn't compete with Conan the Barbarian when it came to paying for TV advertisements. But it must be said that Bustamante managed his campaign with little ink: there were days when he all but disappeared from the headlines, and his relaxed demeanor didn't win over voters who were seeking a strong, decisive leader.

In the end, it was more than Arnold's millions and his campaign advisers—the thing that weighed most heavily in the minds of voters was the inefficiency, indecision, and errors of Governor Davis. What happened in California wasn't so much a vote for Schwarzenegger as it was a vote against Davis. Of course, Davis left a horrible legacy: each of California's 35 million citizens will have to pay $1,000 apiece in order to get rid of the state's budget deficit.

The lessons of the 2003 recall were tough. Despite their growing political power, Hispanics couldn't place a Latino—Cruz Bustamante—in the governor's mansion. Instead, they saw a candidate run—and win—on an openly anti-immigrant platform. It was certainly a wakeup call for immigrant rights groups throughout the nation.

In many ways, Latinos want what everybody else in this country wants: better schools for their children, better jobs for themselves, their own home, more opportunities for personal development, and a peaceful world. But some of these issues take on an added sense of urgency if we note that one out of every three Latinos is under the age of 18, thus making education an especially important issue. Schools and jobs are two of the Hispanic community's greatest priorities. After all, that's why they're here: so that they can have better lives and their children can enjoy a better tomorrow.

But there's more. The situation of millions of immigrants is a constant preoccupation. The discrimination that Latinos suffer—for simply speaking Spanish, coming from another country, or seeing themselves as different—is akin to the African American experience. In times of war, Hispanics are as loyal as any, ready to give their lives for this country despite the fact that many do not even have a U.S. passport. And this country's close proximity—geographically as well as emotionally—to Latin American demands that this part of the world be a focal point of U.S. foreign policy.

So you want the Hispanic vote? Then let's talk about schools and jobs, amnesty, discrimination, Hispanics' sense of loyalty to the United States, and the problems facing Latin America. But we'll take it step-by-step. These, then, are some of the issues that Hispanics are most interested in.

IT'S EDUCATION AND THE ECONOMY, STUPID

What are the two most important issues to Latinos? Without a doubt: education and the economy. Period. There are, of course, other concerns—immigration, medical insurance, social violence, etc.—but nothing takes the place of having a good job and a good school for your children.

According to a Pew Hispanic Center/Kaiser Family Foundation survey, 58 percent of Latino voters rate education as the most important issue when it comes to deciding which candidate to vote for. Among those Latinos who were born outside of the country, that figure rises to 68 percent.[17]

The economy is the second most important issue. According to the same survey, 39 percent of Latinos use it as the determining factor in deciding who to cast their votes for. And the figure rises to 43 percent among foreign-born Latinos.

Other issues such as medical care (23 percent) and Social Security pay (20 percent) occupy the third and fourth tiers in terms of their importance to Hispanic voters.

To paraphrase the watchwords from Bill Clinton's 1992 campaign, "It's education and the economy, stupid." According to the same source, education is even more important to Latinos than it is to African Americans (46 percent) and whites (40 percent), and economic conditions worry more Hispanics than whites (38 percent) and blacks (30 percent).

Almost all Hispanic immigrants come to this country in search of better educational and economic opportunities. But the process of adapting to life in the United States is supremely complicated and doesn't always bring positive results for immigrants or their children.

"The first to arrive are consumed with the logistics of creating a beachhead in the new land," asserts Robert Suro. "In the barrios it is easy to find people who are successful immigrants but failures as parents of American children." Citing the Princeton sociologist Alejandro Portes, Suro suggests that immigrants' children who are poor and victims of discrimination risk "a ticket to permanent subordination and disadvantage."[18]

I personally know a very concrete example of how an immigrant who has done very well for herself in the United States has watched with horror as her son derailed the future that she had laid out for him. The mother came to Los Angeles illegally from Michoacán, Mexico, and after many years of hard work cleaning houses, she managed to bring her son here from Mexico as well. Far from becoming a dedicated student and example, as his mother had wanted, the son began to run with gang members and other delinquents who lived in their low-income neighborhood in south L.A. A few years after his arrival, her son was expelled from school and charged by the police with several minor offenses. Now a teenager, the son lives outside the law: he is here illegally, he hasn't returned to school, he struggles to hold down jobs, and he continues to run with delinquents. His future could take one of three forms: jail, deportation, or poverty. Every time I speak with his mother, she sounds hopeless, wondering if it would have been better to have never brought him here in the first place.

The true tragedy of the immigrant experience occurs when the children are either unable or unwilling to take advantage of the economic and educational opportunities that the United States has to offer. There is nothing more sad for Latino parents than to see their children out of school, out of work, and mired in drugs and gangs. After all, the only reason they and their families made the sacrifices involved in coming to the United States was to have a better future.

School dropout rates are the main indicator that something has gone terribly wrong with the process of adapting to life in the United States. One in three Hispanics drops out of high school, more than double the national average of 15 percent.[19] And the problem doesn't stop there. Only 16 percent of Hispanics go on to get a four-year degree before their twenty-ninth birthday, a terribly low number when compared with whites (37 percent) and blacks (21 percent).[20]

"School segregation is strongly linked to inequalities in schooling opportunities, processes and outcomes," write Marcelo M. Suárez-Orozco and Mariela M. Páez, based on studies done by Luis Moll and Richard Ruiz. "Forced to attend inferior schools, living in deep poverty and in heavily segregated neighborhoods, many Latino children struggle educationally against the odds."[21]

Hispanic Magazine identified five direct consequences of dropping out of school: "functional illiteracy, significantly lower earnings, double the rate of unemployment than for graduates, four times the likelihood of ending up on welfare than that for high school graduates, being at higher risk of becoming a criminal. (Fifty percent of state prison inmates are high school dropouts.)"[22]

What is it that makes Latino students drop out in such high numbers? It's a combination of poverty and the problems posed by cultural and linguistic barriers.

It's much more difficult for a recently arrived student from Mexico or Guatemala to adapt to a new school and learn a new language than it is for someone born here in the United States. Even with bilingual education programs—which, as we've seen, are under attack across the country—there are problems associated with having parents who may not speak English well and therefore can't help their children with their homework. Hispanic students living with their parents usually feel the added pressure to contribute to the family economically, and the need to work can often overpower the need to study, with harmful consequences that preclude their ability to succeed. Indeed, while linguistic and cultural problems are real, the determining factor in a young Latino's decision to drop out of school is poverty.

Four out of every ten Latino children live below the poverty line.[23] Sadly, this terrible statistic has not changed much in recent years. Add to it the fact that one in three Hispanics lacks medical insurance. On average, Latino families have less money than their white or African American counterparts. Poverty and a lack of proper medical care are variables that directly affect school dropout rates.

In 2001, one of the country's largest unions, the United Auto Workers, calculated that a worker had to earn $8.70 per hour to live above the poverty line. A family consisting of a mother, a father, and two children requires a yearly income of $17,960. That same year, the UAW calculated that 40.4 percent of Hispanics fell below this earnings benchmark, compared with 31.2 percent of African Americans and 20.1 percent of whites.[24]

The situation is even more serious when we consider that 21.4 percent of Hispanics live in extreme poverty; in other words, they lack sufficient income to cover even basic necessities. Two out of every ten Latino children can't count on three square meals a day, or a safe place to sleep at night.

How can a family of four live in this country on less than $18,000 per year? Two out of every five Hispanic children do so. Of course, not all Latino families suffer such conditions—in 2001, the average household yearly income for Hispanics was $33,565—but even this figure is well below the national average.

If education and the economy represent the Hispanic community's two greatest concerns, then school dropout rates and poverty levels are the most important signs of failure among Latino families. One in three does not finish high school. Two out of five are poor. Whoever wants to win the Latino vote will have to address these two critical problems. Hiring a mariachi band to play at a political rally is worthless if the rally itself doesn't feature a comprehensive plan for improving the quality of life and the quality of education for Latino children. It's education and the economy, stupid.

COMPREHENSIVE IMMIGRATION REFORM

On March 17, 2003, Secretary of State Colin Powell held a press conference to announce that the United States, Great Britain, and Spain would not be presenting a proposal authorizing the use of force against Iraq to the UN Security Council. The United States would need 9 of the 15 Security Council members to support the measure for it to pass, and it would also need to get around France's veto power. But matters never reached this point, because the United States could count on only four votes: from Spain, Bulgaria, Britain, and itself. This prompted many to ask why wouldn't Mexico—a neighbor, friend, and business partner to the United States—be willing to support the Bush administration at such an important time?

Mexico has a long tradition of peace and nonintervention in the internal matters of other nations and furthermore, President Vicente Fox had nothing to gain by such support: surveys showed that 7 in 10 Mexicans opposed the war. Perhaps Fox would have gone against public opinion if he thought it was truly in Mexico's best interests to do so. Mexico had been calling for an immigration accord with the United States for years, but after the September 11 attacks, President Bush refused to entertain such a possibility. The result? Mexico decided not to support the United States at the UN Security Council, and Fox risked nothing.

The problem with U.S. foreign policy is that it is based on crisis intervention, not on cultivating long-term relationships of mutual benefit. The United States only concerns itself with Latin America when the region is faced with a dramatic crisis, and all but forgets about the region the rest of the time. If the U.S. government understood just how concerned Mexico is on a national level with its millions of citizens living illegally in the United States, then the relationship between the two nations would be dramatically improved. But when your primary business partner—90 percent of Mexican products go to the United States—doesn't pay attention to your biggest concerns, then the basis for the relationship is called into question.

President Fox made the following prediction: Mexico will not be able to reach an immigration accord with the United States until after the 2004 elections, when Bush will be either reelected or replaced. Why, then, would he support such an unpopular move—unpopular both in Mexico and in the world at large—as a war in Iraq?

The immigration issue is not linked exclusively to foreign policy, but for the majority of U.S. Latinos, it's a vital topic. Remember that 7 out of 10 Hispanics were either born on foreign soil themselves or have at least one parent who was. And practically everyone knows, lives, and works with foreigners. As a result Hispanics are generally much more sensitive to immigration issues than the rest of the population. And the statistics confirm this: according to a survey conducted by Hispanic Trends, 70 percent of Latinos are in favor of granting amnesty to undocumented immigrants living in the United States, while 65 percent favor certain legal reforms designed to make it easier for new immigrants to come here.[25]

There's more. Fully 85 percent of Latinos registered to vote favor a proposal that would give undocumented immigrants working in the United States the opportunity to legalize their status, and 62 percent believe that undocumented immigrants help the economy.[26] This latter belief is not a popular one in this county—the very same study shows that 67 percent of non-Hispanic whites and African Americans believe that undocumented immigrants harm the U.S. economy. This is one of the central points of difference between Hispanics and the rest of the U.S. population. Whoever wants to draw the Latino vote will have to understand this.

Republicans weren't able to take advantage of the wave of popular support that followed Ronald Reagan's amnesty bill in 1986. The 1990s marked their party as anti-immigrant and anti-Hispanic. California's Proposition 187, which would have eliminated education and health services for undocumented immigrants in California if it hadn't been declared unconstitutional, and the anti-immigrant rhetoric of Governor Pete Wilson were both identified exclusively with Republicans. It's entirely probable that Bob Dole's failure to garner support among the Latino community during his 1996 presidential run was due not to his own policies but rather to his party's anti-immigrant reputation.

This issue is not going to go away. In fact, the more people try and brush it aside, the more it's going to grow, and become increasingly more difficult to resolve. Politicians have two options: either accept the fact that the United States is a nation of immigrants and that— given the unequal economic condition of Latin America—the immigrants will continue to come; or adopt a repressive posture toward immigrants and step up border patrol forces. This latter option—promoted by ultraconservative leaders such as Pat Buchanan and Congressman Tom Tancredo of Colorado—would require the active and massive participation of the U.S. Army, and would have severe negative repercussions for any party that adopted it. To be anti-immigrant is to be anti-Hispanic.

The choice is there. As Daniel T. Griswold of the Cato Institute wrote, "Conservative Republicans can follow the lead of President Bush, who has sung praises of immigrants and sought to create a more welcoming legal path to the United States for those seeking a better life through peaceful work. Or they can follow the likes of Pat Buchanan, Pete Wilson and Tom Tancredo back into political wilderness."[27]

Some sort of immigrant amnesty or guest-worker program (comprised mainly of undocumented immigrants already in the country) makes sense, both in economic and humanitarian terms. As the analyst Morton M. Kondrake wrote, "From a humanitarian standpoint, the United States ought to stop forcing people to risk their lives sneaking into this country and instead establish an orderly, legal guest-worker program."[28]

According to the National Immigration Forum,[29] true reform would have to include the following elements:

—Expanded legal channels for immigrants to come to this country legally

—A legalization program for hardworking taxpayers already here

—Consideration for families separated by borders or caught in long bureaucratic processing backlogs

—Reasonable and realistic enforcement strategies

—Meaningful worker protection programs for those coming and those already here, whether they be immigrants or not, so that wages are not eroded and workers have rights

—A path to citizenship for those who want to embrace the American dream and become full partners in our shared future, and

—Vigorous support for the bipartisan AgJOBS (which would expand the number of legal farmworkers in the United States) and DREAM Act (that would allow undocumented high school graduates to continue their college education, paying tuition as state residents) proposals pending in Congress

At the beginning of 2004, Bush proposed a set of immigration re-forms, setting in motion an intense debate about how to work with the millions of undocumented immigrants currently living in the United States. His proposal, however, was insufficient; it was not the "comprehensive immigration reform" called for by the National Im-migration Forum. It contained no clear paths to permanent legal status, nor did it propose any long-term solutions to the problems that drive undocumented immigrants to the United States from Latin America. (We'll discuss the specifics of Bush's proposal in more depth in Chapter 7, on "The True Power of Immigrants.")

THE CONGRESSMAN VERSUS THE STUDENT

The case of Jesús Apodaca brought education issues together with the Kafkaesque intransigence of current immigration policy.

It seems hard to believe that a U.S. congressman would use his immense influence and connections to destroy the dreams of a brilliant young 18-year-old immigrant, but this is exactly what happened in Colorado. The case is incredible, both because of the sheer hatred and bitterness evidenced in the congressman's attitude and because of the strength of the Mexican teenager's desire to study and better himself.

This is the story of Jesús Apodaca, the youngest of five brothers, who came from Chihuahua to the United States with his parents in 1997. It's important to note that they brought him here, effectively turning him into an unknowing undocumented immigrant at the tender age of 13.

Jesús was an exemplary student despite his shyness. He made the honor roll in high school and, like any other graduating senior at Aurora High School, decided to apply to college. It soon came to light, however, that he was an undocumented immigrant, and was thus not eligible for the in-state tuition breaks afforded to Colorado residents. He would instead have to shell out some $15,000 a year to attend the University of Colorado at Denver, an unattainable sum for the Apodaca family, as his father was—like many immigrants—a contract laborer on a local ranch.

But Jesús was not going to give up quite yet. He solicited help from the Mexican consulate in Denver and everyone else he could think of. Eventually, his story reached the ears of Michael Riley, a journalist with the *Denver Post,* who broke his story on the front page of the August 12, 2002 edition. In short order, over $2,000 had been donated to his cause, and one donor even offered to contribute $60,000 over the course of his academic career, providing that Jesús maintained a good academic record. Everything was going well until the Republican congressman, Tom Tancredo, got wind of the story.

Tancredo waited until September 11, 2002—the first anniversary of the World Trade Center terrorist attacks—to drop a bomb of his own: instead of offering support as so many other people had done, Tancredo called the INS and asked them to deport Jesús and his family. It's astonishing that an elected member of Congress would dedicate his resources to destroying a student's ambitions. Didn't he have more important things to do? Tom Tancredo had evidently conveniently forgotten that his own ancestors were once immigrants.

And was himself guilty of breaking the law, as the *Denver Post* revealed in an investigation that discovered that undocumented workers remodeled Tancredo's home, even though he says he was unaware they were not legally in this country. Tancredo had employed undocumented immigrants during the remodeling of his home, when he installed a home theater, a billiard room, and an extra bedroom. In other words, one of the most militant opponents of undocumented immigration—Tancredo has advocated sending troops to the southwest border—has himself benefited from their presence here. Nevertheless, Tancredo defended his actions, saying that he had hired a well-regarded contractor to do the work and thus had no reason to question the citizenship of the laborers working on his house.

Like Tancredo the millions of U.S. citizens who complain about the growing presence of illegal aliens also benefit from the work they do here. Immigrants harvest the food they eat, build the homes they live in, and provide their children with day care.

Another ironic twist in the Tale of the Good Student and the Bad Congressman is that the amount of money Tancredo spent on his remodeling—$15,795 according to the *Denver Post*—could have covered Jesús's first year of college. But who could expect such generosity from a man like Tancredo?

This is how things currently stand: the Mexican consulate is treating the Apodaca matter as "a case of protection" and a team of Mexican lawyers is studying ways to legalize their status and prevent the family's deportation. "One of President Fox's goals is to help Mexican immigrants lead easier lives," Consul General Leticia Calzada told me recently. "And the issue of higher education should be part of the trilateral agenda between Mexico, the United States, and Canada."

Apparently, Tancredo's networking skills weren't good enough. The INS never made the case a priority, and have yet to begin deportation proceedings against Jesús and his family. And an unintended consequence of Tancredo's attack is that the plight of the Apodacas has come to represent the situation of the over 7 million undocumented immigrants who make enormous contributions to the U.S. economy and culture each and every day. And Jesús? He's fine. In the fall of 2002 he began his studies in computer science and engineering at the University of Colorado in Denver, and his so-called out-of-state tuition is being paid by anonymous donors.

This case is a perfect example of how education and immigration are linked together. In 1996, the Republican-dominated Congress passed, and President Clinton signed into law, the Illegal Immigration Reform and Immigrant Responsibility Act (IIRAIRA). This law stipulates that undocumented students cannot be considered legal residents for state university entrance purposes unless any legal resident in the entire country is afforded the same benefit. In 2003 Illinois became the first state to pass legislation that circumvents this federal requirement.[30]

Governor Rod Blagojevich signed into law a bill permitting undocumented immigrants to pay the same tuition as other state residents, provided they have studied for at least three years at an Illinois high school.

Similar legislation has been passed in Washington, Texas, California, Utah, and New York, and at least a dozen other state legislatures are considering taking such steps. The difference is whether a student has to pay $5,000 tuition or $20,000. The Urban Institute, a Washington-based economic and social policy research group, estimates that there are between 50,000 and 65,000 undocumented high school students in this country who stand to benefit from policies like the one in Illinois.[31]

The architect of the law in Illinois was Hispanic representative Edward Acevedo, who first proposed the idea in the Illinois assembly in 2000. He argued that the educational system was cheating students by leading them on through elementary and secondary school and then abandoning them. "We made history," Acevedo declared in the papers after his proposal was approved by a vote of 56 in favor to only 1 against. "Students will now have the opportunity to live a decent life and realize their dreams." There are people who close the doors of opportunity, like Tom Tancredo. But there will always be those who help show us the way. Jesús Apodaca is one of these people.

Jesús's case shows how certain specific changes in state and federal laws can help a generation of young Latinos to finish high school and continue on to college. The law currently permits any child or teen to enroll in public school at the elementary and secondary levels regardless of their immigration status. The same ought to be true at the college level. An immigrant student who gets a high school degree should be considered a resident—not an alien—of the state in which he or she completed high school. Such a policy would allow young students such as Jesús to make in-state tuition payments and be eligible for certain grants and scholarships. This simple change would have a profound and positive effect on the lives and educations of thousands of young undocumented immigrants, the majority of whom came here with their families when they were very young. But the law should go one step further.

Here is what I propose: every immigrant student who earns his or her bachelor's degree also earns the right to become a legal resident of the United States, along with his or her immediate family (parents and siblings). This would have impressive results: parents who have spent years as undocumented immigrants would be encouraged to see their children through university, thus reducing school dropout rates while at the same time resolving even the most dramatic immigration cases on the basis of academic advancement.

These two proposals—considering any student who completes

high school to be a state resident and giving legal residence to the family of any student who graduates from college—would cost nothing and yet would have extraordinary consequences for the future of the Hispanic community. If you want to win the Latino vote, then do something concrete for them. Do something for people like Jesús Apodaca.

DISCRIMINATION AND THE ALLIANCE
WITH AFRICAN AMERICANS

Discrimination against Hispanics isn't just a concept; as with African Americans, it is a reality that must be confronted every day. Now, at the dawn of the third millennium, the United States still has yet to accept itself as a multi-ethnic, multiracial, and multicultural society. Many of its citizens seem to think they live in a homogenous country when it patently is not. How many countries on Earth count whites, blacks, Hispanics, Asians, and Native Americans among their populations? Very few indeed. In scarcely more than half a century, the majority in the United States will be "minority" groups. Few, if any, other countries have gone through such a radical demographic change as this. But the sad thing is that the United States still has a long way to go in coming to grips with its own diversity and quashing the iniquities of racism.

The best thing about the United States is its opportunities; the worst thing is its racism. And the effects of discrimination are widely felt throughout the Latino community.

According to the Pew Hispanic Center, 82 percent of Latinos believe anti-Hispanic discrimination prevents them from reaching their full potential in this country.[32] Fully 78 percent consider discrimination to be a problem at their place of work, compared with 64 percent of blacks and 57 percent of whites. Similarly, 75 percent of Latinos worry about discrimination in schools, compared with 55 percent of blacks and 54 percent of whites.

Perceived discrimination is greater among those Latinos who

speak more Spanish than English, and among those who were born in another country or who came to the United States after their tenth birthday. But Hispanics as a whole are very sensitive to the problems of discrimination. It's not just an abstract concept, as these three examples show:

—Latinos are the only group who are not proportionally represented among federal government employees, only 6.7 percent of whom are Latino.[33]

—Of the approximately 16,000 news stories reported by ABC, CBS, NBC, and CNN in 2001, only 99 (0.62%) were about Latinos.[34]

—Only 11 percent of Hispanic students obtain university degrees in the United States, compared with 29 percent of whites and 17 percent of blacks.[35]

Nobody is safe from discrimination—not even the Bush family. During the 2000 Republican National Convention in Philadelphia, I had the opportunity to ask George P. Bush, son of Florida governor Jeb Bush and his Mexican American wife Columba, if he had ever been subject to discrimination. "I have encountered a lot of discrimination in my life," he said, "because in our society, unfortunately, people judge you by the color of your skin." And when I asked him to specify the type of discrimination, he answered, "With words like 'wetback,' or ugly words like 'tar baby' that people say to Latinos."[36]

If it can happen to the president's nephew, imagine what happens every day to millions of ordinary Latinos.

Strom Thurmond never dared to tell the truth. Shortly after he died in 2003, we found out that this senator—this paladin of white supremacy who had defended segregationist ideas and actions, his entire life—had fathered a child with a young African American woman. This secret was faithfully guarded, as much by his black daughter as by his white family. But after his death, this one-time paladin of racial discrimination revealed a profound contradiction that had been hidden his entire life. Without a doubt, Strom Thurmond was a man who caused storms.

On December 5th 2002, when Senate Majority Leader Trent Lott was invited to participate in Strom Thurmond's hundredth birthday party, we saw the true face of their political beliefs. "I want to say this about my state," said Lott, addressing the crowd. "When Strom Thurmond ran for president, we voted for him. We're proud of it. And if the rest of the country had followed our lead, we wouldn't have had all these problems over all the years, either."

Who or what were the problems that Strom Thurmond's leadership might have prevented? In 1948, when he was governor of North Carolina and seeking the Republican Party's presidential nomination, Strom Thurmond vowed, "There's not enough troops in the Army to force the Southern people to break down segregation and admit the Negro race into our theaters, into our swimming pools, into our schools and into our homes."[37] Were blacks and other minorities the "problems" that Trent Lott was referring to in his speech?

A storm immediately ensued. There was one of the country's top public officials publicly defending the segregationist past that many thought we had overcome. Lott, facing enormous pressure and without any support from the White House, was forced to resign his position 15 days later, to be quickly replaced by Senator Bill Frist of Tennessee.

But Lott's comments that December 5 were not the first ones he made on the subject. In 1980, he made the following statement: "You know, if we had elected this man [Thurmond] 30 years ago, we wouldn't be in the mess we're in today."[38] This calls into question the sincerity of Lott's apologies and makes one wonder whether other Republican politicians harbor similar resentments.

I find it surprising that Latino leaders—both in and out of Congress—didn't jump at the chance to stand beside and support the African Americans who came out in droves to denounce Lott's comments. After all, the comments were as offensive to Latinos as they were to African Americans. The strongest criticism came from the president of the Congressional Hispanic Caucus, Silvestre Reyes, who said in a press release dated December 14, 2002, "Millions of Americans, including Members of the CHC, were offended by Senator Lott's comments." Those comments were "reflective of a mentality that no Member of our Congress—the People's Congress—should possess."

But there was no united effort by Hispanic congress people calling for Lott's removal. Nor was there a joint press conference of African American, Latino, and Asian American congress people denouncing the Senate majority leader's comments. Why? Were Hispanics afraid of offending some of the country's top political powers? Was it better to hold ranks than to come out in defense of principle?

Latinos and Asian Americans are somewhat more open to the possibility of voting for a Republican candidate, but this hasn't been the case with African Americans. Republican presidential candidates have historically won exceedingly small fractions of the black community's votes: Ford, 16 percent; Reagan, 11 percent and 9 percent; Bush Sr., 12 percent and 10 percent; Dole, 12 percent, and George W. Bush, 8 percent. With such poor results over the past several elections, it should come as no surprise that Republicans have begun to concentrate their efforts on winning the Latino vote. Nevertheless, racism is an unresolved problem in the United States, and one that affects Latinos and African Americans alike.

George W. Bush himself recognizes this. "Our Constitution makes it clear that people of all races must be treated equally under the law," he said before the Supreme Court regarding the University of Michigan's affirmative action case. "Yet we know that our society has not fully achieved that ideal. Racial prejudice is a reality in America. It hurts many of our citizens." [39]

Bush, more than most Republicans, has tried to recruit minority votes—yet he made these comments in a speech opposing the University of Michigan's affirmative action admissions policy. Through affirmative action, Michigan, whose minority population was extremely low, was able to increase its black enrollment by 8 percent and its

Latino enrollment by 5 percent.[40] For blacks and Latinos, then, Bush's message is a contradictory one: on the one hand, he speaks to the advantages of this country's diversity; on the other hand, he opposes programs specifically designed to help minority students and foster that very diversity.

This contradiction was made explicit when the Supreme Court voted 5 to 4 to maintain the university's affirmative action policy on June 23, 2003. The *New York Times* noted that despite the fact that his administration had opposed the way in which Michigan enrolled minorities, President Bush issued a statement praising the court 'for recognizing the value of diversity on our nation's campuses.' . . . The statement made no reference to the fact that the administration had asked the court to invalidate both Michigan programs as thinly disguised quota systems. . . . Mr. Bush had personally announced in a televised address in January [2003] that his administration was siding against the university." [41] Who do we believe? The president who goes before the Supreme Court to oppose the University of Michigan's admissions policies or the president who says on TV that he favors diversity on our nation's campuses?

One of the central topics of discussion in the black community over the next few years will be that of reparations for slavery. Among the Latino community, the fundamental issue will be how to increase our influence in society while at the same time resolving some important issues, including amnesty, school dropout rates, affirmative action, reducing poverty, discrimination, and resistance to the use of Spanish and other cultural practices. But both groups—blacks and Latinos— are united by similar experiences.

Discrimination in particular is a strong point around which a common alliance can be formed. African Americans have suffered racism and rejection in ways unmatched in this nation's history. Through the civil rights movement of the 1960s and 1970s, blacks showed everyone, Latinos included, how to fight for our rights, to be proud of being a minority, and to insist that we are all Americans. Like

African Americans, Latinos have learned that in order for our rights to be respected, we have to fight for them each and every day—on the bus, at the office, in school, in baseball and football stadiums—because contrary to the experience of many whites, these rights and privileges are not something we can ever take for granted.

But beyond discrimination, African Americans and Latinos share the experience of having a divided identity.

W. E. B. DuBois, who was also the first African American to graduate from Harvard, wrote extensively on how blacks have learned to live with the "double consciousness" of being both African and American, of having skin of a different color from the rest of the country while still being part of that same nation. In his 1903 book *The Souls of Black Folks,* DuBois examines this strange sensation of being two things at once: of being yourself and yet at the same time seeing yourself through other people's eyes. This experience is very similar to that which Latinos live with today.

> It is a peculiar sensation, this double-consciousness, this sense of always looking at one's self through the eyes of others, of measuring one's soul by the tape of a world that looks on in amused contempt and pity. One ever feels his two-ness,—an American, a Negro; two souls, two thoughts, two unreconciled strivings; two warring ideals in one dark body, whose dogged strength alone keeps it from being torn asunder.
>
> The History of the American Negro is the history of this strife,—this longing to attain self-conscious manhood, to merge his double self into a better and truer self. In this merging he wishes neither of the older selves to be lost. He would not Africanize America, for America has too much to teach the world and Africa. He would not bleach his Negro soul in a flood of white Americanism, for he knows that Negro blood has a message for the world. He simply wishes to make it possible for a man to be both a Negro and an American, without being cursed and spit upon by his fellows, without having the doors of Opportunity closed roughly in his face.[42]

DuBois is as forceful and effective at the start of the twenty-first century as he was at the start of the twentieth. So much so, in fact, that his concept of "double consciousness" can now be perfectly applied to Latinos. I constantly hear Hispanics say things like, "I'm Mexican and American." Or "I'm Latino and American." Like African Americans, Hispanics too have a double identity, one comprised of different and at times even contradictory elements.

How, for example, can someone be born in another country but still feel like he belongs to the United States? How can he carry a U.S. passport and pledge allegiance to the flag, yet still feel profoundly Cuban or Mexican? How can you be thinking of two places when you say "my country"?

Both African Americans and Latinos have histories of discrimination, and both identify as members of this nation as well as members of their own minority group. Blacks and Hispanics share a difficult past. This isn't about playing the part of the victim; rather, it's simply about recognizing the fact that both groups have been treated as unequal. Latinos can and should learn from African Americans and their struggles against discrimination and for civil rights in this country. They fought the first battle.

Such an alliance is a natural one, and needs to be explored and studied so that a plan of action can be developed. Its goal? To end racism and discrimination in the United States. Optimistic as it sounds, I believe it is possible.

PATRIOTISM: HISPANICS AND WAR

Around 30,000 Latino soldiers fought in the war against Iraq in the spring of 2003. During my work as a war correspondent, I interviewed many Hispanic soldiers, both on the front lines in southern Iraq and at the Doha and Arefjan military bases in Kuwait. I was struck by how easy it was to find Spanish being spoken in such a war zone. Another surprising thing I came across was the number of soldiers who were born in Latin America and who were not U.S. citizens. Nevertheless, they were ready to give their lives for the United States. I remember two cases in particular: Diana Gonzalez and Cindy Segovia.

Diana Gonzalez, who was only 19 years old when she was sent to the Persian Gulf, decided to enlist—as did her sister—after the terrorist attacks of September 11. I met Diana at a U.S. Army field hospital in Arefjan, very near the Saudi Arabian border. Her big, expressive eyes helped her greatly in work that seemed impossible at times. Diana's job was to talk with wounded soldiers coming in from the field of battle. Some had lost friends, while others had lost arms or legs. All had the shards of war sunk deep in their minds.

When I spoke with her, she was terrified by the threat of a chemical or biological attack. Saddam Hussein's threats that the mothers of U.S. soldiers would be crying "tears of blood" were very frightening indeed. Even after his regime fell on April 9, 2003—when U.S. soldiers toppled a 40-foot statue of the ex-dictator in the streets of downtown Baghdad—she still couldn't bring herself to put away her protective clothing or gas mask.

"I was raised in California since I was two," she told me. "I'm Mexican but I'm 'Americanized.' I've got my green card but nothing else." Diana was born in Jalisco, Mexico, but she knows the hearts of U.S. soldiers better than almost anyone.

Cindy Segovia, 26, was born in Monterrey, Mexico. She'd already begun the process of becoming a citizen when she was sent off to fight in Kosovo. Upon her return, she restarted the paperwork, but had to put things on hold once again when she was sent to Kuwait. "What is a Mexican woman doing fighting for the United States?" I asked her. "I think of myself as being an American, since I've lived in the United States my entire life," she answered, before making a clarification: "I'm Mexican and I feel Mexican, but I'm an American too." "But are you ready to give your life for the United States?" I pressed. "Yes, of course," she responded without a moment's hesitation.

But besides cases like Diana's and Cindy's, most of the Latino soldiers who fought in Iraq were U.S. citizens. Sergeant Rafael Fernandez, born and raised in Cuba, is proud of serving in the Marines.

When I spoke with him, he was in Kuwait recovering from an accident in which a heavy machine gun fell on his right foot, crushing one of his toes. Ironically, this happened after he had withdrawn from the front lines, where he had fought in at least three battles inside Iraqi territory.

I had to ask him, "Did you ever think that you were about to die?" "All the time," he replied. "In war, you never know what's going to happen next." Contrary to what I had expected before arriving in Iraq, the majority of soldiers whom I interviewed were honest about their fears of war and death. The difference between these people and the rest of us is that they are aware of this danger at any given moment, and they are trained to both survive and kill.

It's no secret that many Latinos decide to enlist in the U.S. Armed Forces not because of any desire to see combat, but rather because of the educational opportunities and programs that come with the job. Before September 11, the risk of having to go to war for the United States was relatively small. But ever since President Bush declared the "war on terror" and the "axis of evil"—Iran, Iraq, and North Korea—as priorities, the chances of seeing combat have multiplied.

Commander Mario Reyna, who was born in Coahuila and became a naturalized citizen in 1987, has seen a steady increase in the number of Latinos enlisting in the army, the navy, and the air force. "There are many opportunities today for Latinos to excel in the armed forces," he told me with a certain amount of pride. "They're looking to better their lives; a lot of them join up to get money for college."

Sergeant José López's parents were born in the Mexican states of Durango and Nuevo Laredo. "I was born an American but my heart is Mexican," he told me. Sergeant López joined the Armed Forces "first so I could go to school, but I stayed out of pride. I love the army a lot." "Is it hard being a Latino soldier?" I asked him in Kuwait. "No," he said. "Most of the army is Latino like me." Well, not exactly; the figure is around 9 percent. But it's easy to understand why he feels this way. If José hadn't joined up, he would never have been able to finish his studies.

The choice for Manuel León, who was born in Los Angeles to

Mexican parents, was much more clear: join the army or join a gang. "I grew up on the streets of L.A., and things weren't good," he told me at Camp Doha, northeast of Kuwait. "I joined [the army] to change my life, and it turned out better than I imagined."

Still, there are those Latinos who had other reasons for joining. "The United States has done a lot for us," explained José Fernandez, who was born in Mexico and came to the United States as a child. For him, joining the army "is a way of thanking the United States for how it's helped us."

Hispanic soldiers are no different from other Hispanics who identify themselves primarily with their countries of origin. "What do you consider yourself," I asked Araceli Renderos in Kuwait, "Salvadoran or American?" "Salvadoran," she said. "I may be a [U.S.] citizen now, but I'm Salvadoran through and through." Armando Urriola feels the same way. "Since I was little I've had a great admiration for the U.S. Army," he told me. But when I asked him about his identity, he said "Panamanian" without a bit of hesitation.

Other soldiers have divided loyalties as well. Mauricio Montalvo was born in Barranquilla, Colombia, and could have joined either of two armies: that of Colombia or the United States. He decided on the latter because "the benefits are a lot better." But when I ask him to define himself, then he said: "I'm Colombian and American. Both."

Pedro Echeverría of El Paso, Texas, is married to a woman from Ciudad Juarez, Mexico, and faces the same dilemma as Montalvo. When asked which country he identifies with, he said "I'm part of both." Mexico and the United States.

Less fortunate was José Gutierrez, an immigrant from Guatemala who entered the United States illegally when he was 14. Having lost both his father and his mother, he joined the army a year before the war with Iraq began, and was among the first U.S. soldiers killed in combat in southern Iraq. As a posthumous honor, the United States granted him citizenship. José was 22 years of age.

Clearly the U.S. Armed Forces include many servicemen and servicewomen born on foreign soil who are nonetheless risking their lives—sometimes even sacrificing them, as in the case of José

Gutierrez—for the United States. I only hope that the same recognition won by these Hispanic soldiers in times of war can be extended to them, to their families, and to other immigrants in times of peace. It's about time.

Despite the above examples of patriotism, Hispanics are more skeptical about the U.S.-led war on Iraq than the rest of the country's population. One month before the war began, only 48 percent of Latinos agreed with invading Iraq to oust Saddam Hussein.[43] This contrasts sharply with those polls that put U.S. support in general in the 60 to 70 percent range. Why the difference?

To begin with, Hispanics have access to information that the non-Spanish-speaking population doesn't. The major Spanish-language media in the United States were reporting—before, during, and after the war—on Latin America's enormous opposition to the use of military force. In other words, U.S. Latinos were exposed to arguments that were either lost or simply did not exist in the English-language media. After a bit of preliminary hesitation, President Vicente Fox of Mexico and President Ricardo Lagos of Chile made it quite clear that they would not support a new proposal from the UN Security Council authorizing the use of force against Iraq. The position of Mexico, Chile, and many other Latin American nations was very similar to that of France, Germany, Russia, and China, who wanted to give the UN weapons inspectors more time to do their work. Information such as this was widely disseminated across Spanish-language media in the United States, but was ignored by the English-language channels and stations.

To this we have to add the long, sad history of U.S. invasions and military operations in Latin America, from Chile to the Dominican Republic, to Panama, Grenada, Haiti, and Nicaragua. This history of occupation and violence remains immediate and clear in the collective memory of Latin America—and in the history books as well. Such a history makes it difficult to generate much Latino support for any new military operation, whether in Latin America or not.

Many families still have relatives living in Latin America, and, thanks to phones, e-mail, and airplanes, these relatives can have a significant influence on Latino opinions. Most Latin American nations base their foreign policies on the principle of nonintervention in the interior matters of another nation, and on maintaining a long tradition of pacifism. For example, one survey conducted by the company Televisa found that 9 out of every 10 Mexicans opposed the war. And every time a Mexican American speaks to one of his or her relatives in Mexico, he or she may hear some antiwar sentiments. This can have a certain amount of impact.

There was the perception that more Hispanics would be killed (proportionally) in this war than soldiers of any other ethnic group. One Mexican congressman even contended that 70 percent of the U.S. Army was composed of Latinos—a figure that was quickly refuted and corrected by the U.S. Embassy in Mexico City. But however false, the notion persisted that Latinos would be the first to die in the war.

On April 28, 2003, the death of Edward J. Anguiano was confirmed. He had disappeared on March 23 when he and his maintenance unit were attacked by Iraqi forces outside Nasiriya. His remains were identified by DNA testing. With the confirmation of his death, the number of Latino soldiers killed in the war rose to 24 out of a total of 130 U.S. casualties.[44] In other words, at that point, 18 percent of U.S. casualties were Latinos—double their representation in the ranks. Faced with statistics such as these, it is difficult to refute the perception that a disproportionate number of Latinos die in U.S. wars.

For these three reasons—more comprehensive information, family members in Latin America opposed to the war, and the fear that more Hispanics would be killed than soldiers of other ethnic groups—Latinos were more skeptical than other segments of the U.S. population about the need to go to war.

But once troops were committed, support for the invasion increased, among Latinos as among all segments of the population. The results of a survey conducted by the Pew Hispanic Center between April 3 and April 6, 2003, indicate that 61 percent of Latinos then supported the war against Iraq, and that support was higher among U.S.-born Hispanics (75 percent) than among those born in other countries (52 percent). Still, however, 61 percent was lower than the 70 percent figure that a CNN/Gallup poll reported for the population in general. Ultimately, both before and during the war against Iraq, Hispanic support was distinctly less than that of the country at large.

Most people consider Jessica Lynch to be a hero. But Latinos have other heroes as well—heroes like Edgar Hernández and Shoshana Johnson.

Edgar Hernández, the 21-year-old son of Mexican parents, was one of seven prisoners of war to be rescued, safe and alive, days after Saddam's regime fell. A mechanic who enlisted in the armed forces after finishing high school, Edgar had been shot in the elbow. Shoshana Nyree Johnson, born in 1973 on the shores of the Panama Canal, had also been ambushed by Iraqi forces and shot in both ankles. She'd enlisted in the navy because she wanted to become a first-class chef.

Both were part of Maintenance Unit 507 when they were taken hostage amid fierce fighting in the city of Nasariya. Three weeks later, Shoshana, Edgar, and five other soldiers were rescued.

Jessica in English, Edgar and Shoshana in Spanish. Parallel stories. But why the difference in coverage? The simple fact of their families' origins. Edgar and Shoshana's dedication to the U.S. flag is as strong as Jessica's, and it's impossible to question their valor or loyalty simply because their parents were not born in the United States. Both Hernández and Johnson—who had become symbols of Hispanic soldiers' valor—had to face an uphill battle throughout their childhood and adolescence in the United States. And there are many more Edgars and Shoshanas in the U.S. Armed Forces.

Hispanic or Latin American soldiers have fought for the United States throughout its history. "In every way and on every battlefield, Americans from Spain, Mexico, the Caribbean, and Central and South America have risked their lives in defense of the United States," [45] wrote Colonel Gilberto Villahermosa, chief of NATO's Combined Joint Task Force in Holland. Colonel Villahermosa documents well the participation of Hispanic troops in U.S. wars: 10,000 in the Civil War; 200,000 in World War I; 500,000 (mostly of Mexican origin) in World War II; 148,000 in Korea; nearly 80,000 in Vietnam; 20,000 in the 1991 Persian Gulf War, and 30,000 in the war against Iraq.

Before this most recent conflict, 39 Latinos had received the congressional Medal of Honor for bravery in combat. This includes Alfred Rascon, who was peppered with bullets as he used his own body to shield that of a wounded soldier during a battle in Long Khanh in Vietnam in 1966. Sadly, Rascon did not receive recognition for this heroic act until 34 years later, when President Clinton invited him to the White House and presented him with his Medal of Honor.

Despite acts of heroism like those of Rascon and Edgar Hernández, despite the widespread participation of Hispanics in U.S. wars, and despite the presence of over 1 million Latino veterans, there are relatively few Hispanics among the military's top brass. Other than Richard Cavazos (who in 1982 became the first Hispanic four-star general), we have only Luis Caldera, a West Point graduate who was designated Secretary of the Army 16 years after Cavazos's ascension. No Latino has ever been Secretary of Defense. The Hispanic population's lack of representation in politics evidently extends to the military world as well. In fact, according to the Pentagon, only 4 percent of the officer corps is Latino and there have only been four Hispanic generals in the army's history.[46] Eighteen percent of the deaths, 9 percent of the soldiers, but only 4 percent of the officers—Hispanic soldiers are in strong supply where it hurts the most, but in short supply where it counts the most. Latinos can't help but care about this issue.

FOR THE UNITED STATES, IS LATIN AMERICA INVISIBLE?

Latin America is not a priority of US foreign policy. It should be.

Naturally, Latinos are particularly concerned with what's going on in Latin America. After all, that's where they come from, where many of their relatives live, and where many of their hard-earned dollars go to. But historically this focus on Latin America has not been shared by the U.S. government. And these days are no exception.

"What does the United States think about Latin America?" a Spanish investor recently asked me. "The United States, today, doesn't think much about it at all," I replied. "In fact, at the moment, as far as they're concerned, Latin America doesn't even exist."

This conversation took place shortly before United States bombs began to rain down on Baghdad. But it reflects one of the most frequent complaints that Latinos make about the U.S. government: that it only pays attention to Latin America when there is some crisis or conflict to deal with, while the rest of the time it's as if the entire region ceases to exist.

A week before the September 11 terrorist attacks, President Bush visited the Guanajuato ranch of President Vicente Fox. There he said, "The United States has no more important relationship in the world than our relationship with Mexico."[47] A few days after making this declaration—on September 20, to be precise—Bush pushed Fox aside when he addressed a joint session of Congress, saying that "America has no truer friend than Great Britain."[48] Apparently, Fox was Bush's best friend for three weeks.

The relationship between the United States and Latin America is a continuous string of embraces and snubs. Sometimes the United States squeezes Latin America so tight it can barely breathe; other times, it pays no attention to the region. At the moment, we're living in a time of distance and unconcern.

The same mistakes that the United States made with regard to Osama bin Laden are now being made in Latin America. The United States ignored the Al Qaeda menace until it was too late. The same thing is currently happening south of the border: when the United States suddenly decides to intervene decisively in some conflict, it's usually because action should have been taken sooner and the situation has spun out of control. I refer equally to the new and most intense wave of immigration from Cuba and Mexico, rising poverty in the region, and even the fragility of democracies faced with insurgent or criminal organizations.

The specific consequences are evident: Mexicans are upset about the unwillingness of the United States to negotiate an immigration treaty; Colombians want the United States to play a larger role in combating narcotraffickers; Venezuelan dissidents want a firmer stance against Hugo Chavez's authoritarian government; Argentines still haven't come out of their state of shock at being denied emergency financial aid in 2002.

All this is compounded by the fact that the United States doesn't seem to have any consistency with regard to its foreign policy. To Americans, not all dictators are created equal. The Iraqi dictatorship had to go; China's, on the other hand, could stay. They have devoted much time and energy to the North Korean regime, but not the Cuban one. And Fidel Castro has taken advantage of this.

While U.S. planes were bombing Iraq, Castro skillfully and cruelly organized one of his strongest waves of repression since the 1970s. Thus, while all the world's eyes were on Iraq, he executed three people—whose crime was attempting to steal a boat with which to flee the island—and sentenced 75 dissidents, independent journalists, and political opponents to a total of 1,500 years in prison.

One of the Cuban exile community's greatest frustrations is that Castro—despite his proven links to terrorism and the drug trade—has not generated the same sense of urgency among U.S. administrations as have Osama bin Laden or Saddam Hussein. In fact, one of the principal complaints of congressional Cuban American Republicans—Ileana Ros-Lehtinen, Lincoln Díaz-Balart, and Mario Díaz-Balart—is that the White House has not attended to their requests for a harsher policy against Castro's regime. And in an unusual statement to the press, Ros-Lehtinen said, "I feel frustrated, but I'm not going to give up; I'm going to keep fighting, even against a Republican administration, to denounce tyranny."[49]

It seems the United States has not known how to take advantage of the gradual yet steadily changing attitudes of Latin American governments toward Cuba. It hasn't sought a multilateral, continental approach to removing Castro from power, even though now would be the perfect time to do so. For a time, Castro was a source of Latin American pride, based on his staunch resistance to the United States. But his constant violations of human rights have turned him into a pariah. One survey of attitudes in seven Latin American countries revealed that 69 percent of respondents have a negative opinion of Castro, while only 31 percent see him in a positive light.[50] In Panama, 82 percent view him negatively; in Guatemala, 73 percent; in Nicaragua, 66 percent; in Peru, 66 percent; in Venezuela, 65 percent; and in Mexico, 63 percent. The Cuban dictator is denounced. Why wouldn't the United States take advantage of this widespread sentiment and do something decisive against his dictatorship?

Beyond the issue of Cuba, in my opinion the United States has to understand the three main tendencies that currently affect all of Latin America's citizens. These three tendencies are an ambivalent attitude toward the United States, the resurgence of leftist and populist movements, and threats to fledgling democracies. Without attention, the United States will one day find the problems in Latin America at crisis levels.

AMBIVALENCE TOWARD THE UNITED STATES

How can we reconcile the fact that millions of Latin Americans use U.S. products every day and would jump at the chance to move here to live, while at the same time remaining vehemently critical of its conduct and policies? How can we explain millions of Latin Americans' hatred of U.S.-led wars while still desiring to become citizens?

Latin Americans have conflicted feelings about the United States. On the one hand, they admire its medical and technological advances, try and pattern themselves after its efficiency and organization, watch its movies and TV shows, and long for its freedoms and high standard of living. But they also detest its military and economic arrogance, denounce its racism and maltreatment of immigrants, and—above all—

they resent the way the United States acts as if the rest of the world doesn't matter.

Despite the fact that millions of Latin Americans have made the United States their new home, one thing remains clear: Latin Americans do not want to give up their origins, their customs, and their native lands. But, clearly, they wouldn't mind sharing in U.S. freedoms and quality of life.

The United States is a constant presence in the minds of most Latin Americans. Latin America uses the United States as a benchmark to define itself. But Latin America barely shows up on the U.S. radar. Regardless of attitudes and perceptions, the fact remains that the United States and Latin America occupy the same hemisphere; they are condemned to be neighbors and will someday have to forge a more mature and fruitful relationship.

This seems so obvious, but has been all but impossible to achieve over the course of our common history. The frequent U.S. military interventions in the region (Nicaragua, Guatemala, Cuba, Puerto Rico, Haiti, Panama, Grenada, Colombia, Chile . . .); the annexing of half of Mexico's land; the often fascistic presence of U.S. companies in Latin America; the tacit, sometimes overt support of corrupt governments, assassins, and dictators; and the feeling that the driving force behind such actions is "in the best interests" of the United States as opposed to the development of Latin America—these have all had their negative impacts on our relationship. And if it is true that the official U.S. political agenda over the past two decades has been one of promoting democracy, respect for human rights, and open markets, then the results of this strategy are still not being felt by the majority of Latin Americans.

To say that the relationship between the United States and Latin America is a complicated, tortuous one is a blatant oversimplification. It's a relationship that has had its bright and its dark moments, and is still trying—albeit without much conviction—to become a working business relationship. But that makes Latin America's dilemma very clear: How can it be treated as a business partner by the world's only superpower? How can fair and equal negotiations be conducted when the United States has the power to impose its will at any time?

The differences between the northern and southern continents are abysmal. The Río Bravo/Grande not only marks the physical point where Spanish starts to give way to English; it is also the place where our two cultures, economies, and politics collide like two plates of the earth's crust. Again, Latin Americans do not want to be just like the Americans, but nor does the United States want to completely open its world up to us.

When President-Elect Vicente Fox suggested in the summer of 2000 that the United States and Mexico could erase their border in an instant just as the 15 founding members of the European Union had done, there wasn't a response from Washington at all. None. The idea fell so far outside the U.S. political field of vision that it was discounted before it even had a chance to be seriously considered. Latinos remember this.

The United States and Latin America don't seem to want the same future. Parallel destinies, perhaps, but not together.

The war with Iraq did little to help resolve the differences. Latin America's noninterventionist tradition clashed with U.S. unilateralism. Nothing has affected inter-American relations more in recent years. The "disappointment" that the U.S. government officially expressed at the lack of UN Security Council support from Mexico and Chile contrasted sharply with Latin America's complete rejection of the use of military force.

Despite the modicum of symbolic support that the Bush administration received from some countries—El Salvador, for example—there were constant protests outside U.S. embassies in several major Latin American cities. Not one single survey there showed support for the war. Not one.

But it would be a mistake to think that war is the only thing that causes anger. Mexico still can't understand U.S. resistance to an immigration accord. Nothing could do more to unite each and every inhabitant of North America. It is in the best interests of U.S. national security to pass such an accord. But still, the government refuses to make it happen.

There were other sources of frustration as well. Chile, along with four Central American countries (Guatemala, El Salvador, Honduras, and Costa Rica), had to wait for more than a decade for talks to begin around a free trade agreement. And the artificial 2005 deadline for the Free Trade Association of America (FTAA) negotiations to come to a close seemed to speak more to the populist theoric of certain politicians than to the slow rhythm of hemispheric conversations.

If we add other sources of frustration to these—such as the forced dollarization of the Ecuadoran economy, the emergency financing package that was denied to Argentina, the presence (until 2003) of the U.S. Navy in Vieques, the reluctant admission by Secretary of State Colin Powell that the United States did indeed participate in the 1973 overthrow of Salvador Allende—we realize that, at best, the relationship between the United States and Latin America is an ambivalent one that will only begin to improve with the help of politicians sympathetic to the concerns of Latino voters.

THE RESURGENCE OF LEFTIST AND POPULIST MOVEMENTS IN LATIN AMERICA

In recent years, we have seen more and more Latin American politicians speaking out on behalf of the poor and dispossessed—the "underdogs," as Mariano Azuela put it—and they promise to fight for them using populist methods, which, by definition, are doomed to failure. But even so, these politicians are winning elections.

Democracy hasn't been a magic wand for Latin America. With the exception of Cuba, it has solved the problems of legitimate representation, but it has left the problems of poverty entirely intact. Leftist movements arise in Latin America as a reaction to poverty.

Latin America, tired and fed up with existing poverty and despair, the institutionalized corruption, crime, and kidnappings, the lack of opportunities, and the inequalities in income, had clearly turned to the left. Despite differing circumstances and nuances, the presidents of Brazil, Argentina, Chile, Uruguay, Venezuela, and Ecuador were elected democratically due to their Leftist platform.

All of them, in one way or another, presented themselves as an alternative to the traditional political trends and neo-liberal, privatizing ways. Why? During the last two decades, the majority of governments in the region had mainly managed to produce unemployment, emigrants willing to move to the United States to find jobs, and poverty. In 2003, 44 percent of Latin Americans were poor, according to figures from the Economic Commission for Latin America (CEPAL).

The turn to the left was also notable on a more local level. The mayor of Bogotá, "Lucho" Garzón, was of the Leftist group Democratic Pole (Polo Democrático). Toward the end of 2004, the Sandinista Party's candidate was elected for mayor in Managua. Also during that time it could be discerned that the popular mayor of Mexico City, Andrés Manuel López Obrador, of the Democratic Revolution Party [Partido de la Revolución Democrática (PRD)] would have a clear advantage in the 2006 Mexican presidential election. They represent a whole new generation of leftist and populist politicians who are moving in to fill the void left by the failed neoliberal policies of the past two decades.

Neoliberal policies—the so-called Washington consensus—resulted in healthier, more fiscally responsible governments, but they have failed to reduce the levels of poverty (except, perhaps, in Chile). There is greater poverty in Venezuela today than when Chávez took office in 1999, and in Mexico, 1 million new workers enter the job market every year, while the country's economy grows at a rate of less than 5 percent—well below the 7 percent figure promised by President Fox during his campaign.

This is "leftism lite." The new movements that we are seeing in Latin America in recent years aren't ablaze with Marxist slogans; they do not promote class struggle or workers' uprisings. But they do represent a struggle—albeit a modest one—against hunger and poverty. Lula has said that he would consider his presidency a success if, by the end of his term, every Brasilian could have three square meals a day.

Kirchner, who took office on May 25, 2003, after defeating Argentina's president Carlos Menem, opposed the war in Iraq (as did Lula) and has made several statements condemning big business and the International Monetary Fund. But, as in Brasil, it will take more pragmatism than ideology to move his country's economy forward.

We're talking about a leftist movement that's even afraid to call itself one. "Do you consider yourself a man of the left?" I asked Ecuador's president-elect, Lucio Gutierrez, in January 2003. "I'm a pragmatic man," he replied. "I don't have the ideological mindset of a leftist." And to prove it to me, he told me that his plan for combating poverty—70 percent of Ecuador's 12 million citizens are poor—includes the creation of new jobs with the help of business. Gutierrez won the election on the basis of his anticorruption message, despite having participated in the 2000 military coup against President Yamil Mahuad. Unpopular, yes, but legitimately elected.

Hugo Chávez also reached the presidency nearly seven years after a failed military coup in February 1992. With a decidedly populist message, Chávez told me during a December 1998 interview in Caracas that he didn't want to nationalize any industry. "No, absolutely not. We're even prepared to provide facilities for private, international companies to invest in here," he said. "I'm not the devil."

Chávez's promises to the people of Venezuela have since gone up in smoke. He is responsible for at least two civilian massacres—on April 11 and December 6 of 2002—and he's breaking his campaign promises now that he seems intent on staying in power at least until 2013.

The Venezuelan people swallowed Chávez's promises hook, line, and sinker. And ultimately they are to blame for voting him into the presidency. On Election Day, December 6, 1998, 56 percent of the people voted for him. And in the December 15, 1999 referendum, 71 percent of them approved a new constitution that would permit Chávez to be reelected for a second six-year term. On July 31, 2000, 60 percent of the people did, in fact, reelect him under the terms of the new constitution. It's the Venezuelans—and nobody else—who put Chávez where he is today. But Chávez duped them all with lies and false promises. He is a clear example of the dangers that fragile young Latin American democracies face from opportunistic, populist politicians. And American politicians need to take heed.

THREATS TO FLEDGLING DEMOCRACIES
IN LATIN AMERICA

Latin America's fledgling democracies are under attack from all sides. During a speech in Washington in April 2003, Secretary of State Colin Powell said that the two main problems that Latin America is facing were weak governments and inefficient institutions. Seen in perspective, this is a big step forward when we consider the dictatorial regimes and human rights violations that dominated the region until only a few decades ago. Nevertheless, this observation comes as no relief to the millions of Latin Americans suffering from hunger and weak, corrupt governments; their daily lives are plagued by narcotraffickers, paramilitary forces, and guerrillas, and their children are not guaranteed better lives in the future.

The Institutional Revolutionary Party (PRI) was finally voted out of power in Mexico after 71 years, but this did not instantly solve the problems of corruption and poverty. Democracy has not been synonymous with increased justice in Guatemala—where Alfonso Portillo's government was accused of collaborating with narcotraffickers—or in Nicaragua—where President Arnoldo Alemán was charged and imprisoned for embezzling funds. Democracy has not brought social peace to El Salvador, where crime, kidnappings, and gang warfare are part of daily urban life. And while Argentina followed its constitution to the letter, this did not prevent the succession of several temporary presidents before Eduardo Duhalde took office in 2003.

The survival of fledgling democracies is not at all sure. When Ecuadorans dislike their president, they disregard their constitution to replace him with one they find more palatable. For example, Abdalá Bucaram was forced from power after being declared "mentally unfit" by Ecuador's congress, and later Yamil Mahuad was removed from office. Both won in legitimate elections, and both fell from power through political trapdoors. The idea that if you don't like your president you can simply exchange him for another is beginning to take hold in Latin America, and this represents a serious threat to democracy in the region. Democracy must go hand-in-hand with justice and constitutional law. Democracy is more than just being able to vote for your leaders; it also demands respect for rights and regulations.

The second major threat facing Latin American democracies is that a strong tradition of military-based political power still persists there, and it lacks anything to counterbalance it. Democratically elected presidents begin to feel all-powerful shortly after they take office. Hugo Chávez is the best and clearest example of this phenomenon, which academics have dubbed "delegative democracy." But the problem isn't just with presidential power, which has historically monopolized governmental authority; it also has to do with the courts and legislatures, which are far from exercising any sort of vigilance over the executive branch of the government and instead become simple tools of the president.

The third and most pressing concern is that Latin American democracies are constantly under attack—overtly or covertly—from powerful groups whose erosive tactics put their very existence in danger. Local governments are often at risk from organized criminals who employ such tactics as kidnappings, robberies, and assassinations without fear of reproach. Narcotraffickers, paramilitary forces, and guerrillas control entire regions of certain countries, and when the state lacks the resources and ability to restore peace and guarantee the safety of its citizens, then democracy finds itself teetering on the edge of disaster. And while Colombia is the country that has been most victimized by these forces of late, no Latin American nation is safe from the threats of narcogangsters and armed insurgents.

There is a new political current in Latin America, one that is driven by leftist and populist forces seeking to deal with the havoc left in the wake of the failed neoliberal policies of recent years. Democracy is still facing constant threats in this part of the world.

But what's certain is that the region is changing, and the United

States isn't paying attention to this transformation. Meanwhile, the northern migration of Latin American citizens remains steady. One out of every five Mexicans now lives in the United States, and one out of every four Salvadorans. There are more Guatemalans in Los Angeles than in most cities in Guatemala. . . .

Why should a politician in Arkansas, Wisconsin, or Iowa worry about what's happening in Latin America? Because U.S. politicians must understand that the Latino vote is inextricably linked to current events happening south of the border. And thanks to the growth of Spanish-language media, many Hispanics here can get news from their native countries just as easily as they get local news. This concern that Hispanics have for what's going on in Latin America is one of the best examples of the globalization of information. And any politician who forgets this runs the great risk of alienating Latino voters.

CHAPTER FIVE

THE SECRET LIFE OF LATINOS

"DON'T AIR YOUR dirty laundry" advises a popular proverb. In this chapter, besides pointing out some of the Hispanic community's shortcomings, I want to lay our differences on the table and, yes, air our dirty laundry.

The Hispanic community is not homogenous. While Cubans are worried about Fidel Castro, Puerto Ricans endlessly debate their political relationship with the United States, and Mexicans pray for an immigrant amnesty. Salvadorans haven't gotten along well with Hondurans ever since the so-called Soccer War led to a military confrontation in 1969. Haitians and Dominicans have their own differences, and the increasing migration of Dominicans to Puerto Rico, is putting a strain on that relationship as well.

These differences have occasionally generated strong political face-offs. In late 1993, for example, when NAFTA was being fought out vote by vote, Congressman Bill Richardson complained about the lack of support for the trade agreement from Cuban American congressmen Lincoln Díaz-Balart and Ileana Ros-Lehtinen. "My frustrations were compounded by an unwillingness of many . . . in the Cuban American community to consider arguments for NAFTA outside the narrow and stormy Mexican-Cuban bilateral relationship," he said publicly, referring to the different outlooks in foreign relations priorities for both groups.[1] He didn't have to wait long for a response. After noting that 200 other congressmen were also not supportive of the trade agreement, Díaz-Balart and Ros-Lehtinen asked, "Why has Richardson chosen to show his displeasure only with Cuban Americans?"[2] In the end, the accord was passed. But the staunch debate in

Congress between the Mexican American and the Cuban Americans left its bruises.

Beyond politics, there are also marked differences in the ways Latinos manage their money. More Cubans have credit cards (71 percent) than Mexicans (47 percent). Similarly, Cubans and Colombians are the two Latino groups most likely to keep their money in bank accounts (79 percent), compared with 60 percent of Mexicans.[3] The reasons? Cultural practices and a more favorable migratory status, especially for Cubans.

Differences are apparent in speech patterns as well. You'll often hear a Mexican say *nuestro hijo* while a Cuban will talk about *el hijo de nosotros*. On the computer I'm using to write this book, I can choose from among 20 different types of Spanish: Argentine, Bolivian, Chilean, Colombian, Costa Rican, Dominican, Ecuadoran, Salvadoran, Guatemalan, Honduran, Mexican, Nicaraguan, Panamanian, Paraguayan, Peruvian, Puerto Rican, Spanish (modern), Spanish (traditional), Uruguayan, and Venezuelan. Furthermore, the Spanish spoken in Miami is different from that spoken in Los Angeles or New York.

It's all mixed. As professor Ana Celia Zentella of the University of California at San Diego said in a *New York Times* interview: "When you think that the United States is the fifth largest Spanish-speaking nation in the world and New York has more Spanish speakers than 13 Latin American capitals, you begin to appreciate the dimensions of the linguistic and cultural hybridity that's taking place."[4]

The differences even come out in each group's use of profanities. A Mexican may say *pendejo, cabrón,* or *pinche* to refer to something which a Cuban might call a *comemierda*. A Cuban will tell you to *comemierda,* a Mexican will tell you to go *a la chingada,* and a Puerto Rican will send you off to *carajo viejo.*

But there's more. Even with issues on which there is a solid consensus, we see subtle differences among the different Latino groups. Take discrimination, for example: according to the Pew Hispanic Center, 83 percent of Latinos agree that it's a problem, especially when it comes to education and levels of income. But if we break this down along country of origin lines, we see that fewer Cubans (22 percent) report having been discriminated against than other nationalities, compared to Mexicans (30 percent), Colombians (33 percent), Puerto Ricans (36 percent), and Salvadorans (43 percent).[5]

Independent of the discrimination that Hispanic groups suffer in the United States, there is a distinct brand of discrimination among Latinos themselves. One of the great secrets about Latin America is their history of discrimination and maltreatment of blacks and Indians. Latin American countries continue to suffer from the same sort of class discrimination that characterized the viceregal period, when the whites—the Spanish conquistadors—looked down on Indians, blacks, and mestizos simply because of the color of their skin.

In contemporary Mexico, a society based on class discrimination continues, sometimes subtly, and other times much more boorishly. *Naco, Indio,* and *pinche pobre*—are just three of the many insults heard all too often in Mexico. These social and class-based distinctions have moved north to the United States along with the Mexicans migrating into this country.

This type of discriminatory treatment permeates all Latin American societies. All one has to do is look to countries like Bolivia, Peru, Ecuador, and Guatemala to see just how bad the discrimination against Indians remains. And these same unequal power relationships tend to be replicated among Latinos in the United States. The Spanish-language media is often criticized for not giving enough airtime to journalists, actors, or commentators of black or indigenous roots. And even though there is a greater tendency in the United States to deal with these discrepancies, we still have much work to do before the media reflects the true diversity of the Latino community it serves.

Differences within a country or community can also go beyond social or economic class. For example, Chilangos—people born in Mexico City—are not always well-liked by Mexicans from the provinces, and Cachacos—residents of Bogotá—have tensions of their own with people from Barranquilla or Medellín. Much of this resentment has to do with the centers of wealth and culture in each country.

We can even find clear differences among Mexicans born in the

United States. For example, the Pew Hispanic Center concluded that "Native-born Mexicans from Texas are somewhat more socially conservative than their native-born Californian counterparts on issues such as abortion, homosexuality, and having children outside of marriage."[6]

And to further complicate things, there are patent differences in political participation between Latinos and Latinas. With Hispanics, it seems, gender does have something to do with politics. Mexican women are generally more politically active than Mexican men, while Puerto Rican men participate more than Puerto Rican women, and Cuban men and women are politically active to a very similar degree, according to a study conducted by Lisa Montoya and based on the Latino National Political Survey.[7] Montoya defined political participation as including such things as signing a petition, writing a letter to an elected representative, attending a political meeting or rally, volunteering for a candidate, or making a donation to his or her campaign.

The language that women speak also has some bearing on their political participation. According to the same study, Mexican women who speak only Spanish or are bilingual tend to be less active than those who speak mainly English. On the other hand, Puerto Rican women who speak Spanish or are bilingual tend to be more politically active than those who speak only English. Clearly, a candidate who knows what Latina women want will have an enormous advantage over someone who is oblivious to such things. Whoever thinks that machismo is the only element to consider in Latino-Latina relations, and that Hispanic women aren't politically active, will be left behind in the race.

When considering all of the above, when a candidate speaks about Latinos, we can see why many within the Hispanic community ask themselves, "Who is he talking about?" If there is something that characterizes Latinos and Latinas, it's the fact that they make up a very heterogenous group.

At the political level, nothing reflects the differences better than the Congressional Hispanic *Caucus*—founded in 1976 and currently including 18 Democrats—and the Congressional Hispanic *Conference,* formed by 4 Republicans in March 19, 2003. "Many Americans think the Congressional Hispanic Caucus represents Hispanics, that is not the case," Representative Henry Bonilla, a Texas Republican, told the Gannet News Service. "[It's the] arm of the extreme left of the Democratic Party, the attack dog of the left." [8]

As Congressman Lincoln Díaz-Balart (R-Fla.) explained to me, the Republicans who formed part of the Hispanic Caucus left in 1994 because of the group's refusal to publicly demand the democritization of Cuba and respect for human rights on the island. "It's the least that we could ask for," he told me. The Republicans' break with the Hispanic Caucus occurred after Congressman Xavier Becerra, a Democrat, took a trip to Cuba. But as is to be expected, the Hispanic Caucus's explanation is quite different.

As Congressman Ciro Rodríguez, chairman of the Hispanic Caucus, explained to me in an interview in 2003, the U.S. policy toward Cuba has failed and "should not revolve around Miami." [9] The Caucus functions on a consensus basis. When not all its members agree on an issue—as with Cuba and the political status of Puerto Rico—then the Caucus does not take a public stance.

On a personal level, Rodríguez is against the trade embargo of Cuba, a position that clashes head-on with the Republican Hispanics in Congress, including Lincoln Díaz-Balart. Nevertheless, Rodríguez believes that there is another reason for the Republican split from the Hispanic Caucus: "When the Republicans gained control of Congress," he told me, referring to the 1994 Newt Gingrich–led Republican takeover of Congress, "they didn't need us anymore."

Despite all the differences, the Hispanic Caucus assures us that it's ready to accept the Republican members back into the fold, though it seems that this won't happen anytime soon.

IS MIGUEL ESTRADA HISPANIC ENOUGH?

The case of Miguel Estrada painfully reflects the huge differences within the Latino community. Estrada's physical stature—neither tall

nor strong, with his short, dark hair, boyish face and shy manner—
belies the enormous battle that he's started within the Latino community.

Estrada is a Honduran immigrant who taught himself English,
graduated magna cum laude from Columbia University, and later
graduated with honors from Harvard Law School. He subsequently
clerked for Anthony Kennedy, and the experience served him well.
Bill Clinton named Estrada assistant to the Solicitor General, and there
he won the majority of the 15 cases that he argued before the Supreme
Court.

In 2002, President Bush nominated him to direct the Circuit
Court of Appeals for the District of Columbia. This nomination could
well have been a stepping-stone to the Supreme Court. But in the end,
his Republican supporters couldn't raise the 60 votes needed in the
Senate to stop a Democrat-led filibuster against his nomination. So his
nomination never came to a vote. But why?

The official reason used by the Democrats was that Estrada had
refused to turn over to the Senate certain documents that he wrote
while working for the Solicitor General's office. Many suspected that
Estrada harbored some very conservative viewpoints and was trying to
cover them up. In fact, the most liberal sector of the U.S. political
spectrum stated that his opinions mirrored those of the Supreme
Court's two most conservative justices, Antonin Scalia and Clarence
Thomas. But the White House insisted that the documents not be
brought to light. "They're blocking the vote on this good man for
purely political reasons," President Bush said in February 2003. "Senators are applying a double standard on Miguel Estrada by requiring
him to answer questions that other judicial nominees have not been
forced to answer and that is not right and that is not fair." [10]

Bush publicly promised—in English and in Spanish—that he
would continue to support Estrada until his nomination was approved.
But it was an uphill battle. Democrats disagreed with his conservative
opinions; with Estrada at the threshold of the Supreme Court, legal
abortion was suddenly at risk, and many feared other highly traditional
and conservative positions would be assumed behind the Court's

closed doors. Democrats didn't want Bush to use the Estrada nomination for political ends. Clearly, President Bush wanted to extend his base of support in the Latino community, and nominating Estrada was a perfect way to do that. Nevertheless, this put congressional Latino Democrats in a very difficult position. How could they vote against a Hispanic nominee—however conservative—when no Latino has ever served on the U.S. Supreme Court? Clearly, Bush had beaten them to the punch, as he sought to present himself as more Hispanic than certain Hispanic congressmen.

Was Estrada himself Latino enough? This was the question that many Hispanic leaders began asking themselves. Neither the Mexican American nor the Puerto Rican Legal Defense and Education Funds—two organizations very well regarded for their defense of Latinos' civil rights—supported Estrada. But the U.S. Hispanic Chamber of Commerce and the Hispanic Bar Association did back his nomination. At first glance, it seems obvious that a Honduran immigrant whose native language is Spanish is Latino through and through. But interestingly enough, many Latinos didn't see him as such. If, as his critics argued, Estrada opposed affirmative action programs and defended the interests of big business, then he couldn't be expected to properly represent the Hispanic community at large. To many of his opponents, Miguel Estrada was as unsuitable to represent Hispanics as Clarence Thomas was to represent African Americans. At the end of the day, the question on everybody's mind was, "How do we separate Estrada the conservative from Estrada the Latino?"

Congressman Ciro Rodríguez (D-Tex.) sought to answer that question: "Yes, we are calling for Hispanic representation on our benches. But we want qualified representatives; by giving us a nominee who has nothing in common with our community but a last name, and lacks the necessary qualifications, the Bush administration has given us nothing." [11]

The members of the Congressional Hispanic Caucus made the difficult and controversial decision to oppose Estrada's nomination. Speaking on behalf of the Caucus, Congresswoman Graciela Flores Napolitano (D-Calif.) said: "In our judgment, Estrada is not qualified.

He has never been a judge. He has not done any legal work with the Latino community. He has never joined or supported any organization dedicated to serving and advancing the interests of the Hispanic community. He has never made efforts to increase opportunities to Latino law students. He has no desire or ability to provide a Latino perspective on the judicial bench." [12]

"Ethnic origin is not a free pass to becoming a justice in the United States," declared California Democrat Luis Becerra. Bob Menendez, a New Jersey Democrat, told me something similar in an interview. "The only reason the administration nominated him is because—supposedly—he is Hispanic," he explained. "But there has to be more than just your last name. You have to have lived at least part of the Hispanic experience, you have to have contributed to our community or have an understanding of the difficulties associated with being Latino in this country."

In other words, if Estrada was not willing to openly defend the ethnic diversity agenda that so many other leaders of the Hispanic community are identified with, then he would not receive their support. It was a matter of identity *and* politics. Nobody should be discriminated against on the basis of his or her last name, but neither should someone be nominated to a federal court simply because he or she is Hispanic. And if Estrada wanted to gain some measure of support from congressional Democrats, then he would have to prove to them that he understood, respected, and would defend some of their beliefs.

Sadly, Estrada elected to remain silent, a decision that seemed to confirm his critics' accusation that he really did not represent—or want to represent—the Hispanic community.

But this apparent contradiction was quickly exploited. Raúl Damas, operations director of Opiniones Latinas, a public opinion research firm, wrote in the *Miami Herald* that "Estrada's rejection is only the most recent example of the caucus' placing Democrat Party loyalty over Latino solidarity." [13]

The Estrada case marked the first time in history that the Senate failed three consecutive attempts to bring a federal court nominee to a vote. "The problem comes down to this," said Orrin Hatch, the Senate Judiciary Committee chairman from Utah. "[Estrada] is conservative, and my colleagues across the aisle think this makes him pro-life." [14]

The political problem Democrats were facing was quite clear. If they opposed Estrada's nomination, they would be branded anti-Hispanic by the Republicans. But Congressman Ciro Rodríguez, chair of the Congressional Hispanic Caucus, tried to dispel such a myth: "The [Bush] administration knew they wanted to nominate a Latino," he explained in a televised Spanish-language interview. "They chose someone [Estrada] who is unresponsive [to questions] and then come out and say that this senator [who posed the questions] is anti-Hispanic."

The accusations didn't stop there, prompting the National Council of La Raza, one of the most respected organizations serving the Latino community, to issue a press release containing the following statement: "While NCLR remains neutral on the nomination itself, we urge those who are engaging in name-calling and accusatory language to instead focus on the substantive issues and merits of this nomination. In particular, since the Latino community is clearly divided on the Estrada nomination, we find the accusation that one side or the other is 'anti-Latino' to be particularly divisive and inappropriate." [15] Unfortunately, this call for civility didn't have much effect.

A heated battle along party lines ensued. "From a political perspective, Estrada's future is uncertain, but this is a battle for the Latino vote, and so far Bush is winning," wrote Sergio Muñoz in a *Los Angeles Times* editorial. "Well aware of Latino political ambiguity, President Bush knows that the battle over the Estrada nomination could tip the scales in his favor, and so while he's showing his support for a Latino judicial nominee, he's also painting the Democrats as obstacles to Hispanic progress." [16]

Muñoz's analysis couldn't have been more correct. Some of the top Hispanic spokespeople in the Bush administration began to attack the Democrats—especially congressional Latinos—for opposing the rise of a Latino to one of the highest offices in the judicial system.

The matter came to a close on September 4, 2003, when Estrada himself withdrew his nomination. But the larger debate did not end there. Beyond the party politics and ideological clashes, the Estrada case illustrates the enormous differences that exist within the Latino community. The supposed Latino solidarity, which theoretically should bind together all Hispanic politicians concerned with increasing Latino representation, doesn't always hold true. Hispanics are more heterogenous than many would like to admit.

SALMA HAYEK, FRIDA KAHLO, AND THE RESENTMENT OF SUCCESS

There's a strong tendency to equate Mexicans who live in Mexico with those who live in the United States. After all, they both come from the same place. But there are clear differences—besides the obvious examples of income and geography—between the two groups.

When the film *Frida,* which starred Veracruz actress Salma Hayek, hit U.S. screens in November 2002, the reactions were mixed: Mexicans in the United States loved it, while many in Mexico—particularly intellectuals and film critics—hated it. Why?

Salma Hayek is as well known in Mexico as she is in the United States, and one might guess that her international stardom combined with a film about the controversial life of another Mexican woman, Frida Kahlo, would be well-received on both sides of the border. This wasn't the case.

I saw *Frida* in a San Antonio theater, and liked it a lot. I think it says as much about the actress who interpreted the part as it does about the revolutionary Mexican painter. And just so there are no misunderstandings, before we go on I'd like to make one thing clear: I do not know Salma Hayek personally, I've never seen her in person, never spoken on the phone with her, or swapped e-mails with her. I only enjoyed her movie.

After this film was released, it became difficult—at least in the United States—to talk about Frida Kahlo without thinking about

Salma Hayek. That's what happened, although it bothered a lot of people. Not just because Salma bears a striking physical resemblance to the artist born in 1907, but also because she beat out Madonna and Jennifer Lopez for the lead role. And that, in itself, was no easy task.

Salma convinced Miramax, a division of the Disney Corporation, to produce the film. She convinced her then boyfriend Edward Norton and her friends Antonio Banderas, Ashley Judd, and Geoffrey Rush to participate in the project for less than extravagant fees. And she chose the renowned director Julie Taymor to oversee them all. Nobody could have done all that except Salma. Nobody.

If the applause that I heard as the film came to a close in that San Antonio theater, and the generally good reviews that *Frida* received are any indication, this film succeeded in doing something that many would have thought impossible in the United States: attract attention to a painter defined, in part, by communist ideals, bisexual experiences, and a body shattered by an accident with a trolley car. And this was all thanks to the efforts, dedication, and will of Salma. But here the Hollywood dream ends.

What I never expected was the harsh reception the film received in Mexico, and the cold manner in which Salma was treated there. For sure, Salma doesn't look like a fragile woman. Some journalists I know complained about her distant and perhaps arrogant manner; others say that fame has gone to her head. But the least they can do is recognize that this artist—who left the comfortable world of Mexican *telenovelas*—was able to conquer Hollywood in little more than a decade based on her work, ingenuity, and perseverance.

The main criticism that I've heard in Mexico about the film is that it trivializes Frida Kahlo's life. But people who expected to see a documentary or film biography were mistaken. That's not what this movie is. *Frida* is a film, nothing more. An entire life cannot be captured in a two-hour movie format. Does the film take a certain amount of creative license with history? It does. Does it distill the rich cultural life of post-revolutionary Mexico? Perhaps. Is it a gringified movie? Well, it was made primarily for a U.S. audience. Still, it was a bit bothersome that Frida speaks English and eats enchiladas for breakfast.

First the obvious: the film is a work of fiction. We'll never know, for example, what Frida and Diego Rivera said to each other in bed, or how the whole Trotsky affair was orchestrated. But the film does paint for us—in grand, sweeping colors—a version of one of Mexico's most interesting historical periods. And the important thing is that it revitalizes the image of Frida Kahlo, whose work has not been widely known outside of artistic and intellectual circles. Thanks to the film, Frida's house in Coyoacán is seeing more and more visitors. And just like that, a woman who died in 1954 has suddenly come back into vogue in the twenty-first century.

Now, why was the film so well received in the United States and so poorly in Mexico? To understand this, we'll have to delve a bit into the Mexican psyche. Salma left Mexico City for Los Angeles in 1991, and certainly wasn't the first Mexican to be criticized for leaving, nor will she be the last. There exists in Mexico—and here I will speak from my own experience—a certain resentment toward those who at some point decide to go and live in another country. "Why did you leave?" they ask the 10 million or so of us Mexicans who were born in Mexico but now live in the United States. There's no lack of people who consider us traitors for having gone to seek out better opportunities—economic, artistic, professional—in the north.

When I read the reviews of *Frida* in the Mexico City journals and papers and heard the scathing criticisms on Mexican radio and TV, it was clear that the resentment went beyond the popular expression that the prophet is not honored in his own land. The truly unforgivable thing is to be visibly proud. Leaving Mexico and succeeding elsewhere inevitably calls into question those who either predicted our failure or didn't go themselves. And Salma has certainly been successful on the outside. She was the first Mexican actress to be nominated for a Best Actress Oscar (though the award that year would go to Nicole Kidman).

Mexicans on both sides of the border do have their differences, even when it comes to something as simple and trivial as a film created by and starring a Mexican woman. Sometimes American culture creates invisible borders, and Salma Hayek is living proof of this.

OSWALDO PAYÁ AND THE ART OF FENCING
WITH MIAMI CUBANS

The Cuban exile community is not monolithic. On the contrary. They vote mainly for the Republican Party, but they're not all Republicans themselves. Many of them support the economic embargo of Cuba, but not all of them. Younger Cubans want more contact with the island, but older Cubans do not. Some would return if Castro were not in power. But most would be content to stay in Miami, Orlando, and New York.

An experiment: Put two Cubans in a room and see how long it takes—probably only a matter of minutes or even seconds—before it becomes clear that they cannot come to a consensus over the past, present, and future of the island. The problem isn't just political; it's generational as well.

A *Miami Herald* survey found that only 34 percent of Cubans who left the island in the 1960s support the lifting of trade restrictions against the island, while nearly twice as many—64 percent—of those who arrived here in the 1990s agree with that idea.[17] Why the difference? It's simple. Those who have arrived here recently have more family members in Cuba and more reason to want contact with the island than those who came here 40 years ago.

Another survey conducted by the Cuba Study Group with the help of Bendixen and Associates showed similar results. Only 54 percent of the exiles who came to the United States in the 1960s would be in favor of "forgiveness and reconciliation" as part of a transition to democracy on the island. On the other hand, 70 percent of those who came here in the 1990s would support such a proposal.[18]

The ideas of "forgiveness and reconciliation" with those who remain on the island was being widely discussed among Cuban exiles because of Oswaldo Payá's visit to the United States in January 2003. Payá is probably the best known Cuban human rights activist and dissident in the world. The following ideas are some that he proposed, but clearly not ones everyone accepts.

It was former President Jimmy Carter who—in a 2002 speech broadcast live over Cuban national television—promoted Payá and his proposal for change. "The Varela Project," Payá explained to me, "calls for all Cuban people to be consulted on changes to Cuban law, so that they can exercise their freedoms of expression and association, so that they can free peaceful political prisoners . . . so that Cubans can freely elect their representatives and openly hold elections." At the time of the interview, over 11,000 Cubans had signed the petition demanding a plebiscite.

What Cuban exile wouldn't want such reforms in Cuba? Why wasn't Payá greeted with waves of support in Miami?

In reality, the visit of the Castro opponent rubbed many people the wrong way. And this is not surprising: Payá does not believe that the U.S. embargo has been successful in undermining Castro's dictatorship, nor does he agree with those who support an assassination attempt or other violent end to the regime.

During a long interview I conducted with him, Payá seemed legitimately dedicated to the quest for liberty and democracy in Cuba. Nevertheless, he pushes certain buttons within the Cuban community.

"Is he an infiltrator?" a Cuban woman asked me in a cafeteria. "No, he's not," I replied. But her question reflects the fear harbored by many exiles that the trips Payá has taken to Europe and the United States in 2002 and 2003 have been the result of some bed-sharing with Castro. Payá shifts in his seat and a fiery look comes into his eyes when I ask him, "Why are you allowed to leave Cuba?" "The question one must ask," he answered, "is why haven't they let me leave after so many years?"

The truth is that Oswaldo Payá is allowed out of Cuba because the Castro regime has no other recourse. There was intense international pressure that he be allowed to attend the ceremony where the European Union awarded him the Andrei Sajarov Human Rights Prize. Later, he was received by President José María Aznar of Spain, President Vicente Fox, Secretary of State Colin Powell, and the Pope. No other opponent of Castro—none—has received the attention in recent years that Payá has. And none has been nominated for the Nobel Peace Prize, as Payá has.

To many exiles, the Varela Project seemed naïve, unattainable, a pipe dream. But the strongest argument was that they didn't want to give any validity to the current Cuban constitution by working within and through Castro's system. And to the exile community, the Varela Project somehow gave legitimacy to the Cuban legal process.

"Is this just playing games with Castro?" I asked Payá. "This is not a game; this is a liberation movement against the regime that Castro runs," he replied. "We're not trying to exclude other projects and proposals, but we are against the paralysis of those who claim that we're simply playing games with Castro."

It's very clear to me that most Cubans living in exile want to end Castro's dictatorship. But where there doesn't seem to be a consensus is in the way to do it, in how to best attack it. It was painful for me to listen to Miami radio broadcasts that criticized and lashed out at Payá when he wants the same thing as the listeners.

There are two fundamental issues that separate Payá from the most right-wing Cuban exiles and which explain the rifts in the Cuban community itself: the U.S. embargo and the possibility of a peaceful transition of power. Although the embargo has gradually been losing support, particularly among younger Cubans, it remains a matter of principle for many and a symbol of resistance and dignity.

"Has the embargo done anything to help bring an end to Castro's regime?" I ask. "No," he replies. "It hasn't hurt him in any way?" I press. "It would have already ended the dictatorship by now."

Payá had the theory that the Cuban conflict needs to be "de-Americanized" and remains convinced that "the embargo is not a force of change inside Cuba." Nor does he support violent means of bringing about change.

Contrary to what some of the more radical Cuban exiles think, Payá is against making any attempt on Castro's life. "Death does not foster freedom," he told me. "It's no way to go about liberating Cuba. I don't support it; I refuse to accept it."

What Payá does support is a change from within Cuban borders.

"Listen to me," he said. "We live in a totalitarian regime, like fish in a dirty aquarium." "And change can't come from outside?" I interject, seeking a clarification. "It's not coming from outside Cuba," he replied. "Change comes from within, because that is where the heart of the tyranny lies: inside." It's a strategy similar to the ones Lech Walesa followed in Poland and Vaclav Havel followed in Czechoslovakia, when both countries were ruled by Communist leaders. But the Cuban exile community doesn't appreciate Payá's attitude of irrelevance toward them and their strong views on the Castro regime.

Payá who founded the Christian Liberation Movement and earned only $17 a month fixing medical equipment in order to support his wife and three teenage children, is risking his life to promote the Varela Project. "I fear for my life," he told me. "I could be shot at any time. It could come from one of those security cars that are always following me around. . . . I live surrounded by bugs planted by the state, filming me, watching me."

Cuban exiles fight for the island's freedom from outside. Payá fights from within. This is what makes him different. This is what makes him courageous.

Payá's case makes it clear that even within the Cuban community there are serious and important differences of opinion. After knowing about Payá and after visiting Miami and seeing the wide spectrum of opinion they have of him, nobody can say that all Cubans are the same. They would be stupid to think so.

What do Miguel Estrada, Salma Hayek, and Oswaldo Payá have in common? They are all prominent figures who demonstrate the rifts that run throughout the Latino community. But even more than that, they speak to enormous differences that exist within the groups that comprise the Hispanic identity. Estrada, Hayek, and Payá generate the same sort of passion that, for example, the Puerto Rican champion of independence Rubén Berríos does in his community. If it's true that most Puerto Ricans want the U.S. Navy out of Vieques—a proposal driven and led by, among other people, Berríos and his Independence

Party—it's also true that the Independence Party rarely garners over 5 percent of the votes in elections held on the island. And these differences within Puerto Rico are reflected and paralleled in the Puerto Rican community living in New York.

The next time that someone is tempted to lump all Latinos into the same category, he or she should think of Estrada, Hayek, Payá, and Berríos before doing so. They represent the enormous diversity that runs through the Hispanic community.

The simple solution is to lump all Hispanics into one category. But the correct, true, and fair thing to do is to appreciate and recognize our differences. This is the true secret of Latino life. The more one understands this, the more effective one can be in getting one's point across in the Latino community.

CHAPTER SIX

THE INVADER INVADED

"WE'VE INVADED Manhattan," Erasmo Ponce told me proudly, "with tortillas." And of all the different sorts of invasions one can have, I suppose the tortilla sort is the least serious. Erasmo Ponce is a Mexican who came to New York in the early 1990s. Shortly thereafter he started a tortilla factory with only four employees. He called it Tortillería Chinantla in honor of his birthplace, Chinantla, in the Mexican state of Puebla. Erasmo's small business would eventually explode. Today, it turns out 1 million tortillas a day. One million!

He expanded his business bit by bit. He went to hotels and restaurants personally to pitch his product. A few used them with their Mexican dishes, but most preferred to use them for corn chips or *totopos*. His English wasn't good, and that made it difficult for him to negotiate with the people who supplied his corn meal—the principle ingredient in tortillas—and those who sold him the plastic bags that his tortillas are packaged in. He paid what they charged him. But as he began to learn more English—and with it, the art of negotiation—his profits began to grow exponentially. Today, with 42 employees and two separate factories operating 24 hours a day, he doesn't just control the lion's share of the tortilla market in Manhattan, he also dominates a good part of the New Jersey market and is even considering plans to wage a war—a tortilla war—with the powerful West Coast distributors.

Erasmo is nearly 50 years old, but he appears much younger. He has an easy laugh. Between the making of tortillas, he somehow finds the time to act as a representative to the Mexican government of the millions of Mexicans living in the United States. That's a luxury. When I ask him if he's become a millionaire yet, he pauses for a moment, releases a broad smile filled with pride, and says, "Almost."

The story of Erasmo and his tortillas is only one part of a complicated phenomenon. The United States is indeed starting to feel culturally invaded in the way that U.S. culture has invaded other parts of the world. I invade you and you invade me: the new mantra for globalization.

Nevertheless, Erasmo's company is itself insignificant if we compare it to the 2,600 U.S. companies currently operating in Mexico.[1] One of these is, of course, McDonald's.

I'm not exaggerating when I say that there is a hamburger joint within a short, short distance of every *taquería* in Mexico. Outside the United States there is no more obvious sign of globalization than the mighty golden arches. This is why it was so interesting and supremely symbolic that a group of artists and intellectuals fought against the construction of a McDonald's franchise in downtown Oaxaca, Mexico.

Hamburgers in Oaxaca? Well, this is already as common as tacos in Manhattan, pizza in Tokyo, tapas in Bangkok, and sushi in Madrid. It may seem like some sort of cultural or culinary aberration, but this is the sort of world that we've created for ourselves during the past 20 years or so when "globalization" leapt out of the dictionaries and into our streets, restaurants, bathrooms, offices, and kitchens. The globalization of food, business, politics, human rights is a phenomenon we can no longer stop. We have no choice but to get used to it. Closing borders is a provincial idea, but this is exactly what happened in downtown Oaxaca: they slammed the door in McDonald's face.

In December 2002, the municipal government rejected the proposed construction of a McDonald's restaurant in the city's lovely colonial *zócalo,* or plaza. This is the same place where, as a teenager, I tried my first *mole negro* and my first *chapulines con chile piquín.* The painter Francisco Toledo and a group of Mexican intellectuals led the successful campaign against the restaurant. Certainly, McDonald's will inevitably influence the way Oaxacans eat. "We have values that we have to preserve," said the local government in rejecting the transnational company's proposal, "like our traditions and culture."[2]

They won't be selling any cheeseburgers with fries and a big chocolate shake in Oaxaca's *zócalo.* But almost nothing is pure in this world—not even Oaxaca. This is the sort of planet that we're building: muddy, *mestizo, mezclado,* mixed.

What do Toledo and his friends plan to do with the other 235 McDonald's franchises that have opened their doors in Mexico since 1985? Globalphobic and pseudorevolutionary acts—like the French farmer Jose Bové's attempt to destroy a McDonald's in Millau with his tractor—accomplish little. How to counteract the 15,000 McDonald's restaurants happily scattered across the globe? Definitely not with tractors. But maybe with tortillas. And if you think not, try telling that to Erasmo of Manhattan.

The United States is invading Mexico not only with hamburgers, but with Coke as well. As the *New York Times* reported, "Mexicans drink more Coca-Cola products, 462 eight-ounce bottles a year for every person, than in any other country in the world, including the United States, where consumption is 419 eight-ounce bottles a year per person."[3]

Mexico's strong commercial and labor dependence on the United States is undeniable. But it occasionally sparks strong resistance. In early 2003, a proposal was made to change the official name of Mexico. Since 1824, after Mexican independence, it has been the *Estados Unidos Mexicanos,* roughly, the United States of Mexico. At the time, many Mexicans were looking to the United States of America as the example to follow, not Spain, the colonial power which they had just broken away from. But the new name that was being proposed was just *México,* plain and simple.

But it's unrealistic to think Mexico could survive economically without the United States. Globalization, even with its gross mixing, excesses, and defects, is preferable to returning to a provincial system of closed doors. Closing the border to U.S. products, restaurants, and dollars is not a viable option. That would only create more hunger and poverty.

"Ninety percent of our foreign commerce takes place with the United States; 90 percent of the tourists who come to Mexico come from the United States; roughly 10 percent of our population lives in the United States, and one out of every five employed Mexicans has found that employment in the United States," said former Mexican chancellor Jorge Castañeda during a Univision interview. "The monies that our compatriots in the United States send back to Mexico every year represent the country's most important piece of foreign exchange; one out of every four Mexicans in the field has family in the United States; perhaps 80 percent of foreign investment in Mexico comes from the United States . . . it's not about whether it's needed or not needed, it's the reality of the situation."[4] Ultimately the choice is between a Mexico open to the world or a provincial, timid, isolated Mexico. It's that simple.

For those of you who think that Mexico is turning into McMexico, rest easy: McDonald's is not the devil. The same sort of cultural miscegenation that is currently taking place in Mexico is also occurring in the United States (and, for that matter, the rest of the world). Just as some Mexicans may feel like they're being bombarded with hamburgers, there are also U.S. citizens who are rather uncomfortable with the huge culinary and cultural influence that Mexico is having on the United States.

Some are so worried—including former presidential candidate Pat Buchanan—that they have denounced the so-called reconquest of the territories that Mexico originally was forced to cede to the United States in 1848 and are clamoring for all undocumented immigrants to be booted out of the country. But there are provincially minded folks on both sides of the border. The reality of the situation is that the Mexicanization of states like Texas, California, and Arizona is much more profound than the McDonaldization of Oaxaca.

The Mexican influence on the United States is incredible, overwhelming. Even in the White House. Laura Bush is in charge of the White House and Camp David kitchens. In 2002, she gave her staff instructions on what to prepare for the Christmas dinner menu: enchiladas and tamales. And the Bushes actually know how to eat them; they didn't commit the same egregious error that Gerald Ford did in 1976 when he tried to bite into a tamale during a campaign stunt designed to attract Hispanic votes, but forgot to remove the corn husk wrapper that tamales are cooked in. Ford looked ridiculous, won a mere 24 percent of the Hispanic vote, and lost the presidency.

Dining on tamales and enchiladas is a tradition that the Bush family has maintained ever since George Bush first won the Texas gubernatorial race. And so, in his vacation home at Camp David, George W., Laura, and their daughters Jenna and Barbara had the same Christmas dinner as millions of . . . Mexicans. Yes, that's right. Mexicans.

But Christmas dinners like the one the Bush family enjoys are getting more and more common in the United States. It's not that turkey and cranberry sauce are being replaced by traditionally Mexican dishes; rather, they share table space with foods that only a few decades ago would have been unthinkable or unbearable to a U.S. family.

It's hard to imagine that New Yorkers, Californians, or Washingtonians buy more tortillas than pizzas or bagels, but it's true. Salsa sales have surpassed ketchup: every year, some $700 million worth of *salsa picante* is sold, leaving the famous ketchup in the dust at only $515 million worth, according to Information Resources, Inc.[5]

In other words, the United States, which is rightly considered the number one cultural invader in the world, is itself feeling the effects of invasion. So much so that 27 of the 50 states have felt the need to declare English their official language. It's a ridiculous, ineffective move, though. If the census data is correct, in less than 50 years, there will be nearly 100 million Latinos speaking Spanish in this country.

The United States is feeling invaded. So is the world. I guess we all just have to get used to it. But how?

"Nativists who want to declare English the official language of the United States do not understand the omnivorous appetite of the language they wish to protect," wrote Richard Rodriguez in his book *Brown*. "Neither do they understand that their protection would harm our tongue."[6] If we're talking about invasive languages, then none has a more wide-reaching influence than English. English has all but become the official method of communication across the world—for businesses, sciences, politics, scholarship, and tourism—and it's absurd that some segments of the United States community feel the need to protect it as if it were an endangered species. English is the language of the new empire.

It's hard not to think of the United States as an empire. How can we not, after decisive victories in Afghanistan and Iraq? Or when the United States successfully defied the UN Security Council and the complaints of many other nations? Should we not look at the United States as a military superpower after it toppled Saddam Hussein's regime in 21 days? Could its military not swiftly defeat any other on Earth? How can it be perceived as anything but arrogant when the President tells the world: "You're either with us or you're with the terrorists"?

To much of the world, the United States is the new empire. Official U.S. foreign policy may no longer have as its goal the expansion of its territories and holdings throughout the world, but it conquers with its products and its language and sells its ideas—democracy, open markets, human rights, "the American way of life,"—throughout the world. "We are all Americans," wrote the BBC's political editor, Andrew Marr, in *Newsweek* before going on to explain that all the world's culture is influenced by U.S. products and way of life: "The world is turning bicultural."[7]

U.S. domination has reached such heights that one Spanish writer has gone so far as to call our world "the American planet." Others refer to the "McDonaldization" of the planet and even rechristen it "McWorld." As is the case with any oversimplification, using such terms too loosely will lead us down the path of error and exaggeration. But it is clear that the U.S. presence in the world community is, at times, overwhelming.

A democracy such as the United States will tend to resist being called an empire. After all, the traditional definition of an empire implies such things as the abuse of power and the impossibility of peaceful change from within. But while the United States is indeed a democracy on the inside, the power that it projects externally recalls the empires of old: China, Greece, Rome, Ottoman. Still, the United States presents itself to the world as a new sort of empire, one with very different characteristics than those that preceded it. For example, not only does it hold freestanding elections—it is the oldest democracy on Earth—but it also does not have an overt interest in colonization. It achieves domination and influence without territorial expansion. It's an empire—a new world order—without the historical and geographic connotations of previous empires. It is, as some say, an imperial republic.

According to the definition put forth by authors and scholars Michael Hardt and Antonio Negri, "The concept of Empire is characterized fundamentally by a lack of boundaries . . . an order—this is the way things will always be . . . [and] operates on all registers of the social order extending down to the depths of the social world it inhabits."[8] And the "empire" protagonized by the United States extends itself through its military, its international corporations, world trade, and the exportation of its culture.

In his book *What's So Great About America?* Dinesh D'Souza explains that other empires—such as the Roman, the Ottoman, and the British—were dominant via their military might and left important parts of humanity untouched. "American hegemony is unique in that it extends virtually over the total space of the inhabited earth," he writes. "Once again America is different in that its influence is not primarily sustained by force. This is not to say that America never projects its military power abroad. But these projections of power cannot possibly explain the enormous appeal of the American idea around the globe."[9] It's not just about the enormous influence of U.S. music, movies, or food; it's also the debates surrounding major international political issues that are affected in one way or another by the presence—or absence—of the United States.

This is even apparent in literature. In 1996, an anthology of short fiction by young Latin American writers was published under the title *McOndo.* The word derives from the imaginary town of Macondo, setting of the famous novel *One Hundred Years of Solitude* by Gabriel García Márquez. These writers, all under the age of 35, write in Spanish and yet feel no need to apologize for the influence that the United States has had on their work. "You can call us alienated kids who are sold out on American pop culture," said Bolivian author, *McOndo* collaborator, and Cornell professor Edmundo Paz-Soldán, "but it's the truth of our times. We grew up watching *The Simpsons* and *The X-Files,* and this comes out in our writing." [10]

This phenomenon of ideological and cultural mixing is not exclusive to Latin America. In books such as *The Global Soul* and *Video Night in Kathmandu,* the journalist Pico Iyer has managed to perfectly capture this interplay of U.S. influence on the world and the world's influence on the United States. It also has to do with the interactions between an individual and a world in constant movement. Everything whirls around us at such speeds we never could have imagined only a few years before. But the important thing to bear in mind with regard to this chapter's argument is how the United States—sometimes with force, but other times more subtly—tends to dominate or impose itself on that which is not like it.

Why? Because globalization depends fundamentally on technological advances, and it's the United States and its new inventions that are best equipped to expand the U.S.'s domain, policies, and priorities throughout the world. The United States is currently operating at the center, not the edge, of history; this movement toward the center of things began with its participation in both world wars. If I had to choose a single date on which the world changed decisively, it would be November 11, 1989, when the Berlin Wall fell and the long, protracted Cold War between the United States and the Soviet Union fell with it. Thus began a new world order—one of globalization—and it was ushered in with only one true superpower, the United States, as its leader.

Others, perhaps, will argue that September 11, 2001, was a day of greater import in terms of a changing world. But that day, on which some 3,000 innocent lives were lost, was a reaction to the new world order with the United States at the helm.

The fall of the Berlin Wall was an extraordinary event that marked the fall of many other walls: commercial walls, technological walls, communication walls, political walls, and even geographic walls. When all was said and done, the Soviet Union had broken down into several independent republics. And it's the United States that has the greatest interest in maintaining the current order. As the *New York Times*'s Pulitzer Prize–winning journalist Thomas Friedman wrote, "As the country that benefits most from global economic integration, it is our job to make sure that globalization is sustainable and that advances are leading declines for as many people possible, in as many countries as possible, on as many days as possible."[11] As he puts it, globalization and rapid technological and economic change are "the One Big Thing" going on right now.

Globalization is the United States's way of extending its economic, political, commercial, technological, and cultural power. Terrorism is one violent and asymmetric way of trying to combat this power. But of course there are nonviolent and much more effective ways of facing off with the U.S. empire. That's what makes it so interesting that the most powerful country in history is itself being invaded culturally at the same time as its own culture is spreading across the planet. By opening doors and tearing down walls, globalization makes it possible for people, products, money, and ideas to cross from one side to another, from one country to another, in both directions.

The United States, while reaping the benefits of globalization and the crumbling of so many walls, is also paying the consequences.

"We're getting invaded," an Arizonan bitterly complained to a *New York Times* reporter while discussing the constant influx of undocumented immigrants into the country.[12] His call for the U.S. military to close down and patrol the border is nothing new. During a 1995 television interview, former presidential candidate Pat Buchanan said, "I will stop illegal immigration cold by putting a double-linked security fence along the two hundred miles of the border where millions pour in every year."[13] But one or two fences cannot stop history.

It's silly to think that the most powerful country on Earth is afraid of being invaded. But other examples of xenophobia are abundant:

—Columnist Dame Edna caused an uproar when she wrote the following in *Vanity Fair:* "Forget Spanish. There's nothing in that language worth reading except Don Quixote. . . . As for everyone's speaking it, what twaddle! Who speaks it that you are really desperate to talk to? The help? Your leaf blower?"[14]

—Columnist Jim DeFede of the *Miami Herald* published the following letter he received from a reader tired of hearing about Miami and Cuba: "If you talk to most people here, most non-Cubans, you will not get a favorable opinion of these people. I don't want to be a bigot or anything . . . but this is like living in a Third World, South American country."[15]

—Fox News commentator Bill O'Reilly cited a Fox News Opinion Dynamics survey, which suggested that 79 percent of those surveyed favored putting the U.S. Army along the border to stop the illegal immigration of, in his words, "Mexican wetbacks, whatever you want to call them."[16]

Opinions like these aren't uncommon. Glenn Spencer, president of the organization Voices of Citizens Together, said in the *Los Angeles Times,* "What we are seeing in Southern California is not assimilation, it is annexation by Mexico."[17] But the truth of the matter is that Mexican influence on the United States started before the country's creation and goes much beyond the recent migratory wave.

The border crossed the Mexicans in California, Texas, and Arizona in 1848, not vice versa. As the Mexican poet Octavio Paz wrote in *The Labyrinth of Solitude,* "the United States . . . in one of the most unjust wars of imperialist expansion in history, snatched away more than half our land."[18] After this loss, as author Carlos Fuentes would later write, "the new frontier on the Río Grande became for many Mexicans an open wound."[19]

Today, nobody is calling for the return of lands that formerly belonged to Mexico. But while no fighting is taking place on the military or legal fronts, there is fighting going on culturally. It's the Reconquest.

Latinos are culturally reconquering lands that once were part of the Spanish empire and whose names cry out their origins: Los Angeles, San Bernadino, Monterrey, San Luis Obispo, San Diego. The Spaniards even controlled parts of modern-day Oregon. After the initial war of independence with Spain in 1810, these huge tracts of land fell under Mexican jurisdiction, though they were located far from the seat of the Mexican government. Many of these territories were among those lost to the United States in 1848 while liberals and conservatives were fighting for power in Mexico. It's interesting how many of these places that are now part of the United States still continue to display their Mexican heritage with pride. And with the arrival of each new immigrant, their Mexican traditions and customs—which have never really disappeared—are strengthened.

The influence is felt in both directions. "In effect," wrote Fuentes, "the enchilada can coexist with the hamburger." [20] He then goes on to argue that while the United States continues to ship its culture—its movies, music, books, ideas, journalism, politics, and language—to Latin America, each of these countries is also bringing its own gifts to the United States: gifts like a sense of the sacred, respect for one's elders, and constant commitment to one's family.

But this Latino influence is eating away at areas that were once exclusively in the scope of U.S. businesses. The same Bimbo snacks and pastries that I enjoyed as a child in Mexico can now be found in various California stores—with the same taste! Grupo Bimbo sold $3.7 billion worth of products in the United States in 2002, and it's still growing. "Latinos are becoming a majority in many communities in California and in many western states," said Oralia Michel, spokeswoman for Expo Comida Latina in Los Angeles. "Almost everyone is eating Latino food." [21] Gigante stores, where my mother still shops today in Mexico, are moving into California. In 2002, Grupo Gigante, with annual sales of $3 billion in Mexico, opened four stores in the Los

Angeles area, and plans are in the works to open several more. California is looking more and more like Mexico. So is the world.

The directory of New California Media, an organization founded in 1996, includes "ethnic media" that publish or broadcast in Spanish, Korean, Vietnamese, Arabic, Farsi, Tagalog, Russian, Mandarin, Armenian, Japanese, Hungarian, and Filipino (among many other languages) only in the state of California. Sad as this may be for some to acknowledge, without a shadow of a doubt, California is the future of the United States. It's there that the European, the African, the Asian, and the Latin American are all coming together.

In a 1998 speech, President Bill Clinton said that "within five years there will be no majority race in our largest state, California." And he was right. "In little more than 50 years there will be no majority race in the United States," he said. "No other nation in history has gone through demographic change of this magnitude in so short a time."[22] What's interesting about this statement isn't just that it was made by the president, but rather that it was used by Pat Buchanan in his book The Death of the West. I had the opportunity to debate Buchanan on television two or three times, and it has always fascinated me that the same arguments and statistics that he cites as evidence of the wrong turn that the United States has made with regard to its immigration policy are the same ones that I use to underline the enormous contributions immigrants are making to this country.

"The U.S. lacks the fortitude to defend its borders and to demand, without apology, that immigrants assimilate into society," Buchanan asserts. "But Uncle Sam is taking a hellish risk in importing a huge diaspora of tens of millions from a nation vastly different from our own. And if we are making a fatal blunder . . . our children will live with the consequences, balkanization, the end of America as we know her."[23] But his fatalism and xenophobia simply has no basis in reality. The United States is better off—economically and culturally—thanks to immigrants. But there's little that one can do against those who refuse to see the enormous advantages to this mixing of cultures.

The feeling of being invaded is not new. In 1981, Attorney General William French Smith addressed a joint congressional subcommittee on immigration reform. "We have lost control of our borders," he said. "We have failed to enforce our laws." [24] This was part of a long, protracted debate that culminated in 1986 with the amnesty accord and sanctions against employers hiring undocumented immigrants.

There have been several attempts to restructure the manner in which immigrants from Mexico enter the country. The bracero, or contract laborer, program was in effect from 1942 to 1964, and it brought nearly 5 million Mexicans to work legally in the United States. Agribusiness needed the manual labor, but many in this country still felt like they were being invaded.

In July 1954, Operation Wetback was started, first in California and then in Texas. The INS then claimed that 6 out of every 10 undocumented immigrants were arrested within two days of crossing the border, and the number of arrests made remained relatively low for the next 10 years. [25] But by the early 1970s, with the bracero program no longer in operation, the number of immigrants—both legal and undocumented—erupted.

This latest migratory wave has not stopped even today. But far from being a nationalistic invasion aimed at reclaiming land, it is simply a strong, migratory movement (with causes and consequences on both sides of the border) in an era of globalization where people, products, and money move in unprecedented numbers at extraordinary speeds.

An invasion? No. A cultural reconquest? It could be, at least in part. Things in California and Texas will never be like they were back before 1848. Nor will things ever be the same after this latest wave of immigration—wave that currently shows no signs of slowing down.

Latinos are culturally influencing the United States in ways never before seen, and this leads us to conclude that we're becoming a Hispanic nation. It's no exaggeration to say that several cities like Miami or states like California are already marching to the beat of Latino drums. And once the concentrated Hispanic populations start to filter out of places like Florida, Illinois, and New York into neighboring states, the phenomenon will begin to take place on a national level.

THE DOUBLE INVASION OF LANGUAGE AND SPANGLISH

Our invasion is one of words and means of expression. You invade me and I invade you. The United States may feel invaded by Spanish. But interestingly enough, Spanish-language purists are complaining that their language is being contaminated by English, resulting in a hybrid that has come to be known as Spanglish.

This mixing of the Latino with the non-Latino is also manifested in the way we talk. In the United States, English is infiltrating Spanish just as Spanish is infiltrating it. Sometimes neither language comes out on top, and the result—what comes out of our mouths—is Spanglish. This happens when the invader is himself invaded by a new and different tongue. Those of us who speak Spanish often find that we can no longer speak it properly.

Amherst College professor Ilan Stavans translated the first chapter of *Don Quixote* into Spanglish as a means of demonstrating that even the most respected and revered work of literature in Spanish can be read differently and sound different to those who live in the United States. When it comes to languages, nothing is sacred, and nothing is permanent. Not even El Quixote.

First, a confession: Hispanics speak Spanish pretty poorly. Or, more specifically, we speak a very different sort of Spanish than the one you'll read and hear in Mexico, Argentina, or Spain. In places like Hialiah in Florida, Santa Anna in California, Queens in New York, Pilsen in Chicago, and the West Side in San Antonio, you'll often hear a version of Spanish that not even Sancho Panza would be able to understand.

I know I'm committing a sort of *hara kiri* by launching a defense of improperly spoken Spanish. But I do it first, because it's a linguistic reality for millions of U.S. Spanish speakers, and second, because I truly believe that U.S. Latinos are contributing to the enrichment and expansion of the Spanish language in new and unexpected ways.

I'm not suggesting that we drop Spanish altogether and all start speaking Spanglish. That would be absurd, impractical, and impossible. Nor can we consider Spanglish a new language, seeking to replace either English or Spanish. But what I am suggesting is that many Spanglish expressions—heavily criticized both in and out of the United States—are being incorporated into what we may call a "global Spanish."

Global Spanish is dynamic, innovative, open, and constantly in flux. It's not antiquated, inert, or resistant to outside influence from other languages or new technologies such as the Internet. In other words, it's a living Spanish. And the addition of a bit of Spanglish would only serve to enrich it.

Many purists are scandalized by the fact that Spanglish is making its way, word by word, into Spanish dictionaries. But to be honest, it's really nothing to worry about. It's what gets spoken in the streets and ends up being repeated by Spanish-language media in the United States, especially television.

"You—the journalists—who work in Spanish-language television . . . you have the obligation to speak proper Spanish!" I've heard this on a number of occasions. And when I do, it's easy to counter with, "Which Spanish are you referring to? The one they speak in Mexico City? Santiago de Cuba? Santiago de Chile? Ponce, Puerto Rico? Jujuy, Argentina?"

Yes, it's true, there is a shared lexicon. If there wasn't, nobody would understand a thing. But it's arrogant and pretentious to suggest that there is but one correct way to express yourself in Spanish.

Hispanics aren't even able to agree on what constitutes "proper Spanish." It may not even exist. Which strain should dominate—that of the Mexican majority? The powerful Cubans? The influential Puerto Ricans? What about the rest of Central and South America?

Things get complicated when one particular word or phrase has multiple meanings. In Puerto Rico, *darse un palo* means "to take a swallow." But in Cuba, it means "to hit with a stick." And in Mexico . . . well, better leave that one up to the imagination. Even apparently simple things present challenges: Chileans use the word *corchetera* for what Cubans call a *presilladora,* which is what Mexicans call an *engra-padora,* and some Puerto Ricans call a *clipeadora.* Here in the United States, we say it's a *stapler.*

All of this goes to support a very simple conclusion: the Spanish spoken in the United States is a living, changing, dynamic language subject to outside influences, and trying to resist or counteract this nature is a lost cause. These days, Latinos can do more for the growth of the Spanish language than any other group who speaks it.

This cannot be seen as yet another threat from an alleged English-language imperialism; rather, it is Spanish that is making inroads in the United States.

"This is the first time in history where a community originating outside the United States has not been subject to the homogenizing processes of the cultural melting pot in order to be recognized as 'Americans' " contends the Peruvian writer Mario Vargas Llosa. "Hispanics have not had to renounce either their language or their culture in order to feel assimilated among the Anglo-Saxons. On the contrary, many have taken up positions in defense of their culture." [26]

Spanish forms part of the Hispanic community's cultural identity. Most Latinos speak it at home. Far from fading out, Spanish is gaining strength: some of the radio and television programs that command the largest audiences in cities like Los Angeles, Miami, and Houston are broadcast in Spanish and often beat out their English-language rivals for the top spots in the ratings charts. But we're certainly not talking about a pure, dictionary version of the Spanish language. In fact, one could argue that U.S. Spanish is the most mixed Spanish in the world, not only because of English influences but also because it comes from three major sources: Mexico, Cuba, and Puerto Rico.

American Spanish derives from, many sources. Standardization in the use of grammar, accents, and meaning is now little more than a *guajiro* dream.

I contend that it would be a huge error, and internationally arrogant, to try to get 40 million Spanish speakers in an English-language country to conform to the strict rules of the Royal Academy of the Spanish Language. In reality—and it's sad to say this—very few Latinos know these rules here in the United States, while those that do know them have styled them to the point where they're all but unrecognizable.

Rather than resisting change, our only real option is to welcome it. In fact, most journalists who have been working in Spanish-language media in the United States during the past 20 years have preferred to do their reporting in a way that can be widely understood and appreciated (which means using Spanglish expressions from time to time) rather than purporting to give lessons in a distant, foreign, outmoded form of Spanish.

Spanglish is mixture and change. And it's more alive than ever. Attacking it only makes it stronger. Among U.S. Hispanics, the word *greencard* is more widely used and understood than *tarjeta de residencia*. A professor at Florida International University even went so far as to propose a Spanglish spelling, *grincar,* just as it's pronounced, to avoid any problems. For those who utilize the benefits of welfare, Medicaid, or unemployment, it's much easier to refer to an English word instead of a protracted, incomprehensible Spanish translation.

Then, of course, there are these marvelous and polemical mixtures of Spanglish that have empowered speech. *Ganga* means "gift" in Mexico, but on the streets of East L.A., nobody is going to confuse this word with the chance to buy a cheap souvenir. Most immigrants in Texas, Arizona, and California know that the *bordo or borde* lies to the south, even though signs point to *la frontera. Tener sexo* is frequently used in place of *hacer el amor,* although if you're having it you probably don't care much what term is used. *Hacer lobby* is used like *cabildear. Surfear* is easier than *correr tabla* or *tontear en la Internet. Ambientalista* is shorter and more direct than *defensor del medio ambiente. Sexista* doesn't appear in most dictionaries, but it's a broader term than *machismo.* And *soccer* is even starting to replace *fútbol* in some circles.

At a 1997 linguistics conference in Zacatecas, Mexico, a prominent member of the Royal Academy argued that Spanglish was an affront to the Spanish language. With all due respect, he doesn't know what he's talking about. It's neither an affront nor an obstacle; it's a new branch on which the language can grow.

The late Mexican writer Octavio Paz was a bit less insensitive to Hispanics' cultural influences, but when I asked him in Miami if Spanglish was acceptable, he replied: "I don't think it's a matter of whether it's correct or incorrect; it's fatal. . . . These mixtures are transitory forms of communication among men."

Transitory forms? Without a doubt. But that is no reason to deny the real and definitive effect that Spanglish is having on millions of Spanish speakers. Today, Spanglish is more popular than ever, and much of that is due to the effects of the Internet.

In an article he wrote for the Argentine paper *El Clarín,* Roberto González-Echeverría, professor of Spanish and Comparative Literature at Yale University, wrote that "Spanglish is an invasion of Spanish by English" and that it presents "a grave danger to Hispanic culture and Hispanic progress." He then went on to add that "the sad reality is that Spanglish is basically the language of poor Hispanics, many of whom are all but illiterate in either language . . . some are ashamed of their origins and try to fit in with the crowd by using English words and direct, literal translations of English idiomatic expressions."

I don't agree with the Yale professor in the least. Spanglish poses no danger to Hispanic culture. On the contrary, it's a reflection of the Latinization of the United States and is a direct result of the growth of the U.S. Hispanic community. Far from threatening the culture which the professor is so concerned about, Spanglish promotes and reinforces it.

Nor is it true that "Spanglish is basically the language of poor Hispanics, many of whom are all but illiterate in either language." No. Spanglish is spoken by everyone, from those in the streets to those with Ph.D.s. All you have to do is listen to some of the top Latino executives of major U.S. companies to confirm that Spanglish has established itself at every economic level. In fact, one might even argue that the uses of Spanglish are not as well-known in the more economically underprivileged sectors as they are among those with better educational opportunities.

Professor Stavans is probably the top expert in the nascent field of

Spanglish. His opponents call him "the destroyer of the Spanish language," but Stavans has spent the last few years compiling a Spanglish dictionary, containing over 6,000 entries.

"Talking about maintaining the purity of the Spanish language in the United States is utopian," Stavans told me in an interview. "The purists want to maintain a Spanish frozen in time, as if languages don't change."

"What is Spanglish?" I asked the 40-year-old Mexican-born professor.

"Spanglish isn't a language," he replied. "Nor has it reached the level of a dialect, though it's on its way to becoming one. At the moment, it's a slang or a jargon."

Stavans is convinced that "we are currently witnessing a supremely creative verbal revolution, one that will force us to rethink the way Spanish itself has developed throughout the centuries."

Spanglish can be traced back to 1848 and the Treaty of Guadalupe Hidalgo, when Mexico lost over half its territory to the United States. It was then that groups of Mexicans first found themselves living in U.S.-controlled lands and forced to confront a language and a culture other than their own. According to Stavans, the phenomenon of Spanglish intensified during and after the Spanish-American War, when Spain lost Cuba and Puerto Rico to the United States.

With Spain's complete withdrawal from the American continents, "pure" Spanish quickly found itself under attack. "The phenomenon isn't limited to the United States," Stavans told me. "Spanglish includes Colombian and Venezuelan words . . . and as a matter of fact, Spanglish isn't the same for Mexicans, Cubans, and Puerto Ricans." Despite all its forms and variations—all dependent on the different ethnic groups and places where it's spoken—it wasn't until the second half of the twentieth century that Spanglish surged into our consciousness as something that wasn't quite Spanish but wasn't quite English either.

And now it's official: Spanglish is here to stay. "Spanglish is spoken in the belly of the empire," Stavans observed. "And it's spoken by both educated and uneducated people." He's right. I've heard lawyers and doctors speak Spanglish with their housekeepers, while politicians and civil servants in Texas and California often use it to communicate with many of their voters.

Spanglish has infiltrated every sector of the Latino community, and as a Hispanic journalist who has lived in this country for the past 20 years, I have to recognize that it's often easier to use a word that's technically neither Spanish nor English when I need to communicate and inform people about something quickly and easily.

"There are now more Hispanics in the United States than in the entire country of Spain. It's ridiculous to me that the people in the Royal Academy think that all we need to do is forget how we speak and accept this foreign language that they're trying to impose on us," noted Stavans. "Academics have viewed Spanglish as a defacement and a prostitution of the language for years. What I'm saying is that it's no longer possible to view it in such a negative light.

"I'm no prophet, but I don't think that Spanglish will be disappearing anytime soon," he told me, questioning Octavio Paz's conclusion that Spanglish was merely a transitory form of communication. "I don't see any reason why, in 200 or 300 years, we won't have great works of literature written in Spanglish."

The last word on Spanglish rests, of course, with the millions of people who speak it every day, and the millions more who use it to *emilean* each other over the Internet. It is a marker of how quickly and decisively the cultural reconquest is taking place in this country. Soon, perhaps even a ballot will be marked in Spanglish. At the rate that the United States is being Hispanized, it's not too far-fetched.

CHAPTER SEVEN

THE TRUE POWER OF IMMIGRANTS

Immigration is not a problem to be solved. It is a sign of a confident and successful nation. . . . New arrivals should be greeted not with suspicion and resentment, but with openness and courtesy.

—President GEORGE W. BUSH
Ellis Island, New York July 10, 2001

IT'S A SAD FACT that whenever the country is facing serious problems, immigrants are often singled out as scapegoats. Economic recession, high unemployment, terrorist attacks—it's the immigrants who are to blame. But the vast majority of immigrants now living in the United States are peaceful people who are happy to be here. Immigrants as a whole do not deserve to be held responsible for the enormous failures of the CIA and FBI that allowed four separate planes to be commandeered and turned into flying bombs.

The government should certainly refine its intelligence services and prosecute any terrorists inside its borders. Nobody is questioning this. If the CIA, FBI, and the dozen or so related agencies had done their jobs well, September 11, 2001, would have gone down in history as just another sunny, cloudless day in Washington and New York. But they were wrong. Terribly wrong. Nevertheless, trying to make up for these mistakes by treating any given foreigner as a potential terrorist is akin to going after mosquitoes with a howitzer.

The National Immigration Forum clearly summed up the dilemma faced by many immigrants after the terrorist attacks. "Under the microscope of government scrutiny, immigrant communities across the U.S. are feeling under siege," it stated in a press release. "Unfortunately, the government's actions since September 11—particularly the actions of the Justice Department—seem disorganized, scattershot, and aimed more to create fear and confusion in immigrant communities than to increase the safety of Americans in general."[1]

Fighting terrorism and increasing our safety is vital: everyone who lives in this country wants to feel more secure. But treating all immigrants, foreigners, visitors, and tourists as suspects is counterproductive, exaggerated, and a waste of time.

Immigrants as a body are neither terrorists nor criminals. Nor should anybody feel the need to question the patriotism of immigrants who have decided to make the United States their permanent home. After the September 11 attacks, there were American flags waving in immigrant neighborhoods across the country. People who weren't even legal residents were willing to enlist and fight in the United States Army.

Jesús Suárez del Solar and José Angel Garibay are just two of the many "green card soldiers" in Iraq. Ironically, they were considered good enough for the armed forces, but they wouldn't have been able to get a job working airport security. Could there be some greater display of loyalty than being ready to die for the United States?

High-level U.S. and Mexican officials had hoped to have a concrete proposal on the immigration question in place by the end of 2001. September 11 changed all that. But contrary to what many people may think, there is no better time than now to grant legal status to the 8 to 10 million undocumented immigrants living in the country today. Doing so would identify and locate people who officially do not exist or are invisible to the federal government and its intelligence agencies.

Many people regard undocumented immigrants as criminals. Tom Ridge, in an interview I did with him before he became secretary of Homeland Security, stated: "Technically, they have broken the law. So in a very technical sense as law breakers you could define them as criminals."[2] He went on to say, however, "As Americans we recognize that these are good people trying to support themselves and their families. We also recognize that many of them are very important to the economic success of companies and communities, and actually, while they may have broken the law to get here, they are supporting an enterprise system, a commercial system, once they get here."

By contrast, the same immigrants whom Ridge considers "criminals" were called "heroes" by President Vicente Fox in a public statement.

When I told former Mexican chancellor Jorge Castañeda about Ridge's statements, he observed that the real criminals were the U.S. companies who hire undocumented immigrants. "Since the 1986 accord, it's been a crime to hire anyone without their papers in order," he explained. "But still, tens of thousands of employers hire undocumented Mexicans and Central Americans every day."

Regardless of how we view them, these immigrants are part of our society. They're not going to go back where they came from and they will continue to make substantial contributions to the U.S. economy.

"Data on various aspects of Mexican immigration suggest [that] intensification, over the last two decades, of a trend toward permanent settlement in the United States,"[3] concluded Harvard University scholars Marcelo M. Suárez-Orozco and Mariela M. Páez. Their findings are confirmed by data collected by Wayne Cornelius of the University of California at San Diego: "Mexican immigrants are rapidly moving away from transnational strategies. For example, over time and across generations, Mexicans tend to remit less money, become less involved in Mexican politics and visit there less often."[4]

The increased security along the U.S.-Mexico border, coupled with the semipermanent problem of Latin American poverty, means that immigrants who once shuttled back and forth between the two countries are now doing so less and less frequently. This is particularly true of those who become legal residents and are able to bring their families here to live with them.

Those who come have no desire to leave. That's how it was before September 11. That's how it had been for decades. The cycle of immigration continues, but it no longer turns with the same strength or speed.

BUSH'S IMMIGRATION PROPOSAL

On December 9, 2003, Tom Ridge, head of the Department of Homeland Security, stated: "As a country, we have to come to grips with the presence of 8 to 12 million illegals, afford them some kind of legal status some way."[5] Ridge's declaration, which was surely already being acknowledged in Bush's working plan, took many by surprise and generated much debate around the country. The issue of illegal immigration was begining to gain force. And after Ridge came Bush.

In a Washington press conference on December 15, 2003, Bush said: "Let me clarify something; this administration is firmly against blanket amnesty."[6]

Then on January 7, 2004, Bush invited a group of influential Hispanics to the White House so he could spend 45 minutes describing his plan for modifying U.S. immigration laws. It was the most important such proposal since President Reagan's plan in 1986.

"I propose a new temporary worker program that will match willing foreign workers with willing American employers when no Americans can be found to fill the jobs. . . . This program expects temporary workers to return permanently to their home country after their period of work in the United States has expired."[7] Bush's proposal offered an initial grace period of three years to those undocumented immigrants who had found work. This protection would also include their immediate families, though the applicant would have to pay a fee. Similarly, those residing outside the United States could apply for jobs if and only if there were no U.S. citizens willing to fill them.

Bush made it very clear that he was not in favor of amnesty in any form: "I oppose amnesty, placing undocumented workers on the automatic path to citizenship," he said in his speech. "Granting amnesty encourages the violation of our laws and perpetuates illegal immigration. America's a welcoming country, but citizenship must not be the automatic reward for violating the laws of America."[8]

As was to be expected, Bush was attacked from both sides of the political spectrum. The right accused him of rewarding those who had broken the law, while the left decried it as bait with which to fish for Latino votes.

The Hispanic Caucus issued a press release: "The proposed Bush immigration plan is a modern day rewrite of the 1940's bracero program that tore families apart and stripped laborers of their earnings and their future. The President's program would create a generation of second-class citizens who are baited to work for America with the false promise of ever being able to enjoy the benefits of citizenship."[9] The country's largest union, the AFL-CIO, said that Bush's plan would create a "permanent underclass of workers,"[10] while the National Association of Latino Elected and Appointed Officials (NALEO) stated that "it is our belief that his principles on immigration reform do not focus enough on offering hardworking immigrants a path to citizenship and full participation in our society."[11] Raul Yzaguirre, president of the National Council of La Raza, said: "Hispanic Americans are extremely disappointed with the President's announcement today on immigration policy, which appears to offer the business community full access to the immigrant workers it needs while providing very little to the workers themselves."[12]

During the Summit of the Americas (which was attended by 34 Western Hemisphere nations, Cuba being the only exception) held in Monterrey, Mexico, President Vicente Fox described Bush's proposal as "very important." Clearly, the proposal was taking into account the enormous pressure that his government was exerting in the hopes of gaining some form of legal status for Mexican nationals in the United States. It was also a means of garnering more of the Hispanic vote. Bush's proposal was a good first step; not for what it specifically said but rather because it brought the issue to the national stage. Bush had set the wheel of public debate in motion, and now there was nothing left but to confront the issue.

It's important to note that in his speech, Bush recognized that "the system is not working." He also recognized the enormous contributions that immigrants have made to the history, culture, and economy of the United States. Millions of workers are living in this country in fear, and Bush has said that he's ready to do something about it. He acknowledges that the United States needs the help of foreign workers to continue to grow. And he has declared the need—for both humanitarian and national security reasons—to legalize (albeit in a temporary manner) the status of millions of workers.

Nevertheless, the Bush proposal is unrealistic, because it lacked the most important details, is unilateral, and doesn't offer a long-term solution to the problem of undocumented immigration. Furthermore, it had a distinctly opportunist character in that it lacked specificity and was presented during an election year, clearly to garner support in certain quarters. Let's examine the proposal in more detail.

First, Bush's proposed immigration reform is unrealistic because it only offers *temporary* legal status to undocumented workers and their families. What will they do when their special visas expire and there is no possibility of renewing them? This wasn't made clear; Bush left the details up in the air. It is naive to expect people who have spent years working legally in the United States to move back home when their visas expire. This just isn't going to happen. Any serious proposal must include the possibility of becoming a legal resident and, eventually, a full U.S. citizen—a possibility that doesn't exist under Bush's proposal.

Bush's proposal is also unilateral. He made the announcement himself from the White House, without consulting with any members of the Hispanic Caucus. President Fox can take as much credit as he wants for Bush's proposal, but the fact remains that Bush called him a mere 15 minutes before making the announcement, and then only to advise Fox of what he was going to say. There was no negotiation whatsoever between the two countries, and the proposal is weaker because of it.

Finally, Bush's proposal has no plan for addressing the problem of undocumented immigration in the long term. In fact, it will only delay and complicate matters. Under his plan, millions of workers will gain legal status—perhaps for three years, perhaps for six—only to revert to their illegal status after that time has expired. This isn't going to solve anything.

Temporary legalization could even become something of a trap.

These temporary workers—just like the braceros before them—could easily be exploited and manipulated by the employers who sponsor their work permits, and at the end of their stay, the workers could be deported without much trouble at all, since the new Immigration Service will know exactly where they live and work.

Similarly, Bush's proposal doesn't say anything about the violence going on along the border between Mexico and the United States. On average, one immigrant dies every day along this line. Deaths there outnumber the deaths of U.S. soldiers in Iraq. According to Claudia Smith, director of the Rural Legal Assistance Foundation of California, 409 immigrants died in border-crossing attempts in 2003 alone.[13]

Nor did Bush say anything in his proposal about how he plans to regulate or control the thousands of undocumented workers entering the country every year. It's simply absurd to talk about national security and immigration reform when the southern border of the United States seems more like a colander. The only realistic way of dealing with these illegal border crossings is through an immigration accord with Mexico and Central America. But even still, as long as there is such disparity in wealth between the United States and Latin America, undocumented immigration will continue to come. Therefore, any proposed immigration reform must also include a program of investment, akin to the one developed by the European Union—one that is designed to more or less equalize wages throughout the Americas. With his proposal, Bush is merely skirting the problem. It will neither permanently resolve the situation of millions of undocumented immigrants already in this country, nor will it set us up for a future in which a steady and orderly flow of immigrants can proceed into the United States from Latin America. My only hope—and the hope of millions of immigrants—is that others will expand upon the issue that Bush has set in motion.

IMMIGRANTS ARE GOOD FOR BUSINESS

The United States continues to be a land of immigrants. In 2000, 56 million people in the United States—20 percent of the population—were either immigrants or first-generation Americans. This is a huge increase from the 1970 figure of only 34 million.

FOREIGNERS OR THE CHILDREN OF FOREIGNERS IN THE US [14]	
BORN IN A FOREIGN COUNTRY	28.4 MILLION
BORN IN THE UNITED STATES, TWO FOREIGN PARENTS	14.8 MILLION
BORN IN THE UNITED STATES, ONE FOREIGN PARENT	12.7 MILLION
TOTAL	55.9 MILLION

While the sheer number of immigrants is higher than it has ever been in U.S. history, there have been other points in our history with even higher foreign populations. From 1890 to 1930, over 30 percent of the U.S. population was composed of immigrants and their children—mainly from Ireland, Germany, Italy, and Mexico. Similarly, if we look exclusively at foreign-born populations, the figures were higher in 1870 (14 percent) and 1910 (14.7 percent) than they were in 2000 (10.8 percent).

Immigration is great for business. Immigrants from Latin America are economically essential to combating inflation and keeping prices down. Without immigrants, the cost of food and housing could sky-rocket. Immigrants make it possible for other U.S. citizens to enjoy the high standard of living that they've come to expect. And the United States needs more immigrants to work and pay taxes so that it can support a rapidly aging population.

According to a study conducted by the *Washington Post,* the Kaiser Foundation, and Harvard University, the aging of U.S. society is clearly reflected in its political participation. "If the current trends continue, the number of people 65 and older who vote in midterm elections is likely to exceed that of young adults by a 4-to-1 ratio by 2022."[15] And who's going to pay for the Social Security benefits that the baby boomer generation is expecting? Immigrants.

The Pew Hispanic Center calculates that "between the years 2000 and 2025, the white working age population is expected to decline by five million workers, as baby boomers retire from the labor force. According to the U.S. Census Bureau, the number of working age Latinos is projected to increase by 18 million people."[16]

When the Senate Special Committee on Aging invited Federal Reserve chairman Alan Greenspan to speak, few people expected they'd be hearing a defense of immigrant workers. But that's just what they got. "The aging of the population is bound to bring with it many changes to our economy," he said. "Immigration, if we chose to expand it, could prove an even more potent antidote for slowing growth in the working-age population. As the influx of foreign workers in response to the tight labor markets of the 1990's showed, immigration does respond to labor shortages."[17]

Another study, done by the Center for Labor Market Studies at Northeastern University, confirms the importance of immigrants in the workforce and concludes that "recent immigrants were critical to the nation's economic growth in the past decade. . . . During that decade, eight of 10 new male workers were immigrants."[18]

The results of increased numbers of immigrants in the workforce are changing the way people work in the United States. There is a clear division of labor: there exist certain jobs that nobody other than an immigrant is willing to do, especially in the agricultural, service, construction, and sewing industries. "The American economy absolutely needs immigrants," said Andrew Sum, who directed the Northeastern University study. "I realize some workers have been hurt by this, and some people get very angry when I say this, but our economy has become more dependent on immigrant labor than at any time in the last 100 years."[19]

According to the Urban Institute, immigrants comprise 34 percent of the workforce in the housekeeping field, 23 percent in farming and fishing, 21 percent in assembly and machine operation, and 18 percent in other service industries.[20] The title of the article in which *USA Today* published these statistics couldn't have been more clear: "USA Just Wouldn't Work Without Immigrant Labor."

Even though immigrants are needed to replace retiring U.S. workers, pay into Social Security, and fill certain jobs essential to the overall economy, the debate over immigrants' contributions to U.S. society continues to rage. There is no shortage of arguments that immigrants take more than they contribute to the United States. But the most complete study to date on the issue—done by the National Academy of Sciences—does not support such claims. Immigrants put more into this country than they get out of it.

Tired of hearing arguments for and against immigrants and with no way of determining which side was right, the members of the congressionally appointed U.S. Commission on Immigration Reform asked the National Research Council (the principal operating arm of the National Academy of Sciences) "to examine the effects of immigration on the national economy, on government revenues and spending, and on the future size and makeup of the nation's population."[21] The results released at a May 17, 1997, press conference in Washington, D.C., were convincing: "Immigrants may be adding as much as $10 billion to the economy each year," said James P. Smith, senior economist at the Rand Corporation and chair panel. "The vast majority of Americans are enjoying a healthier economy as the result of the increased supply of labor and lower prices that result from immigration."[22]

It's true that immigrants use state and local services—especially related to education and health care—and these services cost money. State and local governments don't always receive adequate compensation from the federal government for providing such services, and this can sometimes result in serious financial problems.

We'll look at Los Angeles County as an example. According to the *New York Times,* of the 1.5 million people without health insurance who are treated by L.A. County's hospitals and medical centers, some 800,000 of them were undocumented immigrants. This partially explains the $400 million budget deficit that the county is facing for the 2003 fiscal year.[23]

Nevertheless, immigrants do provide an overall positive economic contribution to the United States. The National Academy of Science's "long-term estimates indicated that on a national level, the majority of new immigrants and their descendants will add more to government coffers than they receive over their lifetimes."[24]

But it isn't the only organization extolling immigrants' economic advantages. The National Immigration Forum calculates that the average immigrant contributes $1,800 more to the economy than what he or she receives in public services every year; that over the course of his life he pays $80,000 more in taxes than what he receives from local, state, and federal governments, and that—in 1997, for example—immigrants and their families paid $133 billion directly into local, state, and federal taxes.[25] This figure has surely risen since then.

And though it's true that these figures don't differentiate between legal and undocumented immigrants, the fact of the matter is that immigrants pay taxes, whether they have their papers in order or not. UCLA's North American Integration and Development Center estimates that "the current levels of undocumented migration from Mexico (3 million workers) represents a contribution of $154 billion to the Gross Domestic Product of the United States, including $77 billion to the Gross State Product of California. This is a conservative estimate based on the lower end estimates of the undocumented workforce. More recent higher end estimates of 4.5 million Mexican workers could push the aggregate contribution to approximately $220 billion."[26]

Journalists Peter Jennings and Todd Brewster sum up how important immigrants are to this country: "The American economy depends upon the undocumented worker; indeed, it preys upon him," they wrote in their book *In Search of America*. "It takes Social Security taxes from his income, billions paid into the system that, because of the worker's undocumented status, will never have to be paid out. It withholds federal and state taxes from his paycheck, and perhaps too much at that, since he may not have the will to file a return (fearful that an income tax return would get the INS's attention) and the government may not have to pay him a refund."[27] Is this just? Definitely not.

Besides making substantial contributions to the economy, undocumented workers save U.S. lives. Literally. According to the United Network for Organ Sharing, they account for 2 percent of all organs donated in the United States, while receiving only 1 percent. In 2001, for example, there were 124 deceased immigrants who donated their organs. "Every single day in our country, there are donors who are [undocumented immigrants]," Pam Silvestri, spokeswoman for the Southwest Transplant Alliance, told the *El Paso Times*.[28]

Despite the enormous contributions that immigrants—both legal and undocumented—make to U.S. life, the criticisms continue to come. The Center for Immigration Studies—an anti-immigrant organization—insists that "by historical standards, the number of immigrants living in the United States is unprecedented. Even at the peak of the great wave of the early 20th century immigration, the number of immigrants living in the United States was less than half of what it is today (13.5 million in 1910)."[29] The comparison, of course, is bogus. As we've already seen, in 1910 foreigners made up 14.7 percent of the population, whereas in 2000 they account for only 10.8 percent.

The same organization argues that "by increasing the supply of unskilled labor, Mexican immigration in the 1990s has reduced the wages of workers without a high school education by an estimated 5 percent." The resulting reduction in consumer prices was, according to the CIS, between 0.08 and 0.20 percent over the same time frame, leading to their conclusion that "the impact is so small because unskilled labor accounts for only a tiny fraction of total economic output."[30] Even if these figures were correct and could be independently corroborated, the drawbacks associated with immigrants working in the United States are miniscule when compared with their huge advantages, including paying of many millions of tax dollars, providing essential labor for certain industries, controlling inflation, and supporting a rapidly aging population.

In one of the most complete studies done on immigrants' contributions, Julian L. Simon poses the following question: "How many immigrants, of what kind, should the U.S. admit each year?" His answer is resounding: "More than at present, and chosen more for their economic characteristics and less on the basis of family connections."[31] The conclusion is clear: the United States needs more immigrants.

HOW IMMIGRANTS HELP LATIN AMERICA

Of course, immigrants have benefits that extend far beyond this country's borders. According to the Banco Interamericano de Desarrollo, monies sent from Latinos back to their countries of origin reached $32 billion in 2002.[32] The faster this country comes to terms with this reality, the faster we all can benefit. All of us.

The money immigrants send to Latin America by far exceeds direct U.S. aid to the region. And in the majority of cases, these monies constitute the recipient countries' primary source of foreign investment. According to Public Agenda, "44 percent [of immigrants] send money home at least once in a while."[33]

If we take Mexico as an example, these monies are the country's second highest source of income, behind petroleum and before tourism. Therefore, the United States could help Latin America dramatically, not by sending more money to the region but by granting legal status to the undocumented immigrants supporting their families abroad.

As we've seen, immigrants not only contribute greatly to our economy, they are hugely important to all of Latin America as well. Far from being a burden, immigrants are one of the hemisphere's major economic engines.

Contrary to what many stereotypes suggest, Latino immigrants don't come here to take advantage of U.S. society. According to Public Agenda, "A large majority (73 percent) say it's extremely important to work and stay off welfare," while "Eighty percent of immigrants say the U.S. is a 'unique country that stands for something special in the world.'"[34] Those who think that all immigrants are criminals, terrorists, or just plain lazy don't have the slightest idea how the United States came to be a superpower in the first place. Without immigrants, it would never have happened.

IMMIGRATION ACCORD

The U.S. government has to understand that only an immigration accord—first with Mexico, and then with the rest of the countries in Latin America—will bring some stability to the border. Only then can we rest assured of an orderly, safe, and peaceful flow of workers so vital to the U.S. economy. The wave of immigration isn't going to stop. It never will. What's needed is a way to manage it effectively.

The only people benefiting from the current chaos along the border are the coyotes. In 2004, it was almost impossible to find a coyote who would charge less than $1,000 for smuggling you across the border. They're good at what they do; we have to recognize that. They know where and when to cross without being detected. But some are only there to rob, swindle, rape, and murder immigrants.

U.S. immigration policy is confused, counterproductive, contradictory, and largely ineffective. Instead of helping the economy, it functions as something of a boycott. And instead of protecting immigrants, it forces them into dangerous situations, and even death. And if the goal of current policy is to secure the nation's borders, then it's a near-total failure. Not only does it fail to secure the borders, but it also kills potential immigrants, who would otherwise contribute positively to American society.

Considering all this, it's about time the United States picked up the immigration dialogue between the two countries. An immigration accord and amnesty are two distinct issues, but both are essential to bring stability to the border and dispel the fears of immigrants living illegally in the United States. The former will regulate and administer the stream of immigrants, while the latter will allow millions currently living underground to come out into the sun of the richest nation on Earth. Only an immigration accord between the United States and

Latin America combined with amnesty or some other means of legalizing the status of undocumented immigrants can hope to solve this issue in the long term and put an end to the constant violations on the southern border.

It's no mystery why the Bush administration put the brakes on immigration talks with Mexico after September 11, 2001. Chancellor Jorge Castañeda of Mexico had to recognize in January 2002 that the time frame in which an accord was expected "is not what we had originally expected, given the events that have transpired." [35] It will be a while before Mexico gets "the big enchilada," as Castañeda liked to refer to the immigration accord.

Around this same time, Secretary of State Colin Powell refused to declare the accord dead. "I am determined, the president is determined," Powell said at a press conference in Washington, "to get back to this very important issue of regularizing the movement of Mexicans back and forth. We haven't given up." [36] But few truly believed that the United States was ready to sit back down at the negotiating table. Now that the Bush administration seems to want to restart this dialogue, who knows what the future will bring.

In November 2002, Powell's tone was markedly different. In a visit to Mexico City, President Fox asked him about what distinguishes "those people who arrive in the United States to work and enrich the economy with their labor from those who could represent a threat to the security of the United States." [37] "These things take time," Powell replied. "They are not simple issues." [38] Fox, upset, raised his voice and asked if the United States was unable to do more than one thing at a time. He saw no reason why a new immigration accord couldn't be negotiated while the United States was in the process of implementing a new Department of Homeland Security. The United States' thoughts were elsewhere, though: Afghanistan and Iraq.

Later, Castañeda would resign his office, sending a clear signal that there were not many opportunities for progress with the one issue most central to U.S.-Mexican relations. In the meantime, the lives of millions of undocumented immigrants continue to hang in the balance.

The United States doesn't seem to understand that amnesty and an immigration accord are not at all detrimental to the interests of national security. In fact, an accord would allow the government to know exactly who the new immigrants are, while amnesty would allow it to identify all the immigrants who are actually here. Is this so difficult to understand?

Certainly, though, campaigning in favor of an immigration accord or to support an amnesty for undocumented immigrants could undermine a candidate's support if he doesn't make these things clear to the voting public. Even though Latinos are the swing vote in the elections, they are not—yet—the core of the American electoral system. This is why Colorado governor and president of the Association of Republican Governors Bill Owens felt it necessary to defend the immigration proposals that the Bush administration was considering. "It was never defined as amnesty for illegals," he said, "so much as moving back to legalized work programs."[39]

Neither Bush nor Gore came out in favor of amnesty during their 2000 campaigns. This could be due to the fact that survey after survey showed that most voters were opposed to the idea. A few days before the September 11 attacks, the results of a Harris Interactive poll—released by an anti-immigrant organization known as the Federation for American Immigration Reform, or FAIR—showed that 60 percent of those surveyed opposed amnesty whereas only 29 percent were in favor of it.[40] Regardless of FAIR's methodology or interpretations of the results, the fact is that the concept of amnesty has never been properly and clearly explained nor supported by any politicians on a national level.

On January 7, 2003, Congressman Luis Gutierrez introduced his U.S. Employee and Family Unit and Legalization Act which proposes granting legal status to all undocumented immigrants who had entered the country before January 7, 1998. But his bill lacked sufficient support in Congress.

There has been a certain amount of congressional opposition to granting amnesty and passing an immigration accord if Mexico doesn't bring something to the table as well. NAFTA—which went into effect on January 1, 1994—left two important issues unaddressed: Mexican petroleum and immigration to the United States. According to Carlos Salinas de Gortari, former Mexican president and negotiator of the treaty, the tacit agreement on both sides of the line was that these two issues would not be touched upon. But the question is, for how long?

There are representatives in both houses of Congress who want Mexico to open up its oil fields to U.S. companies in exchange for an immigration accord. But petroleum is intrinsically linked to the concept of Mexican sovereignty. While there are some segments of the Mexican oil industry that would permit foreign companies to participate on a limited basis, the idea of privatizing the Mexican oil industry is, for now, a political impossibility.

The best strategy for success in achieving an immigration accord with Mexico and amnesty for undocumented immigrants is to point out that such an accord will greatly increase national security. That's the approach. But while there may not be enough political support to negotiate something like this at the moment, cracks are beginning to appear in the system. The most obvious one is the growing use of Mexican consular licenses.

Consular IDs are a form of identification given by Mexican consulates to citizens traveling abroad. They're not accepted everywhere in the United States, but by early 2003 they were good at some 60 U.S. banks—including the Bank of America, Wells Fargo, and Citibank—over 800 police departments, and in dozens of cities, including Los Angeles County and Chicago.[41] They were even accepted for entrance into the San Francisco Federal Building. The criticisms, however, were enough to get the experiment stopped after only two weeks.

In this age of terrorism, when it's all but impossible for an undocumented immigrant to obtain a driver's license, a Mexican consular ID is a way of saying, "Look—I'm not a terrorist. I'm not a criminal." Also, with the card, workers are able to open bank accounts, and banks can take advantage of the millions of dollars that undocumented immigrants represent. According to the Mexican consulate in Miami, more than 1 million cards were issued to Mexicans in the United States in 2002.

Not unexpectedly, Republican members of Congress like Thomas Tancredo of Colorado and Dana Rohrabacher of California sent a letter to President Bush in May 2003 complaining about the growing acceptability of Mexican consular IDs. In a Washington press conference, Tancredo and some of the 15 other members who had signed the letter unveiled a poster made up to look like a consular ID featuring a photo of Mexican President Vicente Fox.

For the Mexican Embassy in Washington, this showed "little respect." "I call it anti-Hispanic," said Democratic congressman Ruben Hinojosa in the *Los Angeles Times*. But Tancredo defended his use of the poster. "There is nothing anti-Hispanic about having the picture of the Mexican president superimposed on a Mexican ID," he was quoted as saying in the same paper. Then he sarcastically asked what other kind of picture he should have used, "Somebody who looks like a Swede?"[43] Colorado, in a move that didn't surprise anybody, became the first state in the Union to prohibit the use of consular IDs as valid forms of identification.

The FBI didn't much like consular IDs either. In a June 2003 appearance before Congress, Steven McCraw said that the FBI and the Justice Department had determined that they were not trustworthy forms of identification and could be taken advantage of by terrorists. Specifically, he was worried that they could be used to board planes, transfer funds, or hide terrorists inside the United States.

But despite these accusations, the use of consular IDs will continue to grow as long as undocumented immigrants are prevented from obtaining official forms of identification acceptable to U.S. authorities. And these sorts of complications won't stem the tide of immigration. I don't know of a single person who has decided not to immigrate simply because they wouldn't be able to get a driver's license. Not one.

Of course, today in the United States it is not politically advantageous to propose amnesty for illegal immigrants or to promote an immigration accord with Latin America. It's not even OK to give driver's licenses to undocumented immigrants, which is why Arnold Scharzenegger decided to revoke this right that had previously been granted to thousands as soon as he took office in Sacramento. Nevertheless, there are times when one must make unpopular decisions that can solve problems and humanitarian issues, whether or not they generate votes.

Further, those who want to understand the Latino experience have to understand the importance that Latinos place on gaining permanent legal status in this country. Even those who have already become full-fledged U.S. citizens demonstrate clear support for the ones who have yet to gain a green card.

In times like these, it can be relatively easy to bash immigrants, deny them amnesty, and protest negotiations for an immigration accord between the United States and Latin America. But the Hispanic community—just like any group that's growing in power and importance—is not going to forget those who turned their backs on it when it most needed them. Simply put, it's a very practical question: thousands—perhaps millions—of young, undocumented immigrants could well become important voters in 10 or 20 years. And if they don't, then their sons and daughters will. To oppose the fair and humane treatment of undocumented immigrants today could have counterproductive consequences in the not-so-distant future. From a very pragmatic standpoint, it's imperative that we do something on behalf of the millions of people who currently live in the shadows.

Immigrants are an essential part of this country: they contribute more than they gain themselves, their influence is growing both culturally, economically, and politically, they're willing to learn English and work hard to stay off welfare while at the same time supporting millions of families back in Latin America, they represent future voters, contribute to this country's diversity, and they have no plans of going back to their countries of origin.

Immigrants are going to keep coming, so rather than trying to stop them all at the border—a truly impossible task—we should be managing the flow with the proposed immigration accord based on cooperation and collaboration between the United States and the various Latin American nations. Professor Jagdish Bhagwati of Columbia University wrote in the *Journal of Foreign Affairs,* "If it is not possible to effectively restrict illegal immigration, then governments in the developed countries must turn to policies that will integrate migrants into their new homes in ways that will minimize the social costs and maximize the economic benefits." Penalizing immigrants is not working. Some countries have no other option but to send their workers abroad. "The future belongs to [the] nations [that] will grasp this reality and creatively work with migrants and migration."[43]

Professor Baghwati proposes the creation of a World Migration Organization to supervise and monitor countries' immigration policies and search for mutually beneficial solutions. I wholeheartedly support this idea. But first we'll have to convince the U.S. government—and many European governments as well—that force is not the best solution to a problem that requires dialogue, cooperation, and understanding.

In the meantime, as the Willy Chirino song goes, *"Y siguen llegando"*—they keep coming.

CHAPTER EIGHT

THE LATINO AGENDA

IS IT POSSIBLE to have one single agenda that encompasses all the different groups that make up the Hispanic community? I believe the answer is a categorical yes.

In this final chapter I would like to explore the possibility of creating this agenda for the Latino community, and also try to understand why no single Latino leader has emerged on the national stage. Finally, to balance out this book's theory that a Latino wave is sweeping across the nation, I want to give a little more attention to the opposing current, the Americanization of Latinos and their integration into U.S. society.

The Latino agenda derives from those issues that Latinos face each and every day. From our absence at many levels of authority stems the need for greater political representation; the enormous numbers of undocumented immigrants clamors for the legalization of their status; out of our double identity as North Americans and Latin Americans comes the need to express ourselves in both English and Spanish; the lamentable conditions in which many Hispanics—especially children—live demands that we lift their communities out of poverty; the sad fact that many Latinos drop out of high school begs for a remedy; the injustice of making state colleges unaffordable to so many Latinos points to the need for legalization; our experiences with discrimination and conflicting identities moves us to unite with other minority groups; the failure of U.S. foreign policy to make Latin America a primary concern of must be rectified; and the realization that only one in five Latinos votes in elections calls for us to be more politically active. From the conundrum of who we are and what we want is born the idea of expanding and disseminating the Latino experience.

The Hispanic community's problems are all right there for everyone to see. What we need to do is to define an agenda—one that encompasses all Hispanic groups from all over the hemisphere—that effectively confronts these problems.

ONE SINGLE AGENDA (IN FOUR VOICES)

There are, arguably, four *padres* of the Hispanic world. Latinos pay very close attention to what Raul Yzaguirre of the National Council of La Raza, Harry Pachón of the Tomás Rivera Policy Institute, Roberto Suro of the Pew Hispanic Center, and Arturo Vargas of the National Association of Latino Elected and Appointed Officials have to say. I interviewed each one of them separately.

So, with four voices, we begin our discussion of the Latino agenda. First of all, it exists, right?

Raul Yzaguirre thinks so. "I think there is a consensus on education, I think there is a consensus on immigration, I think there is a consensus on bilingual education," he told me during our interview.

Interestingly enough, in many ways the Latino agenda intersects with issues that concern the rest of the country's population as well. "And in some ways it is very much an American agenda, in the sense that we want better schools, we want safe streets, we want equal opportunity for everybody regardless of color or nationality," continued Yzaguirre, who has been at the NCLR's helm since 1974. "The Latino agenda, at the core, is basically an American agenda. [But] there are a couple of things uniquely Latino that express our priorities (like immigration and bilingual education). With those exceptions we are essentially about what all Americans are about."

Arturo Vargas also believes that the Latino agenda coincides in many ways with what the majority of people in this country want, and that it goes beyond ethnic or geographic differences. "There is this very focused commitment to issues of improving the quality of life for low-income Latinos, in particular. And the three or four issues that consistently occupy the majority of Latino elected officials' time are education, access to health care, access to good-paying jobs, and economic development," he told me. "Now people might well say: 'That's what every American wants.' The difference is the nature of our community, of our population, because we're so young. Education policy affects Latinos more than any other population because of its youthfulness. A larger share of Latinos are affected by the public school system than a comparable share of blacks, Asians, or whites. Because so many Latinos are children, the issues of young people are much more important to Latinos than to other communities."

Harry Pachón agrees with both Vargas and Yzaguirre. "I can get unity on education, I can get unity on procurement, on improving of businesses, and making the naturalization process easier for Hispanics," says Pachón, who helped found the National Association of Latino Elected and Appointed Officials and has served as executive director since 1983. "Immigration issues, such as naturalization and citizenship, are another issue of agreement amongst many Latinos. And eliminating crime in the neighborhoods is another very salient issue."

But the centerpiece of the Latino agenda is education. "As I did surveys across the United States, it didn't matter if they were Cubans, Puerto Ricans, or Mexican Americans, everybody put education for children first," Pachón said.

Roberto Suro agrees. "Education is becoming an overwhelming issue because there are so many Latinos with young children," he observed. Nevertheless, Suro is the most skeptical of the four about the existence of a single, formal Latino agenda.

"I don't think that there is a Latino agenda today that has been articulated and defined as such and that has widespread support and that people could point to and say, Here it is, here are the main points," he mused. "But there could be. There are issues which increasingly are common to a very large part of the population. There are common concerns. And part of that is simply because of demography; such a large part of the Latino population is in the process of raising children. You have a widespread agreement that public schools are in crisis and there is sort of a national reform movement now under way, with No Child Left Behind and federal standards being imposed."

If Suro is right, then why isn't there a formal, structured, universally recognized Latino agenda? "There have been a number of attempts in the last 10, 15 years, by political figures to come to an agreement about what is an agenda, and that hasn't worked in terms of an organized, structural effort," he said. "Henry Cisneros leveled a long effort in the late 1980s and early 1990s to set an agenda and other organizations have tried to articulate one. . . . Nobody is trying to bring everybody together. I haven't seen it happen." But why hasn't it happened? "There are some national origin differences, there are some class differences, there are some political differences; it hasn't really hung together so far," he went on. "That is changing, though. I think we are seeing the beginnings of a change because there's more of a sense of a shared concern, particularly over education, than I've ever seen before."

The Latino community isn't monolithic, a fact that complicates the establishment of a single agenda defended by all Hispanic groups. "There are just very few issues where we differ or where our priorities are different," Yzaguirre said to this point. "Obviously Cuban Americans are more anti-Castro than other Latinos. And of course Puerto Ricans are more concerned about the political status of Puerto Rico than other Latinos. But in terms of equal opportunity, immigration, bilingual education—those very clearly Latino issues—we're enormously united."

Differences between Latino groups go beyond the Big Three. "First of all I think that triad is obsolete," said Vargas. "We can't just talk about Mexican Americans, Puerto Ricans, and Cubans. We have to talk about other communities as well: Dominicans, Central Americans, etc. And even within the Mexican origin community there are those who have been here for generations and those who just got here yesterday." But despite all that, "I think they [politicians, elected officials] don't realize how much in common they have until they actually come together and talk about it together."

There have been several attempts over the past few decades to create a formal, structured Latino agenda which all Hispanics could get behind, including efforts by NALEO and the Congressional Hispanic

Congress. On the legislative level, the National Hispanic Leadership Agenda has taken shape. But this agenda, if it does in fact exist, has not been identified as such, nor has it been universally recognized by Hispanic leaders. There are things in common, sure, but there currently is no conscientious, organized effort to present a single Latino agenda.

Even still, Harry Pachón is optimistic. "What I have seen in the past 15 years is the Latino community has come from being invisible to a point of its emergence as a visible national force," he told me. The Latino agenda "just needs to be articulated and we need to concentrate on issues that unite us rather on issues that we have a difference of opinion."

Despite the consensus and agreed-upon tactics, it seems clear that a Latino agenda—far from being an established document understood by all Hispanics—is, for now, an aspiration and a work in progress.

TEN RECOMMENDATIONS FOR A LATINO AGENDA

In the end, there always seems to be some doubt about what needs to be done to understand the Hispanic experience and to improve the lives of Latinos. Here, then, are 10 concrete suggestions.

1. IMPROVE POLITICAL REPRESENTATION.

Hispanics are not proportionally represented in Congress, the Senate, the Supreme Court, or the U.S. government. They are not even well represented in the army. Latino soldiers make up 9 percent of our armed forces in general, but only 4 percent of its officers. Hispanics must have proper political representation. Greater political representation means more diversity, and that's a goal worth fighting for.

2. STANDARDIZE LATINO IMMIGRANTS' LEGAL SITUATION AND COMPREHENSIVE IMMIGRATION REFORM.

We have to push for amnesty and an immigration accord: 85 percent of Latinos favor some form of permanent legalization for undocumented immigrants, according to a study done by *Hispanic Trends*. And informing the rest of the American population about immigrants' enormous benefits is an essential part of this. Contrary to the rest of the population's opinion, 6 out of every 10 Latinos believe that immigrants have a favorable effect on the economy. And we must deal with issues specifically pertaining to immigrants, for most Latinos are either immigrants themselves or the children of immigrants.

Similarly, it's important that high school graduates get permanent-resident status. We have to allow any undocumented student who finishes high school to qualify as an in-state university candidate; all those who get their college degree should also receive legal status for themselves and their immediate families. This would combat high dropout rates and focus parents' attentions on their children's educations.

3. LEARN SPANISH AND ENGLISH: ONE LANGUAGE JUST ISN'T ENOUGH.

Learning English is essential to achieving success in this country, but at the same time Spanish needs to be kept alive and well. The Spanish language is a direct link Latinos have with their countries of origin, their histories, their traditions, and their families abroad. According to the Tomás Rivera Policy Institute, one in two Hispanics reacts positively when a candidate or politician makes an effort to speak to them in Spanish, while six out of every ten bilingual Latinos prefer to get their news in Spanish. And support for bilingual education is a fundamental part of maintaining linguistic and cultural diversity in the United States.

4. LIFT HISPANICS OUT OF POVERTY: CREATE ACCESS TO BETTER JOBS AND HEALTH CARE.

Most Latinos don't want any handouts. They want what anybody else in this country wants—a good job whose salary can support their family comfortably and access to doctors and hospitals in case of an emergency. Forty percent of Latinos live below the poverty line. This is the true source of many of the other problems affecting our communities. Jobs and health care are the keys to better economic opportunities.

5. ADDRESS SCHOOL DROPOUT RATES.

One in three Latino students fails to complete high school. School dropout rates in California can reach as high as 40 percent. As Robert Suro attests, many Latinos have been successful as immigrants but failures as parents of U.S. Latino children. We must break this cycle if we are to have success both as immigrants and as parents, and it will benefit the greater U.S. society as well.

6. FIGHT CRIME AND MAKE OUR COMMUNITIES SAFER.

Hispanics want many of the same things as the rest of the population. But the lowest common denominator is that Latino children need to be able to walk down the street without fear of being robbed or attacked by a gang. It won't do for our communities to have some of the highest crime rates of any ethnic group.

7. FORGE AN ALLIANCE WITH OTHER MINORITIES.

The objective is to fight the common enemies of racism and discrimination and to study such concepts as double consciousness. The African American community has had a lot of success in its struggle for civil rights, and Hispanics can and should follow their example. The best thing about this country is the opportunity it holds out, but the worst things about it is the persistent presence of racism and discrimination.

8. MAKE LATIN AMERICA A PROMINENT PART OF U.S. FOREIGN POLICY.

Latin America should be the United States's main partner in trade and politics, but it isn't. Now is the time to change this. We're neighbors, brothers, and partners. There is no reason why other regions of the world should receive more interest and cooperation from the United States than Latin America. It benefits us all.

9. STREAMLINE THE PROCESS OF GAINING CITIZENSHIP.

It's natural that more and more Hispanics are becoming U.S. citizens, registering to vote, and participating in elections. This will translate into more political power and better representation for Latinos. Willy Velásquez says, "Register and vote." That's the message.

10. UNDERSTAND THE HISPANIC EXPERIENCE.

Being Latino means having an experience unlike that of any other group in the United States. It implies a history, an origin, and a path all our own. Whoever wants to woo Latinos and win their votes will first have to get to know and understand us. It's not enough to set out some chips and salsa and put on some *ranchero* music anymore.

ONE SINGLE LEADER?

Is it possible to have one single Latino leader who represents all the different Hispanic groups in the United States? Could Hispanic senators Ken Salazar and Mel Martínez become true leaders despite their ethnic origins? Could it be Governor Bill Richardson of New Mexico? Or the top-ranking congressional Latino Democrat, Cuban American Bob Menendez from New Jersey? Why is it so difficult to find a national leader? Why didn't former Clinton housing secretary and mayor of San Antonio Henry Cisneros become such a leader? Why couldn't Cesar Chávez do it? What's preventing Jorge Más Canosa of the Cuban American National Foundation from exerting his influence on a national level? Why hasn't a Puerto Rican leader been able to unite the Hispanic community? Could George P. Bush—the president's nephew and the son of Governor Jeb Bush and his Mexican wife Columba—become this leader?

Many people believe that the unification of the Latino community doesn't depend on the emergence of a national leader. The fundamental problem to finding a single representative leader has to do with the many different nationalities that make up the Hispanic community. Although there is a certain consensus about a Latino agenda, the different interests of the distinct Hispanic groups remain clear.

One of the most interesting things that I came across in my conversations while writing this book is the lack of a strong desire for a national Hispanic leader. On the contrary, the theory of several individual leaders seems much more prevalent. Raul Yzaguirre, Harry Pachón, and Arturo Vargas don't see the need for one single leader, but Roberto Suro does. This is what they have to say.

"I always react negatively to this concept of the one Latino leader," Pachón said. "I mean, we don't have one Anglo leader, we don't have one black leader. Maybe we should be more realistic and think that there should be many Latino leaders. I think this is a healthy sign. We are a community of 37 million people, we have diverse backgrounds, diverse historical experiences. Is it realistic to expect that one person can unify and represent all of the communities 100 percent of the time? I think there are going to be regional Latino leaders, all who would have national stature. Bob Menendez in New Jersey and the East Coast, Xavier Becerra in the West Coast, two congressmen who come to mind as being very significant leaders, Ileana Ros-Lehtinen and Lincoln Díaz-Balart in Florida; that is a healthy thing for the Hispanic community given the diversity and geographic dispersion."

Yzaguirre is also hesitant to defend the idea of one single Latino leader. "We do have multiple Jesse Jacksons," he said. "If you define Jesse Jackson with his ability to connect with his community, his ability to articulate an African American agenda and his ability to be eloquent on issues, I think we've got lots of those kinds of folks. What we don't have is a media that spotlights our leadership, and that's a difference. To put all our eggs in one basket would be a mistake. I think we are fortunate to have multiple leaders. We have very strong leaders. I'm very proud of our leadership, and I'm not sure I would have said that 30 years ago."

"What's changed?" I ask him.

"We support each other," he replies. "I love Henry Cisneros, I love Bill Richardson, we work together. The same thing with Bob

Menendez. We know each other, we work with each other, we support each other. We have some clarity and understanding and cohesion in terms of an agenda."

I ask Vargas why he thinks it's so complicated to talk about a single person to lead all Hispanics. "People identify with leaders," he replies. "And because nationalism is so strong among Latinos in general, I don't see people being able to say, 'Bob Menendez, the Cuban American Democrat from New Jersey, is my leader.' I don't see anyone from El Paso identifying with Bob Menendez. I don't see that happening.

"One leader," he continued, "I think that's impractical and unrealistic and if that's what we are going to wait for, it's never going to happen. I don't see anybody on the horizon right into the point of being the Latino leader, the Jesse Jackson, the Martin Luther King of the Hispanic community. I don't see anybody out there who would have the following to do it, nor do I think that the way our community is structured, that there is a sense at the grassroots level of a commonality to the point that we can all rally behind one person."

Roberto Suro of the Pew Hispanic Center was the only one of the four who did agree with the idea of one national Hispanic leader. "One thing there has not been—and it could make a huge difference—is a national Latino leader. it's the nature of politics, not just in the United States but in the whole world and human history. Leaders not only collect followers, they also shape the way a group evolves."

So why haven't Latinos found such a leader? "Part of it is the fact that you have very important leaders with very specific goals and very specific constituencies. Cesar Chávez would not have been a leader for Cuban Americans any more than Más Canosa would have been a leader for Mexican farmworkers."

Whether it's with one leader or several, one of the main problems facing the Hispanic community is its lack of political representation. Henry Cisneros liked to say that Hispanics had reached a "critical mass" of influence and visibility in the United States. Yzaguirre, borrowing Cisneros's term, agrees. He feels that many of our scholars and business people represent the best in the Hispanic community. But "where we don't have a critical mass is in the political arena. We don't have anybody in the senate or in the Supreme Court. We don't have enough board of directors on Fortune 100 companies. We don't have enough people in the media, in entertainment. There are certain sectors where we don't have a critical mass, but hopefully we're making progress."

The future of Hispanic leadership is presenting us with two options: one with multiple leaders at the head of a fortified, influential community, and another one with a single leader who knows how to capture the dreams and aspirations of the majority of Latinos. Harry Pachón subscribes to this first theory.

Pachón wants the Latino community to resemble the Jewish community more. "What we need to be striving for is to have an organizational, developmental infrastructure in the community that lets our positions be articulated, rather than rely on a charismatic man on horseback. The *caudillo* image . . . maybe we should move away from that. I would love to see us follow the path of the Jewish American community. There are Jewish Americans in many leadership positions; there is not one national leader but nobody doubts the power of the Jewish American community because they can always unite on certain issues. The people who are trying to force a one-leadership model on us do not recognize that it is unhealthy, really, for such a diverse community to have just one spokesperson."

Roberto Suro, on the other hand, has a different vision. He thinks that a single leader on the national stage would bring strength and visibility to a community that is growing larger every day. And this could overcome our geographic and national differences. "I think it's possible to have one leader that rich Miami Cubans and poor Mexicans in Fresno all could have gotten excited about. I think it's possible, I think it's absolutely possible. It hasn't happened yet but there is no reason why it couldn't. It's a matter of the right personality, the right charisma, and articulating a message," he told me. "There is an inspirational message. The people who do marketing to the Latino consumers understand those. This desire *de sobresalir, de superarme* . . . it's very uplifting and is also very successful. . . . You get the right person articulating that message in the right way and it'll take off."

But no matter what form this power takes—whether it comes to rest in one single leader or a group of them—the Latino community is like a torrential river that urgently needs clear direction.

THE AMERICANIZATION OF LATINOS

This book's central argument is that Latinos are changing this country in many significant ways. And yet we haven't dedicated the same space to a parallel argument, the Americanization of Latinos.

"Everyone talks about the Latinization of America, but few people talk about the Americanization of Latinos," Harry Pachón asserts. "It's a two-way street. We are changing America but America is changing Latinos. We are learning English very quickly; by the second and third generation many Latinos have lost their Spanish ability. . . . When you ask Latino parents the language their children watch television in, 70 percent say their children watch television in English. It's a generational shift."

There are clear signs of transformation on the economic front as well. "A college-educated Cuban American, second or third generation, makes as much as, if not more than, a white non-Hispanic in the state of Florida," Pachón offers in support of his argument. But this is not confined to Florida or the Cuban community. "You know the secret? A Mexican American, in the third generation, if he has the same level of education, makes the same as a non-Hispanic white. So mobility is possible. It is there. You see it in California, you see it in Florida, you see it in all the United States. A million Latino families joined the American middle class in Texas and California in just 20 years."

According to a study done by the Tomás Rivera Policy Institute, half of all third-generation Latinos marry non-Hispanic spouses.[1] Specifically, 51.6 percent of Latino men and 49.1 percent of Latina women—the children and grandchildren of immigrants—end up marrying outside the community in which they grew up. In comparison, only about 1 in 10 Latino immigrants—10 percent of men and 11.4 percent of women—marry non-Hispanics. This phenomenon of "outmarrying" is one of the clearest indicators of how the Latino community is integrating into U.S. society at large. The same study emphasized what many already knew: that more Latinos are born in the United States every year than outside.

"Something that we don't talk about is the tremendous amount of intermarrying happening within the Latino community," Arturo Vargas remarked. "You are going to have generations of children saying: 'Well, I come from Puerto Rican and Mexican parents, or Salvadoreño and Mexican parents, so what am I?' I think we are going to have a new generation of children, second and third generation, that is going to increasingly identify with being part of the Latino community [instead of identifying themselves as Mexicans, Cubans, etc.]. I think in the future we are going to see more of a pan-Hispanic identity. But that is going to take time to develop."

The question is whether Hispanics will eventually undergo the same process of assimilation that other, European immigrants went through, or if they will create their own cultural space and unique identity. "No, I don't think they are going to be just like Italians or Germans," continued Vargas. "One is a physical difference. Americans so very much recognize physical features as differences. The darker-skinned you are, you are still not going to be fully assimilated."

Another difference between Hispanics and other immigrant groups is the close geographic proximity we share with our countries of origin. Raul Yzaguirre's family, for example, has been living in what is now Texas since 1748, when that land was still part of Mexico. More than just moving to the United States, the Yzaguirre family found itself here and is still under the same roof. "There is a sense that you're not coming to a foreign country because you have brothers and sisters and cousins and uncles and so on who are already in this country," Yzaguirre reflected. "It's not that kind of drastic immigrant experience which forces you to cut off all communications and shed all that defined you previously and accept a new culture and a new form of living. For us it's an extension of where we were before as opposed to a demarcation line. There are some of us who will seek to assimilate quickly and will do so and Anglicize our names. [But because] of things like Univision, and the radio stations and the newspapers, and *La Opinion,* so far, we have a media that continues to reinforce and sustain a different culture."

The process by which Latinos are integrating into U.S. culture is not a simple one, now that the recently arrived immigrant is being welcomed just as much as families—like the Yzaguirres—who have been here for generations. This points to very different methods of identification and adaptation even within the Hispanic community it-self. "What we have now is a process where in all of our communities you have new arrivals coming in, in one end, with very strong Latino identity and very strong use of Spanish, and then, at the other end, you have people who are becoming Americanized," concludes Suro. "We know, the melting pot never completely melted the people . . . the Hispanic identity is not going to disappear. It's in the process of being formed; we are pretty much in the middle of it. It's very hard to know what shape it'll take in the future."

So if the United States does indeed become a Hispanic nation over the course of the next century, what characteristics will it have? How will we see ourselves? Again, Harry Pachón:

"So for the future, when we talk about this becoming a Latino na-tion, what we really have to say is that America is going to become a little bit darker. Maybe Latinos will put some color in the concept of white, so that white will be darker in America than it will be in Europe."

Will that be a Latino nation? According to Vargas, "Maybe a His-panic nation that is English-speaking. What does that mean? I don't know. It's evolving. We haven't seen that before. . . . So I don't know how it's going to look. If we are going to be one of four Americans within the next 20 years, that's going to have a fundamental effect on what American society is defined as."

What language will we be speaking? According to Saro, "People who come here as adults, Spanish remains their first language and their children are primarily English speakers. The children of immigrants absorb American culture—American popular culture—very quickly. If immigration continues the way it has for the last 10, 20 years Spanish will stay alive, as long as you have a constant influx of half a million or more Spanish-speaking immigrants [per year]. It constantly refreshes Spanish. The evidence to this point is that Spanish falls off significantly from one generation to the next."

How will all this influence the United States? According to Yzaguirre, the United States "is becoming a more pluralistic nation. It's becoming a nation where no single group will be the majority; not now and probably not in the future. It's also becoming a community where there is much intermarriage. So in some ways, becoming a Hispanic, a Latino, in the future will be an option. I didn't have an option. I am a *Mexicano* and if I call myself Italian people will laugh at me. My kids have options. They can become Anglicized, they can become Latino, they can become Mexican, they can become Chicano, and in some ways I've seen them do that."

In other words, the United States is becoming an ever more multiethnic, multicultural, and multiracial country, one where labeling an increasingly diverse population will be an increasingly difficult—and sometimes ultimately futile—task.

THE MOST SATISFYING experience after writing this book was finding many Hispanics in major U.S. cities who were just as convinced as I am—as is evident in the dedication of this book—that the first Latino president of the United States is already born.

In the presentations of this book in Los Angeles, Nueva York, Houston, Dallas, Chicago, and Miami, including many others, many Hispanic families got close in order to introduce to me their children and babies. They would say to me, "Look, this child, Juanito, will become the first Hispanic president." Or, "Take a good look, because this baby named Lourdes will become the first female president of the United States." It should be stated, of course, that neither Juanito nor Lourdes is more than a year old. But the wonderful thing about this experience is the idea that anything is possible in the United States—including having a Hispanic president, a son or daughter of immigrants—has deeply permeated the Hispanic community. And just as Don Quijote would say to Sancho Panza, that is a sign that we advance, not just in numbers, but also in cultural influence and political power.

The future of the United States, however you want to see it, is Hispanic.

The Latino Wave is unstoppable.

APPENDIX: HISPANICS AT A GLANCE

Understanding these figures is like trying to sip from a powerful river: as soon as you touch the water, the current grabs you and carries you off, far out of reach.

HISPANIC POPULATION: 38.8 million, or 13.5% of the U.S. total (288.4 million) on July 1, 2002.[1] The 2000 census showed a 57.9% increase in the Hispanic population over that recorded in the 1990 census.[2]

AVERAGE AGE OF LATINOS: 25.8 years (nearly 10 years younger than the national average of 35.3). Fully 35% of Hispanics are under 18 years of age and not yet able to vote.[3]

AVERAGE HOUSEHOLD INCOME: $33,447 per year (significantly less than the national average of $42,148).[4]

PURCHASING POWER: Hispanics spent $580 billion in 2002[5] and will reach *$1 trillion* in 2010.[6]

HOME OWNERSHIP: Only 46.3% of Latinos own their own homes, compared to the national average of 67.4%. But this is logical, given their lower average age and income. Also, 6.7% of cars are registered to Latino drivers.[7]

NUMBER OF CHILDREN: Hispanic families average just over three children, compared to just under two children per family for the rest of the country.[8] Over half of Latino families—58%—have children.[9] The 2000 census recorded 7.4 million Hispanic families.[10]

NUMBER OF HISPANIC CONGRESSMEN: 22. In the Senate? Zero. In the Supreme Court? Zero. How many Latino governors are

there? Just one, Bill Richardson, in New Mexico. In 2002, some
5,400 Latinos were elected to public positions—but it's still not
enough. We are numerous, but we lack political representation
commensurate with our numbers.

LANGUAGE: 28 million Latinos age 5 and older speak Spanish at
home. This figure, obtained during the 2000 Census, is a marked
increase from 1990, when the figure was only 17 million. Fully
29% of people living New Mexico speak Spanish at home,
27% of Texans and 26% of Californians.[11]

PLACE OF ORIGIN: The majority of U.S. Latinos are originally
from modern-day Mexico or are historically of Mexican
descent. The 2000 census recorded some 20.6 million Mexican
Americans, followed by 3.4 million Puerto Ricans, and
1.2 million Cuban Americans. The interesting thing is that
all three of these figures are lower in 2000 than in 1990: the
percentage of Mexicans dropped from 60.4% to 58.5%;
Puerto Ricans, from 12.2% to 9.6%; and Cubans, from 4.7% to
3.5%. What's the explanation? Immigrants from other countries,
especially Central America (1.7 million), South America
(1.4 million), the Dominican Republic (765,000), and Spain
(100,000) are coming in greater numbers than before.[12]

VOTERS: From 1996 to 2000, the number of Hispanic voters
increased by over 1 million: from 4,928,000 to 5,934,000. And
if the calculations done by the National Council of La Raza are
correct, there will be almost 2 million more (7,484,000) by the
2004 elections.[13]

LATINOS IN THE 2000 ELECTIONS [14]

UNDER 18 YEARS OF AGE	12.3 MILLION	35%
NONCITIZENS	9.8 MILLION	28%
ELIGIBLE TO VOTE	13.2 MILLION	37%
TOTAL U.S. LATINO POPULATION IN 2000	35.3 MILLION	100%

LATINOS REGISTERED TO VOTE [15]

DEMOCRATS	49%
REPUBLICANS	20%
INDEPENDENT	19%
DON'T KNOW/OTHER PARTY AFFILIATION	12%

LATINOS: DEMOCRAT OR REPUBLICAN BY COUNTRY OF ORIGIN [16]

	DEMOCRAT	REPUBLICAN	INDEPENDENT
TOTAL	49%	20%	19%
DOMINICANS	66%	8%	20%
PUERTO RICANS	52%	15%	17%
MEXICANS	49%	19%	20%
CUBANS	14%	54%	25%

U.S. CITIZENS: Fully 72% of people of Cuban origin in the United States are citizens, but only 58% of Mexican Americans and 46% of South Americans carry U.S. passports. Of all Latino voters—in other words, U.S. citizens who are registered to vote—72% were either born outside the United States themselves (41%) or have one or both parents born outside the United States (31%). Further, 1 out of every 8 Latino voters (13%) became a U.S. citizen after 1995.[17]

CONNECTED: According to Public Agenda, 59% of immigrants regularly phone their families abroad.

HISPANIC GOVERNORS IN U.S. HISTORY		
GOVERNOR	STATE	YEAR ELECTED/ASSIGNED
ROMUALDO PACHECO (R)	CALIFORNIA	1875
EZEQUIEL CABEZA DE BACA (R)	NEW MEXICO	1917
OCTAVIANO LARRAZOLA (R)	NEW MEXICO	1918
JERRY APOCADA (D)	ARIZONA	1974
RAUL CASTRO (D)	ARIZONA	1974
TONEY ANAYA (D)	NEW MEXICO	1982
BOB MARTINEZ (R)	FLORIDA	1986
BILL RICHARDSON (D)	NEW MEXICO	2002

HISPANICS IN THE MILITARY IN 2002 [18]

	TOTAL ARMED FORCES	NUMBER OF LATINOS	PERCENT OF TOTAL
ARMY	484,551	46,000	9.5
NAVY	379,457	37,987	10.0
MARINES	173,897	23,192	13.3
AIR FORCE	364,215	19,591	5.4
TOTAL	1,402,120	126,770	9.0

TOP FIVE CITIES WITH LATINO POPULATION [19]

	HISPANIC POPULATION	PERCENT OF TOTAL (%)	PERCENT GROWTH, 1980-2000 (%)
LOS ANGELES	4,242,213	45	105
NEW YORK	2,339,836	25	60
CHICAGO	1,416,584	17	143
MIAMI	1,219,737	57	123
HOUSTON	1,248,586	30	211

INCOME DISTRIBUTION [20]

COUNTRY	WEALTHIEST 10 %	POOREST 10 %
BRAZIL	46.7%	1.0%
CHILE	41.2%	1.2%
MEXICO	41.1%	1.6%
COSTA RICA	34.6%	1.7%
INDIA	33.5%	3.5%

MONIES SENT TO LATIN AMERICA (IN MILLIONS OF DOLLARS)[21]

MEXICO	$14,500
BRASIL	$4,600
COLOMBIA	$2,431
EL SALVADOR	$2,206
DOMINICAN REPUBLIC	$2,211
GUATEMALA	$1,689
ECUADOR	$1,575
PERU	$1,265
CUBA	$1,138
HONDURAS	$770
NICARAGUA	$759
VENEZUELA	$235
ARGENTINA	$184

NOTES

PROLOGUE

1. U.S. Bureau of the Census, Washington, D.C., June 18, 2003.

CHAPTER 1

1. Bush's approval ratings, based on data from polls conducted in August 2004:

	Approval %	Disapproval %
Pew Research Center	46	45
AP-Ipsos	49	50
CNN/*USA Today*/Gallup	51	46
Time	50	46

2. Of the 22 Hispanic congressmen that there were before the 2004 elections, Ciro Rodríguez lost his Democratic primary, leaving a total of 21. But then, Henry Cuellar won in Texas' 28th District, Jim Costa won in California's 20th District, and John Salazar (the brother of Senator Ken Salazar) won in Colorado's 3rd District. Thus, by November 2004, there were 24 Hispanics in Congress. (This does not include California Representatives Dennis Nunes and Dennis Cardoza, who are both of Portuguese descent and therefore not traditionally counted on lists of Hispanic congressmen.)

3. 2004 poll conducted by Edison/Mitofsky and 2000 poll conducted by Voter News Service.

4. Ibid.

5. Ibid. 26 percent described themselves as conservative in 2000, and 33 percent did so in 2004.

6. José de la Isla, *The Rise of Hispanic Political Power,* Archer Books, New York, 2003, pp. 196, 277.

7. Adam J. Segal, "The Hispanic Priority: The Spanish-Language Television Battle for the Hispanic Vote in the 2000 U.S. Presidential Election." Report published by the Hispanic Voter Project at Johns Hopkins University, Washington, D.C., January 2003.

8. Ibid.

9. Ibid.

10. Ibid.

11. Ibid.

12. Eduardo Porter, "Univision Is Cleared to Buy Radio Firm," *Wall Street Journal.* February 28, 2003.

13. Ibid.

14. Louis DeSipio, *Latino Viewing Choices: Bilingual Television Viewers and the Language Choices They Make,* Tomás Rivera Policy Institute, Los Angeles, May 2003.

15. Ibid.

16. *Wall Street Journal.* October 6, 2000.

17. *Los Angeles Times.* August 3, 2000.

18. *Washington Post.* October 26, 2000.

19. *New York Times.* November 12, 2000. Data for 2000 were collected by the Voter News Service based on questionnaires completed by 13,279 voters leaving 300 polling places around the nation on Election Day.

20. Sonia Colín, interview by the author, February 19, 2003.

21. Marcelo Amunátegui, interview by the author, February 25, 2003.

22. Adam J. Segal, "The Hispanic Priority," p. 44.

23. Janet Murguia, interview by the author, February 27, 2003.

24. Guillermo Meneses, e-mail communication with the author, February 24, 2003.

25. U.S. Bureau of the Census, *Census 2000 Brief. The Hispanic Population,* Washington, D.C., May 2001.

26. José de la Isla, *The Rise of Hispanic Political Power,* p. 196.

27. Lourdes Cué, "Election 2001: The Latino Factor," HispanicMagazine.com, January/February 2001. Viewed online at http://www.hispanicmagazine.com/2001/jan_feb/Features/index.html.

28. President Bill Clinton, interview by the author for Univision, May 5, 1997.

29. Jorge Ramos, *The Other Face of America,* HarperCollins, New York, 2002. p. 104.

30. Ibid.

31. Janet Murguia, interview by the author, February 27, 2003.

32. Ibid.

33. Jeffrey Toobin, *Too Close to Call: The Thirty-Six Day Battle to Decide the 2000 Election,* Random House, New York, 2001.

34. Ibid.

35. Sergio Bendixen, interview by the author, March 6, 2003.

36. Jeffrey Toobin, *Too Close to Call.*

37. Sergio Bendixen from Hispanic Trends and Voter News Service.

CHAPTER 2

1. Robert Suro, *Strangers Among Us: Latino Lives in a Changing America,* Vintage Books, New York, 1998, p. 70.

2. U.S. Bureau of the Census, "Census Bureau Releases Fact Sheet in Observance of Hispanic Heritage Month," Public Information Office, Washington, D.C., September 3, 2002.

3. U.S. Bureau of the Census, *Census Hispanic Heritage Month 2002 Facts.* Washington, D.C.

4. Alexis de Tocqueville, *Democracy in America,* Signet Classics/New American Library, 1835/2001, p. 11.

5. Ibid.

6. Ibid., p. 40.

7. Carlos Fuentes, *The Buried Mirror,* Houghton Mifflin, Boston, 1992, p. 343.

8. Alexis de Tocqueville, *Democracy in America,* p. 130.

9. Robert Suro and Audrey Singer, "Latino Growth in Metropolitan America: Changing Patterns, New Locations," Brookings Institution Center on Urban and Metropolitan Policy/Pew Hispanic Center, July 2002.

10. Source: The Brookings Institution, Census 2000.

11. Sara Curran and Estela Rivero-Fuentes, "Current Mexican Immigrants Provide Key Link for Future Migrants." Study produced for the Office of Population Research, Princeton University, May 2003.

12. Alexis de Tocqueville, *Democracy in America,* p. 164.

13. Robert Suro and Audrey Singer, "Latino Growth in Metropolitan America," pp. 7, 10, 11.

14. Alexis de Tocqueville, *Democracy in America,* p. 132.

15. Ibid, p. 41.

16. Steven Camarota, "Immigrants in the United States 2002: A Snapshot of America's Foreign-Born Population." Press release, Center for Immigration Studies, Washington, D.C., November 26, 2002.

17. U.S. Bureau of the Census. "Census Bureau Releases Fact Sheet."

18. Steven Camarota, "Immigrants in the United States 2002."

19. Carlos Villanueva, Asociación Mundial de Mexicanos en el Exterior, October 3, 2002. Viewed at http://www.mexicanosenelexterior.com.

20. "Distribution of Wealth," *Reforma,* February 4, 2003.

21. "Latin American Emigrants Prefer U.S.," Reuters, November 20, 2002.

22. "INS Counts 7 Million Immigrants Living in U.S. Illegally," Associated Press, January 31, 2003.

23. Ibid. "The new estimates are based on the foreign-born population counted in the 2000 Census combined with INS statistics on immigrants admitted to the country, deportations and numbers of the nonimmigrants admitted, such as temporary workers."

24. "U.S.-Mexico Study Sees Exaggeration of Migration Data," *New York Times,* August 30, 1997.

25. Ibid.

26. Ibid.

27. "INS Counts 7 Million Immigrants Living in U.S. Illegally."

28. Figures from 1999 to 2001 are supplied by the INS; figures for 2002 were cited by Mario Villarreal, spokesperson from the Bureau of Customs and Border Protection, in an interview on *Talk of the Nation,* National Public Radio, May 19, 2003.

29. National Immigration Forum. Fall 1994.

30. President George Bush, in a speech at The White House, August 24, 2001.

31. Daniel Rodgers, *Coming to America: A History of Immigration and Ethnicity in American Life,* HarperCollins, New York, 1990.

32. Peter Jennings and Todd Brewster, *In Search of America,* Hyperion, New York, 2002.

33. Immigration and Naturalization Service. Immigration Quota Act of 1924.

34. Immigration and Naturalization Service. Immigration and Nationality Act Amendments of October 3, 1965.

35. José de la Isla, *The Rise of Hispanic Political Power.*

36. "Migrants' Deaths Reverberate at Home," *Washington Post,* May 16, 2003.

37. National Center for Health Statistics.

38. "Temen más ilegales por subsidios," *Reforma,* December 2, 2002.

39. U.S. Bureau of the Census, "Census Bureau Releases Fact Sheet."

40. "Hispanics Pass Blacks as Nation's Largest Minority, Census Shows," *New York Times,* January 22, 2003.

41. National Center for Health Statistics. *National Vital Statistics Report,* 50(5): February 12, 2002. For comparison, 532,249 Hispanic babies were born in 1989, representing 14 percent of the national total.

42. Ibid., Table 7. Live births by Hispanic origin of mother and by race for mothers of non-Hispanic origin.

43. Ibid.

44. UCLA Center for the Study of Latino Health and Culture, "Majority of Babies Born in California Are Latino," February 5, 2003.

45. "The Rise of the Second Generation: Changing Patterns in Hispanic Population Growth," Pew Hispanic Center, October 2003.

46. Half of all Hispanics lived in California (31.1 percent) and Texas (18.9 percent), according to the 2000 census.

47. José Pablo Fernández Cueto, written communication to the author, January day, 2003.

48. Rita Arias Jirasek and Carlos Tortolero, *Mexican Chicago,* Arcadia Publishing. Chicago.

CHAPTER 3

1. Brian Frazelle, "The Truth about Immigrants: Xenophobia Existed in Early America," *Houston Catholic Worker,* 19(7): December 1999.

2. Benjamin Franklin, "Observations Concerning the Increase of Mankind, Peopling of Countries, etc." 1751.

3. U.S. Bureau of the Census, "Spanish Speaking Population: Percent of Population 5 Years and Over Who Speak Spanish at Home by State," *Census 2000,* Washington, D.C.

4. *2002 National Survey of Latinos,* final report released by the Pew Hispanic Center/ Kaiser Family Foundation on December 17, 2002. Viewed online at www.pew hispanic.org/site/docs/pdf/LatinoSurveyReportFinal.pdf.

5. "Hispanic TV Households by Language Spoken in Home," Nielsen Media Research Universe Estimates, 2002.

6. Barbara Zurer Pearson. "Bilingual Infants: What We Know, What We Need to

Know," in M. Suárez-Orozco and M. Páez (eds.), *Latinos: Remaking America,* University of California Press, Berkeley, 2002, pp. 306–320.

7. Patrick J. Buchanan, *The Death of the West,* Thomas Dunne Books/St. Martin's Press, New York, 2002, p. 125.

8. Deborah Kong, "Study Sees Hispanics Choosing Spanish TV," Associated Press, May 21, 2003.

9. Louis DeSipio, *Latino Viewing Choices.*

10. Ibid.

11. Dowell Myers, "The Changing Immigrants of Southern California," Research Report No. LCRI-95-04R, Lusk Center Research Institute, School of Urban Planning and Development, University of Southern California, 1995.

12. *2002 National Survey of Latinos.*

13. Ibid.

14. "Immigrants Dispel Negative Stereotypes," *Public Agenda,* January 14, 2003.

15. Carlos Fuentes, *The Buried Mirror.*

16. Ibid., p. 347.

17. "Revival of State Law Sought. Debate Continues to Rage on Bilingual Education," *Los Angeles Times,* February 10, 1988.

18. Patricia Gándara, "Learning English in California: Guideposts for the Nation," in M. Suárez-Orozco and M. Páez (eds.), *Latinos: Remaking America,* University of California Press, Berkeley, 2002.

19. Ilan Stavans, *On Borrowed Words: A Memoir of Language,* Viking/Penguin, New York, 2001, p. 225.

20. *2002 National Survey of Latinos.*

21. Ibid.

22. "Divided by a Call for a Common Language," *New York Times,* July 19, 2002.

23. *El Nuevo Herald,* August 13, 2001.

24. Peter Kivisto, *Key Ideas in Sociology,* Sage, 1998.

25. "Rand Study Shows Hispanic Immigrants Move Up Economic, Educational Ladder as Quickly as Other Immigrant Groups," News release, May 22, 2003. Viewed online at http://www.rand.org/news/press.03/05.22.html.

26. Ibid.

27. Ibid.

28. Ibid.

29. *2002 National Survey of Latinos.*

30. Ibid.

31. Ibid.

32. Fareed Zakaria, "Bush, Rice, and the 9/11 Shift," *Newsweek,* December 12, 2002.

33. *Pareja Media Match,* October 15, 2002.

34. América Rodríguez, "Made in the USA: The Production of the *Noticiero Univision,*" a report for the College of Communication, University of Texas, August 1994.

35. Hispanic Trends. August 2000.

36. "AOL Time Warner Venture Targets Spanish Readers," *Wall Street Journal,* September 27, 2002.

37. Ibid.

38. "Book Review. *Vivir para Contarla,*" *Los Angeles Times.* February 16, 2003.

39. Ana Celia Zentella, "Latin @ Languages and Identities," in M. Suárez-Orozco and M. Páez (eds.), *Latinos: Remaking America,* University of California Press, Berkeley, 2002, p. 322.

40. Ibid.

41. "Latinos Tune In to Watch George Lopez on ABC," *Wall Street Journal.* December 31, 2002.

42. Ibid.

43. "J. Lo in Love," *USA Today,* November 11, 2002.

44. "Crest's Spanish Ad Raises Eyebrows. CBS, Procter & Gamble put Spanish Ad on Primetime TV," CBSMarketwatch.com, February 24, 2003.

45. This now bears the name "Hispanic Employment Program" and was originally established on November 5, 1980.

46. Peter Skerry, *Counting on the Census? Race, Group Identity, and the Evasion of Politics,* Brookings Institution Press, Washington, D.C., 2000.

47. *2002 National Survey of Latinos.*

48. "Latino, Sí. Hispanic, No," *New York Times,* October 28, 1992.

49. Ibid.

50. Octavio Paz, *The Labyrinth of Solitude.*

51. Ibid.

52. Carlos Fuentes, *The Buried Mirror.*

53. Emilio O. Rabassa, "Entre Morelos y Bush," *Reforma,* November 5, 2002.

54. José Vasconcelos, *The Cosmic Race,* Johns Hopkins University Press.

55. Marie Arana, *American Chica,* Random House, New York, 2001.

56. Ibid.

57. Ibid.

58. Ibid.

59. Ilan Stavans, *On Borrowed Words.*

60. Ibid.

61. Ibid.

62. Ibid.

63. Richard Rodriguez, *Brown: The Last Discovery of America,* Viking/Penguin, New York, 2002.

64. Ibid.

65. Ibid.

66. Ibid.

67. Ibid.

68. Ibid.

69. Edward W. Said, *Out of Place: A Memoir,* Random House, New York, 1999.

CHAPTER 4

1. Statement by DNC chairman Terry McAuliffe to the Pew/Kaiser Latino Survey. October 3, 2002.

2. A.P. Hispanic Voters–New Latino Survey. October 3, 2003. Guillermo Menéses/ Democratic National Committee-Hispanic Outreach.

3. The 19 congresspeople who won reelection in 2002 are Sivestre Reyes (D-Tex.), Charles Gonzales (D-Tex.), Ruben Hinojosa (D-Tex.), Ciro Rodríguez (D-Tex.), Solomon Ortiz (D-Tex.), Grace Napolitano (D-Calif.), Joe Baca (D-Calif.), Hilda Solis (D-Calif.), Loreta Sanchez (D-Calif.), Xavier Becerra (D-Calif.), Lucille Roybal-Allard (D-Calif.), José Serrano (D-N.Y.), Ed Pastor (D-Ariz.), Luis Gutierrez (D-Ill.), Robert Menendez (D-N.J.), Nydia Velasquez (D-N.Y.), Henry Bonilla (R-Tex.), Lincoln Diaz-Balart (R-Fla.), and Ileana Ros-Lehitinen (R-Fla.).

4. Governor Bill Richardson, interview by Luis Megid for *Noticiero Univision,* November 2002.

5. "Exito Chicago. Study Reveals Latino Voting Tendencies," November 21, 2002. Source: National Council of La Raza.

6. José de la Isla, *The Rise of Hispanic Political Power.*

7. "Mobilizing the Vote: Latinos and Immigrants in the 2002 Midterm Election," National Council of La Raza.

8. Governor Jeb Bush, interview with Lourdes del Río for *Noticiero Univision,* November 3, 2002.

9. "Mobilizing the Vote," *Orlando Sentinel,* November 7, 2002.

10. "Pataki Took the Reins of His Campaign to Break from the Republican Mold," *New York Times,* November 11, 2002.

11. Mobilizing the Vote. National Council of La Raza. Source: Voter News Service 1998. Los Angeles Times, 2002.

12. Political State Report. Postate.com. January 17, 2003. Source: Republican pollster Mike Baselice and Southwest Voter Registration Education Project.

13. Suzanne Gamboa, "Increasing Number of Politicians Airing Spanish-Language Television Ads," Associated Press, November 21, 2002.

14. Tony Sanchez, interview with Martín Berlaga for *Noticiero Univision,* November 2002.

15. Menendez, interview with the author, October 23, 2002.

16. Data are taken from the *Los Angeles Times* exit poll, reported on October 9, 2003.

17. *2002 National Survey of Latinos.*

18. Robert Suro, *Strangers Among Us.*

19. Mayra Rodríguez Valladares, "Crisis Among Hispanic Students," *Hispanic Magazine,* December 2002.

20. "For Hispanics, Language and Culture Barriers Can Further Complicate College," *New York Times,* February 10, 2003.

21. M. Suárez-Orozco and M. Páez (eds.), *Latinos: Remaking America,* University of California Press, Berkeley, 2002, p. 28.

22. Mayra Rodríguez Valladares, "Crisis Among Hispanic Students."

23. National Council of La Raza. "Latinos Potent, but Vulnerable, Force in U.S. Economy," July 21, 1997.

24. "Income and Poverty 2001: The Recession Takes a Toll," Research Bulletin No. 4, United Auto Workers, 2002. Viewed online at http://www.uaw.org/publications/jobspay/02/no4/jpe03.html.

25. Hispanic Trends. The polling report was written by Sergio Bendixen, president of Hispanic Trends. 2000.

26. *2002 National Survey of Latinos.*

27. Daniel T. Griswold, "The Immigrant Question: Were Obituaries of the GOP Premature?" *National Review,* November 20, 2002.

28. Morton M. Mandrake, "Pennsylvania Avenue," *Roll Call,* November 25, 2002.

29. National Immigration Forum. January 6, 2004.

30. "Growing Number of States Granting Resident Tuition to Undocumented Immigrants," Associated Press, May 21, 2003.

31. Ibid.

32. *2002 National Survey of Latinos,* p. 70.

33. U.S. Bureau of the Census, Current Population Survey, OPM The Fact Book 2002 Edition.

34. National Association of Hispanic Journalists. December 16, 2002.

35. "Fast Hispanic Growth Probably Will Continue At Least Until 2020, Group Says," Associated Press, October 14, 2003.

36. Jorge Ramos, *The Other Face of America,* HarperCollins, New York, 2002.

37. Bob Herbert, "Racism and the G.O.P.," *New York Times,* December 12, 2002.

38. Ibid.

39. President George W. Bush. December 15, 2003.

40. Source: National Council of La Raza. "NCLR Blasts Bush Opposition to Affirmative Action," January 15, 2003.

41. *New York Times,* June 24, 2003.

42. W. E. B. DuBois, *The Souls of Black Folks,* 1903.

43. "Survey of Latino Attitudes on a Possible War with Iraq," report released by the Pew Hispanic Center on February 18, 2002.

44. "Names of the Dead Confirmed by the Department of Defense," *New York Times,* April 20, 2003. Latino soldiers who died in Iraq as of April 2003: Andrew Julian Aviles, Aaron Contreras, Ruben Estrella-Soto, George Fernandez, Jose Garibay, Juan Guadalupe Garza, Armando Ariel Gonzalez, Jesus A. Gonzalez, Jorge A. Gonzalez, Jose Gutierrez, Francisco Martinez-Flores, Johnny Villareal Mata, Jesus Martin Antonio Medellin, Gil Mercado, Fernando Padilla-Ramirez, Diego Rincon, Duane Rios, John Travis Rivero, Robert Rodriguez, Erik Silva, Jesus Suarez, Riayan Tejeda, Osbaldo Orozco, and Edward Anguiano.

45. Colonel Gilberto Villahermosa. *Army Magazine,* September 2002.

46. "American Tale: Poor Hispanic Rises to Commander in Iraq," *Miami Herald,* June 14, 2003.

47. "Fair Weather Friends?" *The Economist,* September 20, 2001.
48. President George Bush, Address to a Joint Session of Congress and the American People. September 20, 2001.
49. "Critican las postura de la Casa Blanca con Cuba," *El Nuevo Herald,* May 8, 2003.
50. Sergio Bendixen & Associates Survey for the Cuba Study Group. 10,248 interviews conducted in seven nations between April and August 2001.

CHAPTER 5

1. José de la Isla, *The Rise of Hispanic Political Power,* p. 268.
2. Ibid.
3. *2002 National Survey of Latinos,* p. 86.
4. "In Simple Pronouns, Clues to New York Latino Culture," *New York Times.* December 5, 2002.
5. *2002 National Survey of Latinos,* p. 76.
6. Ibid., p. 56.
7. Lisa J. Montoya, "Gender and Citizenship in Latino Political Participation," in M. Suarez-Orozco and M. Páez (eds.), *Latinos: Remaking America,* University of California Press, Berkeley, 2002.
8. Gannett News Service. March 19, 2003.
9. Congressman Ciro Rodríguez, interview by the author, August 29, 2003.
10. Associated Press, February 26, 2003.
11. Democratic National Committee. Press Release, February 5, 2003.
12. Congresswoman Graciela Flores Napolitano from California. March 1, 2003. Hispanic Response to the Estrada Nomination.
13. Raúl Damas, "Why Hispanic Caucus Rejects Estrada?" *Miami Herald.*
14. "Tercer Intento Fallido por Estrada," *El Nuevo Herald,* March 19, 2003.
15. "NCLR Makes Plea for Civility in Debate over Estrada Nomination," NCLR press release, February 12, 2003.
16. Sergio Muñoz, "El Ajedrez Politico de Bush," *Reforma,* March 6, 2003.
17. "Exiles More Amenable to Dialogue with Cuba," Reuters, February 13, 2003
18. Ibid.

CHAPTER 6

1. Associated Press, September 4, 2001.
2. "Mexico: McDonald's Loses Battle with Tradition," *New York Times,* December 11, 2002.
3. "Latin American Coca-Cola Bottlers in Giant Merger," *New York Times,* December 24, 2002.
4. Chancellor Jorge Castañeda of Mexico, interview by María Elena Salinas for *Aqui y Ahora,* Univision, February 6, 2003.
5. "Mexican Dishes Are Becoming One of America's Most Popular Meals," Associated Press News. October 28, 2002.

6. Richard Rodriguez, *Brown.*
7. Andrew Marr, *Newsweek,* June 23, 2003.
8. Michael Hardt and Antonio Negri, *Empire,* Harvard University Press, Boston, 2000.
9. Dinesh D'Souza, *What's So Great About America,* Regnery, 2002, pp. 72–73.
10. "New Era Succeeds Years of Solitude," *New York Times,* January 4, 2003.
11. Thomas Friedman, *The Lexus and the Olive Tree,* Farrar, Straus and Giroux, New York, 1999, p. 352.
12. *New York Times,* June 18, 2000.
13. Jorge Ramos, *The Other Face of America,* p. 26.
14. *Vanity Fair,* February 2003.
15. "In Our Cocoons, Divisions Persist," *Miami Herald,* January 26, 2003.
16. *The O'Reilly Factor.* February 6, 2003.
17. *Los Angeles Times,* November 3, 1995.
18. Octavio Paz, *The Labyrinth of Solitude,* p. 113.
19. Carlos Fuentes, *The Buried Mirror,* p. 269.
20. Ibid., p. 346.
21. "Hispanics Developing Their Spending Power," HispanicBusiness.com, September 24, 2002.
22. Pat Buchanan, *The Death of the West,* St. Martin's Press, New York, October 2002.
23. Ibid., p. 127.
24. Thomas Weyr and Tom Weyr, *Hispanic U.S.A.: Breaking the Melting Pot,* Harper-Collins, New York, 1988.
25. Ibid., p. 19.
26. Mario Vargas Llosa.

CHAPTER 7

1. National Immigration Forum. August 29, 2002.
2. Tom Ridge, interview by Jorge Ramos for Univision, April 2002.
3. M. Suárez-Orozco and M. Páez (eds.), *Latinos: Remaking America.*
4. Wayne A. Cornelius, "Ambivalent Reception: Mass Public Responses to the 'New' Latino Immigration to the United States," in Ibid.
5. Tom Ridge, Secretary of the Department of Homeland Security. Miami, December 9, 2004.
6. George W. Bush. Press conference in the White House. December 15, 2003.
7. George W. Bush. January 7, 2004.
8. Ibid.
9. "Bush Proposes 21st Century Bracero Program," Congressional Hispanic Caucus, January 7, 2004.
10. "Bush Immigration Plan 'Creates a Permanent Underclass of Workers,'" AFL-CIO, January 7, 2004.
11. NALEO. January 7, 2004.

12. National Council of La Raza. Raul Yzaguirre, President of NCLR.

13. *La Opinión,* January 9, 2004.

14. "Foreign Born in U.S. at Record High," *New York Times,* February 7, 2002.

15. "Study Finds a Graying of the American Electorate," *Washington Post,* October 20, 2002.

16. "Latinos in Higher Education: Many Enroll, Too Few Graduate," report released by the Pew Hispanic Center on September 5, 2002.

17. Statement of Alan Greenspan, Chairman, Board of Governors of the Federal Reserve System before the Special Committee on Aging, United States Senate, February 27, 2003.

18. *Washington Post,* December 2, 2002.

19. *Contra Costa Times,* Walnut Creek, California, December 10, 2002.

20. *USA Today,* July 23, 2001.

21. National Academy of Sciences. "Overall U.S. Economy Gains from Immigration, but It's Costly to Some States and Localities," May 17, 1997.

22. Ibid.

23. "Los Angeles Weighs the Budget Cost of Illegal Immigrants," *New York Times,* May 21, 2003.

24. "Overall U.S. Economy Gains from Immigration."

25. National Immigration Forum. "Immigrants and the Economy," February 18, 2003.

26. UCLA's North American Integration and Development Center. "Comprehensive Migration Policy Reform in North America: The Key to Sustainable and Equitable Economic Integration," August 28, 2001.

27. Peter Jennings and Todd Brewster, *In Search of America,* p. 239.

28. "Illegal Aliens Donate More Organs Than They Get," Associated Press, March 3, 2003. Source: *El Paso Times.*

29. Center for Immigration Studies. "Immigrants in the United States—2000. A Snapshot of America's Foreign-Born Population," January 2002.

30. Center for Immigration Studies. July 12, 2001.

31. Julian L. Simon, *The Economic Consequences of Immigration,* Basil Blackwell, Cambridge, Mass., 1989, p. 337.

32. "Remesas Récord a América Latina," *El Miami Herald,* February 28, 2003.

33. "Immigrants Dispel Negative Stereotypes," *Public Agenda,* January 14, 2003.

34. Ibid.

35. "Diálogo EEUU-México Muestra Pocos Avances," Associated Press, January 10, 2002.

36. Mexican Immigration Again on Agenda," *Arizona Republic,* January 7, 2002.

37. "Mexico Leader Presses U.S. to Resolve Migrant's Issues," *New York Times,* November 27, 2002.

38. Ibid.

39. "GOP Governors Back Bush on Illegals," *Washington Times,* November 25, 2002.

40. "Poll Finds that Majority of Americans Oppose Illegal Alien Amnesty," U.S.

Newswire. This was based on a nationwide sample of 1,017 adults surveyed between August 15 and August 22, 2001.

41. Bernardo Mencez, press consul, Mexican Consulate in San Francisco, January 7, 2003; "A Card Allows U.S. Banks to Aid Mexican Immigrants," *New York Times,* July 6, 2003.

42. "Congressman's Tactics Under Fire," *Los Angeles Times,* May 23, 2003.

43. Jagdish Bhagwati, "Borders Beyond Control," *Foreign Affairs,* January/February 2003.

CHAPTER 8

1. Tomás Rivera Policy Institute. Whither the Latino Community? Alternative Perspectives for Latinos in the United States. 2003. Exogamy Estimates for Ethnic Groups by Couples 1996–1999. Source: Jeff Passel, Urban Institute.

APPENDIX

1. U.S. Bureau of the Census, June 18, 2003.

2. U.S. Bureau of the Census, *Census 2000,* Washington, D.C.

3. Ibid.

4. U.S. Bureau of the Census, "Money Income in the United States: 2000," Washington, D.C.

5. "Hispanics Developing Their Spending," HispanicBusiness.com, September 24, 2002.

6. "The Hispanic Consumer Market in 1999 and Forecasts to 2020," Standard & Poor's, January 2001.

7. Joint Center for Housing Studies of Harvard University. "The State of the Nation's Housing 2001." And R.L. Polk & Co. Survey of Hispanic Registrations 1990–2000. August 2001. 908,451 vehicles out of a total of 13,516,730.

8. "The Hispanic Consumer Market in 1999 and Forecasts to 2020."

9. Nielsen Media Research Universe Estimates.

10. U.S. Bureau of the Census, "Fact Sheet in Observance of Hispanic Heritage Month 2002," Washington, D.C., September 3, 2002.

11. Ibid.

12. Ibid.

13. National Council of La Raza, "Mobilizing the Vote: Latinos and Immigrants in the 2002 Midterm Election."

14. National Council of La Raza, based on results from the *Census 2000.*

15. "Political Party Self-Identification among Registered Latino Voters," 2002 National Survey of Latinos, Pew Hispanic Center/Kaiser Family Foundation, October 2002.

16. Ibid.

17. "The Latino Electorate," 2002 National Survey of Latinos, Pew Hispanic Center/Kaiser Family Foundation, October 2002

18. These figures do not include the 2,481 Latinos who make up 6.7 percent of the U.S. Coast Guard.

19. The Brookings Institution; Census 2000.

20. "Distribution of Wealth," *Reforma,* February 4, 2003.

21. "Money Sent Home by Mexicans Is Booming," *New York Times,* October 28, 2003.

BOOKS BY JORGE RAMOS

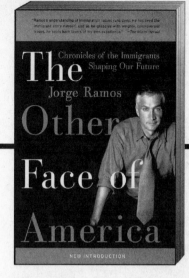

NO BORDERS
A Journalist's Search for Home
ISBN 0-06-093826-9 (paperback)

ATRAVESANDO FRONTERAS
*Un Periodista en Busca de
Su Lugar en el Mundo*
ISBN 0-06-055929-2 (paperback)
SPANISH EDITION

From his childhood days in
Mexico, to his experience with
censorship by government owned
Mexican media companies, his
student years in L.A., and his
early beginnings as a journalist in
the U.S., Ramos gives a personal
and touching account of his life.

"An insightful memoir."

—*Booklist*

THE OTHER FACE OF AMERICA
*Chronicles of the Immigrants
Shaping Our Future*
ISBN 0-06-093824-2 (paperback)

Focusing on the personal plight
of the Latin American immigrant,
Ramos listens to and explores the
stories of dozens of people who
decided to change their lives and
risk everything—families, jobs,
history—in order to pursue a
better, freer, wider future in
the United States.

"As [Ramos] grapples with
weighty, controversial issues,
he peels back layers of his own
experience." —*Miami Herald*